What the critics said in 193.

Cheapjack lifts the tent flap on a score of th   ₁ ₁ess innocent rackets practised on the punter by tick-offs, grafters, fly-pitchers and crocuses ... an exhilarating, happy-go-lucky book.   Roger Pippett *Daily Herald*

It is brisk and lively and colourful and human – even if its humans are not always admirable – and its people and its little world are always and profoundly English, as English as Dickens.   *New York Times*

We will advise anyone who is interested in the fairs of England to read this book in the certainty that they will never get a better or more amusing guide.
                        W. H. Davies   *Sunday Times*

A book that is stuffed full of bizarre happenings and queer characters ... He has explored an England that most of us have only glimpsed and brought back a joyous and exhilarating report.   Howard Spring   *Evening Standard*

Anyone who enjoyed *The Good Companions* will find here the raw material of that masterly effort in the picaresque.
                                                                        Everyman

The book is amusing and engagingly honest; it is thoroughly good entertainment and extremely well done.
                                        Ethel Mannin   *Daily Mirror*

Odd personality. Worries friends by relapsing into incomprehensible jargon of fairs, using such words as 'monkery', 'chavvy', 'gelt', 'groiny', 'tosheroon.' Fortunately his autobiography *Cheapjack* contains a glossary for the unenlightened.   William Hickey   *Daily Express*

As 'tick-off', 'knocker-worker' and 'mounted pitcher' Mr Allingham was a success and he would be equally successful, we feel sure, as a 'mug-faker' or a 'windbag-worker.'
E. B. Osborn *Morning Post*

There is a vigorous freshness as well as a ring of authenticity about this autobiography of a penniless young man.
Daily Telegraph

A most entertaining account of the strange people who make their living by their wits at these fairs. *Daily Sketch*

Cheapjack is certainly a book that is well worth reading. Its humour is excellent ... We must forget all about it, however, when we go to the fairs – otherwise Mr Allingham's former companions will have a thin time. J. Bilibin *Observer*

Charming and candid ... Mr Allingham ... is out not to defend but to describe his grafter's life. He makes a good job of it, loading his open-air narrative with a fresh and airy charm that is never literary, and avoiding like the plague that jovial, picaresque note that one would naturally, and in terror, look for.
Clifton Fadiman *New Yorker*

A surprising and delightful book ... It is just the simple but vividly told story of how a young man who couldn't make his living in the ordinary routine of business life, branched out for himself to cultivate the only talent which Nature had given him, and in doing so found romance and adventure, privation, good fellowship, bed-bugs, and an entire new world within this old one, yet one which is essentially England. *Tatler*

We can do no better than recommend you to read it yourself.
Robert Lynd *News Chronicle*

CHEAPJACK

To
MY CLIENTS
THIS HISTORY IS
AFFECTIONATELY
DEDICATED

HAVE YOU READ "CHEAPJACK" YET?

The most amazing autobiography of the year! Widely praised, vivid, exciting: a glimpse of a romantic England known to few of us. Selling Everywhere. 7s. 6d.

2nd Ptg. Already . . . HEINEMANN

Publisher's advertisement in the *Daily Telegraph*, June 5th 1934.

CHEAPJACK

BEING THE TRUE HISTORY OF A YOUNG MAN'S
ADVENTURES AS A FORTUNE-TELLER
GRAFTER, KNOCKER-WORKER, AND
MOUNTED PITCHER ON THE
MARKET-PLACES AND FAIR-
GROUNDS OF A MODERN
BUT STILL ROMAN-
TIC ENGLAND

BY
PHILIP ALLINGHAM

Foreword by Vanessa Toulmin

Introduction by Francis Wheen

GOLDEN DUCK

First published in Great Britain in 1934 by William Heinemann Ltd and in
the USA by Frederick Stokes & Company

This edition published in 2010 by
Golden Duck (UK) Ltd.,
Sokens,
Green Street,
Pleshey, near Chelmsford,
Essex
CM3 1HT

www.golden-duck.co.uk

Copyright © The Margery Allingham Society 2010

Foreword © Vanessa Toulmin 2010

Introduction © Francis Wheen 2010

Afterword © Julia Jones 2010

ISBN 978-1-899262-02-1

Design by Roger Davies
rogerdaviesdesign@btinternet.com

Enquiries in the USA and Canada should be addressed to
The Crum Creek Press,
484 E Carmel Drive # 378,
Carmel, IN 46032

www.crumcreekpress.com

Printed and bound in Great Britain by
CPI Antony Rowe, Chippenham, Wiltshire

FOREWORD

PROFESSOR VANESSA TOULMIN

PHILIP ALLINGHAM'S adventures as a grafter and pitcher on the British fairgrounds offer a rare insight into a closed society that, in many ways, remains unchanged from the 1930s. The life of the showman appears romantic and carefree and *Cheapjack* frequently resembles an exotic travelogue with the showmen, hawkers and Gypsy travellers characterised as colourful characters living on the edge of society. 'Once a grafter always a grafter' is the phrase utilised by Allingham in the first page of his narrative but, although Allingham is expressing his personal commitment to the travelling life, yet, paradoxically, this same phrase reveals the extent to which his book was destined to remain an outsider's account. The showman, not the grafter, is at the centre of the fairground – as Allingham would later recognise.

Cheapjack was published at a critical time in the history of British fairgrounds, with the Showmen's Guild of Great Britain, the trade association of British showpeople, gaining strength and power, a power that would be consolidated with the outbreak of World War II. Without membership of the Guild it would become virtually impossible to break into the fairground fraternity and the 1930s were the last time when one could operate on the fairgrounds without this membership. Allingham was chronicling a way of life that he could never really be part of. The fairgrounds were changing. They were becoming more modern and the world of the grafter and sideshow hawker would soon disappear as modern rides, greater technology and the outbreak of war would bring changes to the society that Allingham describes so poetically.

Some things remain unaltered. The *World's Fair* newspaper that Allingham used to aid him in his work is still published weekly from Oldham and remains the trade paper for fair people. The grafters' slang – a mixture of Romany, cant, palarie and local dialect – is still prevalent within the travelling society, and many of the expressions and phrases listed in the glossary and used quite naturally by Allingham, are common terms today.

Cheapjack is more than an interesting curiosity and a lively read: it is an important historical record of a way of life that was in transition, a society that was secretive and one that would ultimately close its doors to outsiders by the 1940s.

National Fairground Archive,
University of Sheffield Library.

Detail from Pip Youngman Carter's dust jacket for the first UK edition 1934.

INTRODUCTION

FRANCIS WHEEN

'And so you're one o' these as goes wi' t'tides – fairs – like?'
'That's me! My name's Jackson. What's yours?'
'Oakroyd. Jess Oakroyd.'
'Oakroyd. Good enough! Well, mine's Jackson – Joby they call me – Joby Jackson. Everybody in this line o' business knows me...Done everything – you ask anybody – Joby Jackson. Boxing shows, circus, try-your-luck games, everything. I've run shows of me own – Human Spider and Wild Man o' the Amazon. You can't name a place where they 'ave a fair or a race-meeting I 'aven't been to, you can't do it. I know 'em all. England, Scotland, Wales, Ireland, Isle o' Man, Isle o' Wight, you can't lose me. Marvellous!'
– J. B. Priestley, *The Good Companions* (1929)

PHILIP ALLINGHAM (1906-1969) grew up in a household of writers – what his father called 'my little fiction factory'. No great surprise, then, that having forsaken the factory to become an itinerant fortune-teller and fairground huckster he should write a book about it.

That wasn't his intention, however – which may explain the enduring and exhilarating vividness of this memoir (though his famous big sister Margery also deserves some credit, as Julia Jones reveals in her afterword to this edition). What makes *Cheapjack* such a delight, more than 75 years after its first publication in 1934, is its apparent artlessness. In his *New Yorker* review, Clifton Fadiman praised the *al fresco* narrative for having 'a fresh and airy charm that is never literary, and avoiding like the plague that jovial, picaresque note which one would naturally, and in terror, look for'. As Fadiman concluded: 'Several well-born Englishmen have extracted cash from the plebs, but never with Allingham's frank directness.'

Dozens of young middle-class authors in the late Twenties and early Thirties went 'slumming', but most were driven by political or artistic (or even sexual) imperatives. Tom Driberg worked as a washer-up in a Soho cafe-cum-brothel after leaving Oxford, sprucing himself up every Saturday afternoon to attend Edith Sitwell's tea-parties. Henry Green's novel *Living* emerged from his stint as a manual worker at his family's foundry in Birmingham. George Orwell, the ragged-trousered Old Etonian, reported on his ventures into the *terra incognita* of proletarian and sub-proletarian life in *Down and Out in Paris and London* and *The Road to Wigan Pier*. In Orwell's novel *Keep the Aspidistra Flying* (published two years after *Cheapjack*), Gordon Comstock's socialist friend Ravelston takes him to working-class pubs as 'part of a lifelong attempt to escape from his own class, and become, as it were, an honorary member of the proletariat'. But Comstock and Ravelston were political tourists. 'Like all slummers,' Valentine Cunningham argues in *British Writers of the Thirties*, 'they were "going over", but with their bags perpetually packed for the journey back...Even Orwell – especially Orwell, perhaps – was never less than consciously a migrant with a return ticket.'

Similar journeys were undertaken by posses of Marxist poets, Fabian novelists and Mass Observation investigators, but the people with whom they identified – 'the people of the abyss', in Jack London's phrase – didn't always appreciate their sympathetic attentions. 'The men down here, in fact all the people down here, have grown very, very sensitive about the

INTRODUCTION

enormous number of people who have come down here from London and Oxford and Cambridge, making inquiries, inspecting places, descending underground, questioning women about their cooking, asking men strings of questions about this and that and the other,' says one of the men interviewed by James Hanley in his account of deprivation in industrial South Wales, published under the uncompromising title *Grey Children: A Study in Humbug and Misery* (1935). 'They object to all these people coming down and asking questions. That's all. They're not animals in a zoo.'

For all the earnest nobility of their intentions, there is something inescapably comic about these slummers, especially when they try to disguise themselves. Some reporters for Mass Observation, striving to be 'unobserved observers', impersonated drunks or tramps. Christopher Isherwood ate boiled sweets by the bagful in the hope of wrecking his 'good bourgeois teeth', a dead giveaway. George Orwell affected a fake Cockney accent which fooled nobody. ('It was not easy,' he admitted. 'I imagined – notice the frightful class-consciousness of the Englishman – that I should be spotted as a "gentleman" the moment I opened my mouth.') Ravelston in *Keep the Aspidistra Flying* is found out when he orders double whiskies for himself and Comstock:

> The navvy smiled flickeringly under his moustache. '– ignorant toff!' he was thinking. Asking for whisky in a – beer 'ouse!' Ravelston's pale face flushed slightly. He had not known till this moment that some of the poorer pubs cannot afford a spirit licence.

Orwell's friend Rayner Heppenstall may have had him in mind when he wrote mockingly of bourgeois artists who 'wear peaked caps, cultivate an accent, smoke very foul tobacco...and cease to wash'.

No wonder the *New Yorker*'s critic found *Cheapjack* so refreshing. Whereas the slummers strove to look shabby, Philip Allingham chose a top-hat and tails as his working clothes with no hesitation or embarrassment. Unlike those anguished intellectuals who tiptoed into gutters and ditches to expiate their bourgeois guilt or expose the privations of the poor, he did so purely because wayside hustling seemed more congenial and lively than nine-to-fiveing at an advertising agency in Piccadilly Circus. The shoals of odd fish with whom he now swam – The Ugliest Woman in the World, The Darkie Kid, Peter the Whistler, Flash Jackson, Madame Sixpence – were not mere exotic specimens to be scrutinised and dissected; they were his companions and chums. There's no sermonising, no didactic subtext in *Cheapjack*. The headline on a *Daily Express* news story about Allingham in May 1934 may make him sound like another posh boy flirting with bohemianism – 'Public Schoolboy: Knocker Worker: Now Cheapjack – At £50 a Week' – but the report itself confirms that this is someone who has found his vocation. 'My people, of course, want me to go back to London and lead a normal life,' he tells the paper. 'But well – I like this job.'

The longer he works at it, the more he likes it. Everyone visiting a fair is in holiday mood, hunting feverishly for a good time, and this unflagging carnival spirit keeps him cheerful even when business itself flags. Skint or flush, he remains invincibly happy-go-lucky. 'I had only a few shillings in the world, and something had to be done,' he writes early in his story. 'I had not made much progress, although somehow I felt that I had only to hit on the right idea when everything would be all right...' Many months later, on a brief return visit to

INTRODUCTION

London, he is walking along Tottenham Court Road late at night 'with exactly a shilling in my pocket...I seemed to think better when I was walking, and I felt that now was an ideal moment for me to plan out something for the future.' The talent of grafters such as Philip Allingham – whether selling palm-readings or hair-curlers – is to suspend the punter's disbelief about who is likely to get more out of this transaction. The irony of the trade, as he notes on the very first page, is that no punter is half so gullible as the grafters themselves. In the winter they mutter about finding a steadier way of life but as soon as the weather improves they're back on the road, thinner and more threadbare and yet brimming with optimism that this time they'll make their fortune.

W. H. Davies, the poet and sometime super-tramp who reviewed *Cheapjack* for the *Sunday Times*, marvelled at Allingham's 'extraordinary innocence, right from the beginning to the time he leaves off...If he had been less innocent he would not have had so much success'. The most startling proof of this innocence is his account of picking up a penniless 13-year-old girl from South Shields and taking her on his travels as a showman's stooge – with the grateful blessing of her parents, and no interference from the police. 'Was it,' Davies wondered, 'because it all happened at the fair, and that that place was regarded as the home of freedom and hilarity, where anything could be done except murder?'

The milieu of Gypsies and tramps and spivs is a world apart – or at least a *demi-monde* – with its own customs and morals and unwritten laws, and even its own newspaper in the form of the *World's Fair*. It also has a separate lingo, a semantic stew of Yiddish tags and Cockney rhyming slang and underworld argot, translated in Allingham's glossary at the back of the book. Some of the jargon which he thought it necessary to explain to readers in 1934 has since passed into common parlance. Look up 'bevvy' (to drink) or 'bird' (a jail sentence) or 'busk' (to perform in the street) in the *Oxford English Dictionary* – or 'punter' or 'on one's tod' or 'gezumph' (now usually rendered as 'gazump') – and you'll find *Cheapjack* cited as a source. With 'rozzer' (a policeman), the *OED* compilers seem to have missed his usage in 1934, citing instead a line from *Flowers for the Judge*, a crime novel published two years later by his sister Margery. ("Aven't seen 'er since she went off with a rozzer.') Since she worked on the manuscript of Philip's book, however, one can hazard a guess as to where she found the word. Sometimes she was ahead of him: 'scarper' (run away) and 'whizz-boys' (pickpockets) are both attributed by the *OED* to Margery, in novels published two or three years before his memoir, but she may well have picked them up during the wayward sibling's occasional detours to her house in Essex.

Philip Allingham's publishers, Heinemann, who also published Margery's novels, advertised *Cheapjack* as 'an astonishing autobiography of an English gentleman turned county fair mountebank'. As a pitcher himself, Philip would have understood that one must allow the facts some elasticity when trying to make a sale (his huge canvas banner at travelling shows informed punters 'that I was Society's Leading Palmist and that I had been patronised by the nobility, and quite a lot of other things not strictly true'), but he wasn't quite the pristine gent presented in the sales-pitch. Readers of Margery Allingham's Campion novels will know of her fascination with misfits and drop-outs who refuse to play the game by society's official rules. Philip's father, Herbert, seldom missed an opportunity to work Gypsies into the hundreds of serials he wrote for popular magazines in the late Victorian and

INTRODUCTION xv

Edwardian eras. There was even a family belief that the Allinghams themselves had Romany ancestry. It may have been a myth, but one senses that this beguiling legend is in Philip's mind as he stares out of his office window in chapter one, wondering what to do with his life. 'I had tried my hand at almost every job I could think of,' he writes. 'Suddenly it dawned on me – and the relief at the discovery was extraordinary – that there was nothing at all to prevent me from earning my living reading the future in other people's hands...I decided to steal out of London as quickly and as quietly as possible and join the Gypsies.'

Not so much slumming as coming home. Heinemann's copywriter had the essential point bang-right: *Cheapjack* was an extraordinary autobiography. It still is.

Philip and Margery Allingham
as children, circa 1912.

Allingham
pitching at night.

CONTENTS

Foreword by Vanessa Toulmin page vii

Introduction by Francis Wheen page ix

List of Illustrations page xxii

Note on the text page xxiii

CHAPTER 1
In which I explain myself : Relate how I had my Idea, and then set out in my silk hat to tell fortunes in London.
page 1

CHAPTER 2
I turn professional grafter : Visit Southall Fair : The misfortune which there overcame me.
page 13

CHAPTER 3
I meet Spike, the Darkie Kid, and spend the night in a boxing booth : I return to London and, after a dispiriting experience, set out to visit Southend.
page 21

CHAPTER 4
I meet an unpleasant woman : Am gently rebuffed at a large hotel : I find a new friend with a mug-faker : He tells me his sad history : I take several sea trips.
page 28

CHAPTER 5
I return to London, where I observe some ladies of the town : I meet a man with a cat in his bonnet.
page 44

CHAPTER 6
I spend August Bank Holiday at Hunslet Feast, where I find a friend in a bowler hat : I meet my first Gypsies and am led into a dissertation on my friend Ezra Boss, head of his tribe.
page 51

CHAPTER 7
I go to Bradford with Sammy York : We visit Whitby : I meet the Little Major, Doncaster Jock, and Sheeny Louie : Parny on the Tober : I am initiated into the mysteries of the R.O. and have leisure to observe the London Mob : I go to Sleights, where I find a different punter.
page 59

CHAPTER 8
I meet the Church Militant.
page 78

Chapter 9
I experience my first big fair : I come to grips with the Law : The truant policeman : Madame Clarissa advises me to go to Llandudno.
page 88

CHAPTER 10
I meet Mr. Dell and his family : I join their fair and learn Mary Ann Bevan's story.
page 103

CHAPTER 11
My friend Clarry introduces me to his future mother-in-law's extraordinary ménage : I become a part of it : I fall in love with a Gypsy queen and Clarry acquires a pair of boots.
page 111

CHAPTER 12
I go to Llanfairfechan and visit No Name, where I am tempted by my anger to become dishonest : I return to Mold, where I part from my love and meet a Napoleon : The apple with a shilling in it : I spend a strange night, and in the morning, on hearing of the fruits of dishonesty, become dissatisfied with Wales and decide to follow love to Hull.
page 120

CHAPTER 13
I take part in Hull Fair and meet many strange and interesting people, including Mad Jack, Peter the Whistler and Madame Sixpence : I am invited to become an orthodox Jew, but decline and leave Hull.
page 148

CHAPTER 14
I have fifty pounds and decide to go to London : London has a bad effect on me : I meet my conscience in very strange disguise and part with my fortune to two men in gloves.
page 163

CHAPTER 15
I return to the grafters and discover that the sun does not always shine : I meet London Joe, who persuades me to join him and his strange friend : I sell the cockernen and find Cross-Eyed Charlie a difficult colleague.
page 175

CHAPTER 16
I make three new friends, and we are all faced with a pressing problem : We solve this problem and rid the City of Manchester of a pest.
page 188

CHAPTER 17
I think of changing my vocation : Meet an unlovely person and am introduced to his unhappy partner : I decide to become a pitcher.
page 200

CHAPTER 18
I start as a pitcher at Slough and visit Newbury, where misfortune overtakes me and a young woman with bobbed hair : I meet Alfie Holmsworth and am introduced to his Academy : The disastrous history of Gloria Eve, alias Miss Smith.
page 211

CHAPTER 19
I visit Newcastle Town Moor, where I become a mounted pitcher : I get into serious difficulties with a belligerent mob, from which I am rescued by my good friend Ezra Boss and his valiant tribesmen: I witness the stand of a Napoleon.
page 224

CHAPTER 20
I make money and go to South Shields, where I meet Sally : Sally adopts me.
page 243

CHAPTER 21
Sally and I go to Whitby, where the Little Major recounts to me his great plan to make our fortunes : The advent of the motor-car : The reappearance of Three-Fingered Billy, and the ancient secret of the Bugfat.
page 255

CHAPTER 22
I am lost without a model : I acquire the Citroën and Sally returns: We observe Three-Fingered Billy selling nerves of steel for a shilling : We meet Brother Adam : The service he did us : The Little Major and London Joe reappear and I hear a story, an explanation and a business proposition.
page 269

CHAPTER 23
Sally and I go south : The weather improves : I buy a new car and become 'Professor X, the Mystery Man from the East': The winter again : I am tempted by security and fall.
page 284

CHAPTER 24
I take Sally home : I pause to say good-bye and meet two very old friends : I hear of new fields to conquer : I am tempted : Sally knows best.
page 296

Glossary of Grafters' Slang
page 303

Afterword by Julia Jones page 310

Acknowledgements page 324

Philip Allingham's Psychological Reading of You Page 325

Notes on the Contributors page 328

LIST OF ILLUSTRATIONS

Unless otherwise stated, all illustrations are reproduced by kind permission of the Margery Allingham Society. Their archive is held in the Albert Sloman Library, University of Essex. We are also very grateful to the National Fairground Archive, University of Sheffield Library, for permission to use photographs from their collection. Thanks also to Simplon Ship postcards and to Southend Central Museum (Padgett Collection).

page iv Publisher's advertisement in the *Daily Telegraph,* June 5th 1934.

viii Detail from Pip Youngman Carter's dust jacket for the first UK edition 1934.

xv Philip and Margery Allingham as children, *circa* 1912.

xvi Allingham pitching at night.

xxiii Allingham working as a mounted pitcher.

xxiv Allingham as a young man.

20 A Wild West show at Hull Fair, circa 1930.
National Fairground Archive

27 Boxers at Nottingham Goose Fair.
National Fairground Archive

43 The *Princess Maud,* an excursion vessel off Southend circa 1930
www.simplonpc.co.uk

43 The view from Pier Hill, Southend, late 1920s
Southend Central Museum

77 Allingham and assistant with umbrella

147 Endpapers drawn by 'Grog' (A. J. Gregory) for the first UK edition, 1934.

174 Punters at Nottingham Goose Fair, *circa* 1930.
National Fairground Archive

187 Fair on Newcastle Town Moor, early 1930s
National Fairground Archive

199 Three-Fingered Billy at work

247 Nottingham Goose Fair
National Fairground Archive

295 Punters at Hull Fair, 1935
National Fairground Archive.

301 Headline in the *Sunday Express,* May 20th 1934.

307 Showpeople at Hull Fair
National Fairground Archive

308 – 309 ALLINGHAM FAMILY PHOTOS

323 Francesca and Joyce Allingham with actress Enid Stamp Taylor.

328 The Author

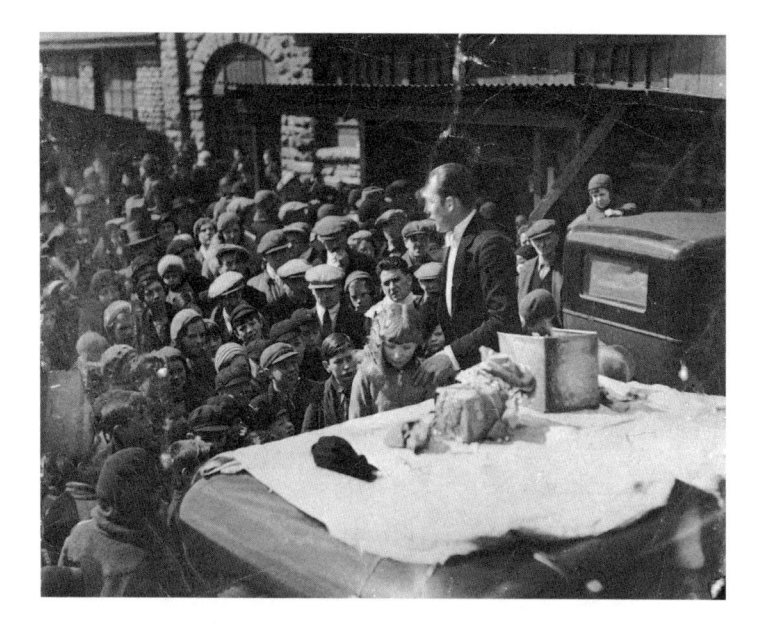

'Instead of talking to one person at a time, I thought, it must surely be more profitable to talk to a hundred.' Allingham working as a mounted pitcher.

A NOTE ON THE TEXT

The text of *Cheapjack* has been photographically reproduced from the 1934 US edition and is therefore exactly as it appeared then. It contains a few epithets that are no longer used or accepted; in the context, however, it is clear that Allingham intended no offence.

'… although my heart was willing, my hand, or perhaps my head, was weak.'

CHEAPJACK

CHAPTER 1

In which I explain myself: relate how I had my Idea, and then set out in my silk hat to tell fortunes in London.

It's a queer life, on the whole a good life, and if by practical standards it leads nowhere in particular, at least we can always make a fresh start, or we think we can.

This last is probably the snag in it. There is a saying among the Fair People, "Once a grafter, always a grafter," and of course sayings have a disconcerting habit of proving true.

In the winter most market folk decide to get out of the business forever, and a home, security and respectability become more than vague terms of contempt.

But as soon as the weather improves you find us on the road again, a little threadbare, a little thinner, but full of that extraordinary optimism which makes us what we are, the arch "punters"—or, as the Americans say, "suckers"—of the world.

Our lives are so much of a gamble that boredom is impossible. However successful we may be for a time, at the back of our minds there is always the knowledge that one day we shall be short of a night's lodgings and one day we shall be rich. Really rich: for who is so affluent as the man who has sixty or seventy pounds and no responsibilities in a new and exciting town?

However, if I had known some years ago, when my education came to an abrupt end, that I should be a "mounted pitcher" on a market at twenty-five, or earning my living by telling fortunes on fair-grounds at twenty-two, I should not have been encouraged, save that it would probably have been a relief to me to know that I should be earning a living at all at any future date.

My education came to an end on the day that the Provost of an Oxford college pointed out to my father gently but very firmly that my chances of passing Responsions at any date were less than small and that my work was too weak all round for any tutor to waste his time on me.

After this I worked for many people, but all of them formed, sooner or later, the same opinion of me as had the Provost at Oxford, but some of them naturally expressed themselves less gently than he had done.

I tried my hand at practically everything it was considered dignified for a son of my family to do, but although my heart was willing, my hand, or perhaps my head, was weak.

At last, when I was twenty-one, I sat one morning in an office in Coventry Street, the window of which looked over the Corner House restaurant. I had plenty of time to stare out of windows, for my job at the time was practically non-existent.

I had the room rent free in the offices of a publicity agent, in return for which I helped him whenever he was exceptionally busy. This was extraordinarily seldom.

I am not sure now, nor was I then, exactly what I intended to do with this room, and, save that it gave me the feeling that I was there on the spot should anything ever arise for me to do, it really was not of very much use to me.

Apart from a few odd guineas which I earned from writing occasional articles and a few very minor publicity jobs, I was earning nothing at all.

It was while I sat in this office, looking across the street at the huge popular restaurant, that I decided to become a professional fortune-teller.

Whenever I had had an idea before there had always been something to prevent me from putting it into action. It is most difficult to start doing anything on one's own with no capital at all, and I had tried my hand at almost every job I could think of, but the fortune-telling idea was different.

Suddenly it dawned upon me—and the relief at the discovery was extraordinary—that there was nothing at all to prevent me from earning my living reading the future in other people's hands. Sitting up there, I thought it might be very profitable, and for almost the first time in my life I was quite right.

I have always been able to tell fortunes.

By that I do not mean that I am at all psychic, but years earlier I had discovered that I could talk to strangers about themselves to their enjoyment and that I could make pretty accurate guesses about their types and dispositions, and thence by a process of natural deduction to their pasts and probable futures.

This is, after all, not difficult, if one brings one's mind to it, for if you consider the subject, most people's lives pan out in a more or less logical way.

I had always been more interested in people than in things or ideas; and considering the matter in my lonely office, this interest seemed to me to be my only asset, and it now actually appeared that it might be a realizable one.

I had had some experience of fortune-telling, although I had never charged a fee, of course, but, realizing that most people like to hear themselves being intelligently considered, I had told a few fortunes while I was at a crammer's in Chancery Lane, and later, when a cub reporter on the Cambridge *Daily News,* I had discovered that certain people to be interviewed, actresses especially, told me much more about themselves if I told their fortunes instead of asking direct questions.

Again, when I was a copy writer at Selfridge's, I had often read people's hands, and a buyer once invited me into her office to ask my advice about a husband of whom she had neither seen nor heard for a couple of years.

The same sort of thing had happened at Dorland's Advertising Service, and, in fact, everywhere I worked.

Thinking it over, I felt sure I could satisfy my clients, but I was a little vague as to how to go about it. Telling a girl's fortune for the privilege of holding her hand is, after all, one thing, but to ask her to part with her money for the experience is quite a different caper.

I realized this and spent a long time thinking about it.

In the end I paid threepence for a copy of the *World's Fair* and employed myself for the rest of the day thinking my project over.

There were difficulties. In spite of my succession of failures in every occupation I had yet essayed, I felt somehow that, whatever I did by way of fortune-telling, it would not be considered exactly a brilliant move by my relations and the people I knew in London. I foresaw all sorts of opposition from my parents if they should discover what I was about to do, so I decided to steal out of London as quickly and as quietly as possible and join the gypsies.

That the gypsies would not be too keen to have me did not then occur to me; but this was fortunate, for I left the office that evening determined to make a break in my life and joyously enthusiastic about the whole scheme.

After all, I had acquired something out of the afternoon's thought which I had not had before. I had now two definite aims: one, to make money; the other, to escape.

I knew London pretty well and I quite liked the West End, but everywhere I went in London I was sure to find myself in some place which reminded me of some previous failure, and I wanted to get away from them all.

That night, after I left the office, I went to my

combined room in New Compton Street, for which I paid twelve shillings a week and which was as near to the West End as any one could desire.

Next door was a café frequented solely by colored people, and practically opposite Jimmy's Club, one of the few establishments of the kind in London which had never been raided.

The curious mixed smell of garlic and cabbage water always haunted the stairs which led to my room, and the landlady, who was an Italian, was too fond of cats, but by watching my step I reached my room without inconvenience and changed carefully into full evening kit.

Apart from its being the best suit of clothes I possessed, I felt that I required some sort of uniform for this new venture. Moreover, I had found that policemen were apt to treat me differently when I was thus arrayed. I still hold the belief that they are more gentle with you when you are drunk thus clad and less likely to be suspicious when you are sober.

It was June, so there was no need to wear an overcoat, and, setting my tall hat at an angle, I went off in search of some one who might possibly require information about his future.

I did not hope to make much money, fortunately, but I wanted to gain a little experience before I burnt my boats behind me and set off on my new career in earnest.

A pub seemed the best place to begin.

My first job was to find a house where I was not known, and, after wandering round the West End in a rather aimless manner, I found myself in Whitehall.

Entering the saloon bar of a public house near where the Whitehall Theatre stands today, I ordered a whisky-and-splash. I did not like whisky, but I thought it would make a better impression than beer.

The man in shirtsleeves who served me looked like the proprietor.

"Oh, by the way," I said, trying to sound as natural as possible, "I happen to be a professional palmist. I don't suppose you'd mind me approaching some of your patrons?"

The landlord was polishing a glass at the time, and he gave me one quick look.

"There's a notice outside," he said. " 'No Hawkers Allowed in this Bar.' "

I wanted to get outside, but the door seemed a devil of a long way from where I stood, so I swallowed my drink hurriedly and ordered another.

This was not too good, I thought, for a start. But the two whiskies had given me a certain amount of confidence and I decided to try somewhere else.

Further along Whitehall, towards Westminster, I came to another house, and here I was more fortunate.

The saloon bar was a cosy little apartment, and seated at several tables were a number of people, both men and women.

I had only a few shillings in the world, so I ordered half a pint of bitter and hoped for the best.

Here the man hurried to get my order and eyed my boiled shirt approvingly as he wiped the counter before putting down my tankard.

"Lovely evening, sir," he said briskly.

I agreed, and there was a long pause. It was not

exactly stage-fright, but the way he said "sir" had disarmed me. Although I didn't want to be treated like a hawker, I was made uncomfortable at being accepted as a "gent." I was not quite sure how a palmist should expect to be treated, but anyhow I was afraid that I was going to disillusion him and I think it was his disappointment and probable embarrassment which I most feared.

At last I plunged into it and introduced myself as I had done before.

He looked rather surprised, and stepped back a pace to have a good look at me. Then he grinned.

"What exactly do you mean?" he asked, quietly enough. "D'you want to read their 'ands, Guv'nor?"

I concurred that this was my idea.

"You see," I lied hastily, "I've been the professional at the Silver Slipper Club, but I'm always on for a little extra work, and it suddenly occurred to me that I might entertain your customers. I make the nominal charge of one shilling, and, of course, I know how to approach them without giving offense."

The barman was still grinning. He was a nice chap.

"Well, you'd better wait a moment till I've seen the missus," he said. "But I should think it'd be all right."

It was all right, and the good lady came along herself to have a look at me.

I walked over to the table where the most likely lot of people were seated and introduced myself again. There were three women and two men, and they obviously had no idea what I was talking about when I first approached them.

They seemed more surprised than the barman had

been and obviously thought it was all very unusual. But when I had explained everything to them very carefully and told them my fee, one of the party, a plump middle-aged woman who was drinking Guinness and wore a wedding-ring, decided to have a bob's worth.

She ordered another round of drinks, included me in it, and paid for them. The fact that she paid for the round at once told me that her husband was not among the party, and also that she was not a "pick-up."

The men offered no protest to her paying, and, when one of them offered to settle with me for her reading in advance, she called him by his Christian name and told him that it would be unlucky if she didn't cross my palm with her own silver.

This was obviously a superstition invented on the spur of the moment, and it gave me a very useful insight into her character.

I told them that I never accepted a fee until after the fortune had been told, and this rule I adhered to ever afterwards.

When I had finished her fortune, every one else at the table decided that they would have to have theirs told, "just for fun."

I was quite successful. But one of the odd things was that while I was reading the first woman's hand some one nudged my knee whenever I hit on a lucky guess. Obviously he thought it was the knee of my client, and on many occasions afterwards similar unconscious prompters have proved most useful guides.

Later, when working in a tent, I used to arrange

things so that I could feel the slightest movement under the table, and on some occasions, when two women have been together at a sitting, I have received such violent and painful jabs that it has been as much as I could do to disguise my feelings.

"Just a minute, old boy," called the barman when I had finished the first table. "The lady would like to see you. Would you come through this way?"

I was shown into a cosy little room at the back of the bar, and there I was soon joined by a woman who had once been very pretty. She had jet black hair dressed in a most complicated manner, and although she was rather too plump she looked very pleasant, I thought.

I saw that she had been upstairs to attend to her make-up. Her cheeks were slightly over-rouged and her lipstick looked fresh, although the atmosphere around her indicated that quite a quantity of spirits had recently passed her lips.

She greeted me in a more or less formal manner and looked me up and down approvingly.

"There is something I particularly want to know," she said, "and I hope you can help me."

I took her left hand, which had far too much jewelry upon it, and started to talk rapidly. I had always found that as long as I kept talking I was making headway, since I was bound to hit on something true sooner or later. Besides, while I was talking a client was more likely to say something which might give me a lead.

Now I very seldom ask a direct question. By continually talking I can usually induce a client to let down his guard. If it is a woman she will not remain silent for long, however intently she tries to do so.

"You should guard against a woman," I suggested. "She seems to lie between you and your real happiness."

"I thought as much," said my client savagely. "What's she like?"

I ignored this question, but dwelt upon a few of her own characteristics, which I knew would not interest her, but which gave me time to think about my next important point.

The publican had been so decent to me that I didn't want to cramp his style by confirming any suspicions which the dear lady might have about one of his admirers.

However, I was anxious to satisfy her, so I continued.

"There is a woman," I said. "Blonde, I think. Probably a little younger than yourself."

Since she was a brunette it seemed only likely that her husband would be attracted to an opposite type if he desired a change.

"She's not to be trusted, I'm afraid."

"That's the bitch," said my client suddenly. "But she's not much younger than I am, young man. And what's more, she doesn't look it."

Poor landlord! I felt I wasn't quite playing the game.

"But there's nothing to fear," I continued hurriedly, "provided you are on your guard. She is in love with some one in whom you are interested, but this person is a married man, I think. Whatever happens, he will be true to his first love. He may be slightly infatuated for a time, of course, but deep in his heart it is his home in which he is interested. Right will conquer wrong," I added fatuously, "and where he really belongs, that is where he will eventually be."

"You mean he will never leave his wife for long?" asked my client. Her voice was unusually quiet, and she was looking at me in a rather peculiar way.

"Of course," I went on with courage. "This other woman is clever. She is dangerous, remember. But the man I see is some one who would never . . ."

I hesitated. I was thinking of some suitable quality yet trying to avoid making a direct reference to the man outside.

"He will never leave his true love, you understand," I said at last. "His home, his wife, his . . . I think I see children. They all mean more to him than just a passing fancy."

My client interrupted me.

"A passing fancy?" she said, and her voice was not friendly. "Let us get this quite clear. This fair-haired woman you've described sounds exactly like his wife."

I didn't bother to have a drink at the bar before I left. It seemed to be time to move on.

CHAPTER 2

I turn professional grafter, and visit Southall Fair. The misfortune which there overcame me.

SEVERAL NIGHTS AFTER this I repeated my psychic pub crawl with some cards I had had printed. On these I described myself as a clairvoyant and adviser. I felt very professional.

Occasionally a drunken man wanted to have an argument with me, or a light-hearted lady delighted in knocking off my silk hat, but on the whole my perambulation was successful.

There was not much money in it, of course, and directly I got a few shillings together I wanted to start off on the Fairs in real earnest. I was still anxious to get out of London for my original reasons, but the main one was because I was determined to become a real palmist and I did not feel like the genuine thing at all while I was knocking about the West End.

I bought another copy of the *World's Fair,* and studied the advertisements.

All sorts of showmen were advertising space, and one of them gave a 'phone number in Ealing. His announcement was in connection with a two-day carnival and gala at Southall. I rang up the showman right away.

"A tent for palmistry?" he said. "Yes, I'll be able

to fix you up. See me on the ground sometime on Friday."

It seemed very simple. I had no idea what the charge would be, but I had three pounds on me and when Friday arrived I set off early, full of big ideas.

It was very hot, and, as it was in the morning and I was wearing evening clothes, I had to don an overcoat. My only opera hat had been completely ruined in a public house some nights previously, so I carried my silk topper in a brown paper bag.

I had little difficulty in finding the show-ground, and when I caught sight of it through the trees I decided to walk back to Southall and buy a couple of cigars. I thought a cigar might be a good introduction to the showman, and when I had bought them I walked around for a bit while I smoked one. A half-smoked cigar would look better, I thought.

Men were still busy building up the roundabouts when I arrived, and although most of the coconut sheets and hoopla tables were ready for business there was no sign of any visitors.

A girl was washing some clothes in a basin which rested on the steps of a living-wagon, and a few people obviously belonging to the show were standing about idly. I approached the girl.

Her slight curiosity she did not attempt to disguise, but she was not very interested. She was perspiring freely, and her attitude towards me, if any, was aggressive.

"Mr. Gay?" she repeated slowly. "It'll be Bill you're after. He's that finger yonder by the machine." She jerked her head towards the roundabout. "Ask any of the lads for the gaffer," she said, and went on with her washing.

The man I wanted was a thick-set, tough-looking fellow with a nose which looked as though it had been trodden on. He was wearing a heavy gold watch-chain, a bowler hat, and a large silk handkerchief, which had once been scarlet, was tied round his neck.

He took the cigar I offered readily enough, but me he regarded with suspicion.

"Yes, I get you," he said. "You were talkin' to me on the telephone at my 'ouse."

He looked me up and down very slowly.

I discovered later that all show people are like that. They are very open in everything they do, and when they see anything that interests them they have a good look at it.

I suppose I must have interested him, for he took plenty of time taking stock of me, pulling at one of his ears as he did so and then rubbing his chin slowly as if he were exceptionally deep in thought. But I do not think he was, really.

"Well, I can fix you up," he said at length. "You can build up yonder by the gate. Where's your joint?"

He eyed my brown paper bag. It seemed to fascinate him.

He was not an easy man to talk with, and it took some time to discover that by a "joint" he meant my tent. I had thought that he was going to supply this, but I was very wrong.

I also discovered that Friday was devoted to building up, and that it would be useless for me to attempt to start business until Saturday.

I had a look round before I left for London, and I thought that they were all going to an unusual amount of trouble just for a one-day show.

I was getting short of funds, but I bought a garden shelter at Gamage's for thirty-five shillings. I also purchased an incense holder, some incense, and a number of eastern trays from Woolworth's, and when I had draped some cloth across the open front of my shelter it made a pretty good fortune-telling booth.

I carried all this paraphernalia along with me to Southall on the following day, together with my silk topper in its brown paper bag, which was getting rather the worse for wear.

I also had a card painted with the single word: "Palmist."

It was the first week in July and one of those days when people walk about with their waistcoats unfastened and some of the more unconventional carry their jackets on their arms.

I sat in my tent for a while, waiting for some one to come in, but I had not allowed for any ventilation, and the sun, shining on the low canvas roof, made it like an oven.

The incense didn't help things either.

At two o'clock the organ on the roundabout started to play, so I decided to have a drink at a hostelry nearby where I had previously borrowed a small table and a couple of chairs.

Several show people were in the bar.

"You're working the tick-off, aren't you?" said one of them, and although I did not know quite what he meant I thought it advisable to agree with him.

It was several drinks later that I discovered that "tick-off" was the fair-ground slang for "fortune-teller."

The show people seemed to be talking a foreign language. They invited me to have a "bevvy" with them and ordered me a drink, and when they suggested we should go back to the fair-ground they said: "I think it's time we scarpered back to the tober now."

Business did not really start until after six o'clock, but at that hour the whole place suddenly became alive. All the showmen on the various side stalls began to shout at the top of their voices, while the organ on the roundabouts seemed to play louder than before.

The whole ground was soon thronged with people, and a party of four girls stopped to ask me my fee.

I had decided to charge a shilling and two-and-sixpence until I knew more about the business, and they all squashed in somehow for a reading.

I discovered later that most palmists insist on having only one person in at a time, but I had had good practice on my pub crawls at reading hands in front of an audience, and as I did not expect much money I did not mind a crowd. The more, the better, I thought.

I did not have to go out again for a long time, because I had a crowd waiting to see me. Most of my customers appeared to be thoroughly satisfied, and some of them decided to have a half-dollar reading when I had told them all I could think of for a shilling.

Towards the end of the evening, when things had quietened down a bit, I counted my money out on the table and I discovered that I had taken exactly four pounds and twelve shillings.

While I was arranging the money in neat little piles two women entered. Their profession would have been obvious to any one, since it was part of their business to make it so. Their clothes were ordinary enough, but, apart from their peculiar make-up, they had a style about them which was recognizable at once.

They both decided to have a half-crown reading to start with, and they asked me if I minded if they smoked.

It was a little difficult to vary the readings sufficiently, as it would have been pretty safe to suggest that both of them had had a broken romance, been married, or should have been, and had experienced difficulties with relatives and home life generally at an early age.

I was getting desperate towards the end of the second woman's reading and I worked off the old story.

"You know, your profession is like mine," I said. "It's been ruined by amateurs."

She laughed. "Cut out the trimmings," she said, "and tell me if you see any money in my hand."

I told her that I saw an unexpected sum of money in the near future, and that although there were so many men in her life that it was difficult to describe him, a man who would be connected with this windfall was then not far away. And I told her a lot of other things as well.

"What's the full strength of your game?" she asked suddenly. "I bet it's a lot of piffle really."

Of course I protested.

"Aren't you satisfied?" I asked.

"Oh, I'm satisfied all right if it comes true," she said. "Tell us some more about the future. Am I going to have a baby?"

Her companion laughed and told her not to be silly.

I pointed out that this eventuality was entirely at her own discretion.

"As a matter of fact," I added, studying her hand, "you should already have had one."

"You're really not at all bad," she said, and after collecting their money I ushered them outside, where we stood talking for a bit.

One girl went off, but her friend remained.

"It's a pretty good game, isn't it?" she said.

"It's all right," I agreed cautiously. "And yours?"

She grinned. "I hope to get that sum of money you talked about. Have a cigarette?"

Show people were still doing fair business, but the rush for my tent was over. People were throwing confetti about, and squirting themselves with water from little tubes they bought from a woman who stood near my tent with a basket of them.

Everybody was too excited and unsettled to bother about the future at this time of the evening. I wondered if I should be in time for a drink and hoped that my late client would depart.

"You know you must meet opportunities halfway," I said. "There's money indicated, all right, if you keep a look-out for it."

She laughed and puffed a cloud of cigarette smoke into my face.

"That's just what I'm doing, love," she said. "So long."

She walked off hurriedly and was soon lost in the crowd. Not a bad sort, I thought. She had treated me as some one on her side of the counter, anyway. I was no longer a customer, a sucker, but one of the great crowd of entertainers.

I stooped down into my booth, and the first thing that caught my eye was a neat rent in the back of the tent. It was just large enough to allow a hand to pass through, and was low down, just out of the radius of light cast by my candle on the table.

I gaped at it for several seconds. My day's takings had vanished.

I swore a good deal, but nobody heard me.

I had two satisfied customers at Southall, anyway, and at least one of my prophecies had come true.

'I was one of the great crowd of entertainers.' A Wild West show at Hull Fair, circa 1930. *National Fairground Archive*

CHAPTER 3

I meet Spike, the Darkie Kid, and spend the night in a boxing booth. I return to London, and, after a dispiriting experience, set out to visit Southend.

M<small>R.</small> GAY, WHO OWNED THE roundabout, and who appeared to be running the whole show, charged me a pound for my day's rent.

I discovered afterwards that this was his usual fee, although I thought it a bit heavy at the time.

Fortune-tellers are usually charged more than any one else on the fair-ground, considering the space they occupy. Realizing that it is a pretty profitable business, several showmen have put their wives in fortune-telling tents, but, generally speaking, "tick-offs" belong to a class of their own and are only just tolerated by the majority of show-ground proprietors.

For a small tent occupying only four feet frontage a tick-off worker often pays more than a man who has twenty feet of shooting range or a darts stall.

The fortune-tellers themselves are probably to blame for this, because they have gradually raised the rents all round by outbidding each other for special positions, and sole rights at some fairs.

Another reason is that the show people, especially at small fairs, are all related to one another, and if an outsider wishes to come in he must pay for it.

"Had a good day?" Mr. Gay inquired when he came to me for my money.

"I can't grumble," I told him.

I lied, of course, but there were times, I decided, when there was nothing to be gained by telling the absolute truth, and this I felt was one of them.

That night I slept in a boxing booth.

With me was a colored boy known as "The Darkie Kid, the Demon of the Ring." Every one called him "Spike," and the others who shared our sleeping quarters considered him their leader.

There were five of us altogether: Spike and myself, a north country boxer and two cockney boys.

I struck up acquaintance with Spike as I was pulling down my joint, and he told me that he had a brother who was working my game somewhere in South Wales.

"You may as well kip in with us tonight," he said, "if you haven't fixed anywhere. We've got a sleeping-wagon, but it's more 'ealthy in the booth this weather. We won't be pulling down till morning."

He did not look older than I was, and showing under his blue jersey were the muscles of a giant. His face was scarred in several places, but these were not at once noticeable because of his black skin.

"I say, that's awfully decent of you," I told him.

I had less than thirty shillings in the world, and it was too late to get back to London that night even had I desired it.

" 'S all right. Pleased to meet you, I'm sure," said Spike. " 'Ave you got a tab on yer?"

The only tabs I knew were connected with the theater, but I discovered later that "tab" is a common name in the north for a cigarette.

Spike made himself clear to me, and, after I had handed him a packet of Gold Flake, we got on very well together.

In the booth that night he tried on my silk hat, and the others agreed that he looked "a right collar and cuff."

This observation seemed to delight them, but Spike was not so pleased.

"No one ain't a collar 'ere," he said. "And if you think a gent's titfer can make me look like a sissy I'll give any one a sock in the lug that'll make 'em look like a blinking dog's dinner."

"Spike's off again," said one of the others sullenly. "Can't you take a joke, Spike?"

"I can allus take anything that's coming to me," replied Spike, looking at him. "And you're getting a ruddy sight too cocky lately."

Then he looked at my clothes and said that he thought my clobber was real dandy.

No one made any comment, and his aggressiveness vanished as quickly as it had come.

Using the cover of my tent as a ground sheet, and my overcoat and everything I could lay my hands on as blankets, I spent my first night under canvas.

"You can't beat the booth this weather," remarked the north country boxer before going to sleep. "There ain't so many jumpers 'ere as in the wagon."

"A jumper'd find you anywhere," said Spike. "They like soft meat."

A few minutes later I heard him snoring.

I was awake at dawn and every one was out and about. I was glad to get up, because, although the others had slept in their clothes, I had taken off my suit, since I wanted to preserve it as much as possible, and it had become cold in the night and I had not slept really soundly.

I was in London before nine o'clock, and London on a Sunday always depressed me. As I sat in one of the little cafés in Old Compton Street which cater to waiters and the foreigners who work in hotels, I tried to decide what to do next.

If I could find somewhere to work six days out of seven, I thought, I should probably earn about thirty pounds a week.

This sounded all right, and, since I had little more than a pound on me, the more I thought of it the better it sounded.

At a news-agent's opposite, whose window was occupied mostly with cards advertising rooms to let, and who seemed to stock every publication from *La Vie Parisienne* to *The Catholic Times,* I bought a copy of the *World's Fair* and again studied the paper.

There were so many fairs advertised that I found it difficult to choose among them. Now and again I read "Tick-offs need not apply," and I presumed that some one had already obtained the sole rights. But this was probably quite wrong.

A week's fair advertised to open the following day at Dartford appealed to me. This was no doubt because I had never been to Dartford.

That afternoon I walked through what I thought must be one of the biggest fair-grounds in the country.

It reminded me of Barnet, which I had visited as a punter years earlier.

Huge canvas coverings hid most of the attractions from me, but quite a dozen enormous roundabouts occupied the most prominent positions, and nearly fifty island stalls were ranged around them.

On either side of the fair-ground was a wall of side attractions, and at the far end I found the living-wagons.

"There's no room," the head man told me when I approached him.

"But I only want about six feet somewhere," I protested.

He looked at me for a fraction of a second and then turned his back and walked towards his wagon.

"There's no room for *you*," he repeated, but he did not turn to see if I had heard him.

I had, though, and I decided that there was nothing to do but to move on.

I discovered later that he was a fairly big man on the Showmen's Guild, and all Guild members had agreed not to have fortune-tellers on their grounds. They were not supposed to have any one who was not a member of the Guild, and as fortune-tellers could not become members it was a case of "Tick-offs need not apply."

Fortunately for me, however, all showmen were not so loyal to their society. Some of them preferred gelt to the guild, "gelt," I found out later, being the general term for money.

I did not know all this then, but I saw that to work

six days a week on the fairs was not as easy as I had imagined.

So when I saw a space for palmistry in a fun arcade at Southend advertised in the *World's Fair*, I set off to Fenchurch Street to book a ticket.

The train was crowded. The other people in my compartment looked like day trippers, although this could hardly have been so, since it was a late Sunday train. They were probably all people off for their summer holidays, and I regarded them all as prospective customers. They looked charming to me.

They were a noisy, good-natured crowd, full of their own affairs, but decidedly matey.

When the train jerked forward on leaving the London station we all swayed forward in perfect unity, since we were so completely wedged together.

The men might all have belonged to the same family, although they had probably never seen each other before.

There were four of them, and they wore rather creased blue serge suits, while two had very pointed and uncomfortable-looking light brown boots. All were rather bewildered-looking little men. Three were wearing silver watch-chains on which hung two or more shield-shaped medals, which I felt convinced they deserved.

There were a number of children. These sucked oranges, fingered large brown paper parcels, and struggled continuously to get away from where they happened to be at any given moment.

The women who belonged to the men were without exception very large, very hot and very tired. Now and again they appeared to wake up, and suddenly shook, spanked or kissed one of the orange suckers according to the demands of the occasion.

Although none of them would probably come my way again, they all looked like people who were out to have a good time and who would certainly have to have their fortunes told during the holiday. To be among them was exhilarating. It was a holiday train.

As we left the suburbs of London behind us the little men became more assertive and much more confident. They looked more important, or rather as if they felt more important, and they explained the various things which could be seen from the carriage windows to the excited children and not very interested women.

I was glad I was on this train. We were all off on an adventure.

'That night I slept in a boxing booth.' Boxers at Nottingham Goose Fair
National Fairground Archive

CHAPTER 4

I meet an unpleasant woman, am gently rebuffed at a large hotel, and find a new friend with a mug-faker; he tells me his sad history. I take several sea trips.

MISS BLOUNT WAS MY landlady at Southend. Her smile was mechanical, and whenever it appeared she displayed an eighth of an inch of pinkness between her teeth and her lips which her dentist had optimistically intended to represent gums.

Her hair, too, looked as if it were false. She took me in to oblige, and wanted my money in advance.

The room in many ways resembled her. It was stuffy, yet managed to be cold although we were in the height of summer. The wallpaper was faded, and, apart from a rather unpleasant conception of The Crucifixion and one other picture of a small girl grasping an unhappy kitten round its middle, there was little attempt at decoration.

Oilcloth covered the floor, and the only chair was a basket affair which was none too safe and not at all comfortable. The place was very dusty. Smuts speckled the wash-basin and a collection of grit had silted up the bottom of the water jug. The lace curtains were passably clean, but they looked mournful and suggested the respectability which is associated with uncharitableness.

I was not critical, though. I was tired and I wanted somewhere to sleep. I was honest enough to tell Miss Blount that I did not know the length of my stay, so she made me pay three nights' rent in advance. I gave her twelve shillings, which was very nearly all I possessed, and was soon in bed and asleep.

But this was not for long. I woke with an unpleasant irritation on my chin and it seemed that some sort of rash had broken out on my neck and on the small of my back. It was not until I felt something crawling on my neck that I got out of bed and lit a candle.

I soon discovered the trouble. It was the first time I had ever seen this variety of insect, but when I pulled back the bedclothes and threw aside the pillow I felt my education on the subject was complete.

It was a wretched night, and even after I lay down at the foot of the bed with my overcoat as a covering I didn't get much rest.

In the morning I interviewed Miss Blount and had time to observe her better.

She was middle-aged, shapely in the wrong places, and had arrayed herself in a brown satin frock which was covered with lace and decorated with innumerable little brown beads.

As soon as I saw her in this costume I was reminded of my visitors of the previous night. There was something very evil and unpleasant about her, I thought.

"I say," I said, "I don't like to mention this, but your bed isn't clean."

I was angry, but also I was acutely embarrassed.

"Not clean?" she repeated, looking at me as though I had pinched her leg or tried to smack that part of her body which protruded most. "What exactly do you mean, young man? My beds are all spotlessly clean. I'm most particular who I have in my house . . . as a rule," she added as an afterthought.

"Well, there are bugs in the bed," I blurted out, now thoroughly fed up with the whole business.

"Bugs?" echoed the offensive old woman. "Bugs in my beds? Good gracious, what next!"

She walked over and threw back the clothes.

"I can't see anything. I think you must have been mistaken. I've never had a complaint like this before. Why, I have all the very best people in my house; people who come to me year after year. Only last week I had two of the leading performers from the theater."

I began to dislike the woman intensely and I disliked her bed.

"Well, there are all sorts of performers," I said rudely. "What did they perform with? Fleas?"

I think she disliked me too. Her face was flushed and I thought she was going to hit me.

"I'm not going to be insulted in my own house," she said, raising her voice and getting very short of breath. "How dare you! I've been in this house for twenty years, and never, never in all my life have I been treated like this. If there's anything in that bed you brought it in with you. I should have known better than to take you in last night. This is a respectable house and it's a clean house—spotlessly clean."

I had an old Gladstone bag and she pounced on this suspiciously.

"That's where they get," she said. "People like you carry them about in their luggage."

She walked over to the bed again and had another look.

"It's clean—perfectly clean," she said defiantly.

"Well, I wish you'd sleep in it tonight," I told her.

Miss Blount swung round to face me. Her bosom heaved and for some reason she kept her mouth shut. The heavy breathing through her nose made a terrifying sound. Her personality, unpleasant as it was, rather overpowered me.

"You common, common man," she said at last, and walked out of the room.

Quite unconsciously, I seemed to have given her an opportunity to make some sort of dignified exit, and of course she had not missed it.

A few minutes later the maid, a poor timid little creature, tapped at my door.

"Miss Blount will require this room today, sir," she said, and looked at the bed in terrified fascination.

"Tell Miss Blount that I require twelve shillings before I go," I said.

As it was the only money I possessed it seemed important.

I packed the things I had with me, although most of my luggage I had left at the station.

It was some time before the little maid returned to tell me that Miss Blount would see me downstairs.

It was not a pleasant interview, although I was greeted with one of Miss Blount's smiles, but she certainly knew more about beds, bugs and lodgers than I did, and as long as she did not give me an opportunity to lose my temper I was at a distinct disadvantage.

Eventually I agreed to accept eight shillings, and Miss Blount and the other occupants of her house passed out of my life.

Even though my experience of the fortune-telling business was small I realized that the position advertised in the amusement arcade was no good to me as soon as I set eyes on it.

The arcade was an empty shop in which a number of automatic machines had been installed. Moreover, it was situated in the poorest part of the town and at some considerable distance from the main thoroughfare.

Most of a fortune-teller's clients are women, and I very much doubted if any of the sex would even visit the place.

It was early when I called, but the place was so small that it could not hold many people at the best of times and it obviously catered to youths about eighteen years old.

I was offered a position here for three pounds a week, but I did not take it.

I had only a few shillings in the world, and something had to be done. I was dressed in full evening kit and I was wearing my topper. My overcoat I had left with my luggage at the station. The weather was ideal. It was one of those July days when the sea is a real attraction.

I wandered along the front and reviewed the past few days. I had not made much progress, although somehow I felt that I had only to hit on the right idea when everything would be all right and I should be able to make up for lost time.

When I found myself near the Palace Hotel I decided to see if I could do any business there. I asked to see the manager, and, waiting in the reception hall, tried to look as little self-conscious as possible.

This was not easy, because the place was crowded with young people in white flannels and tennis frocks, and my evening clothes, although immaculate, were decidedly out of place.

The manager approached me, looked hurriedly around him, and invited me to go with him to his office without asking me my business.

I had difficulty in keeping up with him; he almost ran.

"Now what can I do for you, sir?" he said when the door of his office closed behind us.

He looked at my clothes and smiled broadly. He seemed to be less agitated, and looked like a man who is about to perform some service which he knows he will enjoy.

I was not feeling too good. I had decided to walk into the hotel on the spur of the moment and I had kept walking in spite of a temptation to turn back. I think if I had had any money I would have booked a room and had my things sent on from the station, but of course I had very little more than my eight shillings, and I had to say something.

"I'm a professional palmist," I said, talking very quickly. "I wonder if you would care for me to entertain your guests? I see you have a thé-dansant this afternoon. I thought I might sit at one of the tables, where they could consult me if they liked."

The manager was a very decent sort of fellow. He was not much over thirty, and, although wearing a black jacket and striped trousers, was not really conventional. He seemed to have hit on the same idea of a uniform which had occurred so happily to me.

He was surprised, but he still smiled.

"I don't think you'd do much good here, old man," he said at length. "Besides, I'm only the manager. I couldn't possibly give you permission."

But I was not kicked out—that was the main thing —although he did show me out of a side entrance.

We shook hands warmly when I left and I went on feeling quite encouraged.

But more or less the same thing happened at the Queen's at Westcliff and at a number of private hotels. Here people wanted to make appointments. These were all for several days hence, and although I booked them they were not of much use, for of course it was the ready cash I needed.

It was afternoon by the time I had exhausted my hotel idea, and I was feeling a little weary. I was back in the neighborhood of the Kursaal at Southend, and, attracted by a large public house, I decided to have a drink and see if I could do the same sort of thing that I had done in London.

Outside in the road a lot of women were dancing and making a tremendous amount of noise with rattles and toy trumpets. They wore paper hats and were singing at the top of their voices.

Inside it was even more boisterous, and it was some

time before I could edge my way to the bar. I thought it hardly necessary to ask the permission of the publican, and, when I had had a drink, I approached a group who were standing near me.

"What's that, love?" one of the women cried. "You want to tell me fortune? 'Ere, what're you going to stand us?"

"That's right," shouted another. "Stand us a drink and we'll tell you everything you want to know."

She then seized my hat and tried to put it on her friend's head. Some one else flung her arms round me and told me we were dancing.

It soon dawned upon me that telling fortunes in public houses was not the idea in Southend. There were far too many other attractions, and fortune-telling was no novelty.

I got away as quickly as I could and ordered another drink in a different part of the house.

Next to me was a small man with a large camera. It was one of those things which take old-fashioned tin-type photographs while you wait.

"This is real 'oliday beer," he said, putting down his half-empty glass and wiping his hand across his lips. "There's one 'op to a pint of water, but I suppose it's good enough for these bastards."

He emptied the glass and then looked at me again.

"You in the Kursaal?" he asked.

"No, I haven't fixed anywhere really. I'm working the tick-off," I told him, wondering if he would know what I meant.

"Well, if you ain't fixed I'll tell you something for nothing. Get out o' Southend just as soon as you can.

Of all the bloomin' carsies I've ever struck, this 'ere takes some beating. They ain't got a sausage, son, not a sausage. I've taken more in a couple of hours on a Sunday in the rag market than I'd take here in a couple of weeks. Gawd blimey, I've known the time when I could take a couple of quid as easy as kiss yer 'and with this 'ere mug faker of mine."

I then discovered that a "mug faker" was the general term for a camera or any one who works it. It also appeared that "smudge" was another word for photograph.

He turned away from me for a minute to order a drink and then continued breathlessly.

"Why, I've took more money in a cemetery than I 'ave 'ere," he said with a seriousness which demanded belief. "'Ere I've been workin' for thrummers. Threepence a smudge! Can you beat that? O' course, as you know, you have to drop the bat a bit round the Smoke these days. When I get away I 'ope to work for denars, and when you get bobs they soon mount up. But you can't get sprasers 'ere. Believe me, you can't *give* the smudges away! The place is beat. 'Ere I've been, working all the bleedin' morning for a few lousy bob. I ask you, what can you take in thrummers?"

"No, you can't take much," I agreed wisely, and wondered what he was talking about.

I gathered that a "thrummer" meant threepence and that a "denar" was a shilling.

Some time later I found out a lot more about this language. A penny is a "clod," and "sprasy" means sixpence. A shilling is also a "hole," and a two-shilling-piece is a "two-ender." A half-crown is a "tosheroon" and a pound is a "phunt," a "bar" or a "nicker." A ten-shilling-note is a "half-bar" or "half a nicker." A fiver is a "flim" and a tenner is referred to as a "cockernen."

"The Smoke," I had early discovered, meant London.

"I'm back to the Smoke tonight," said the little man, "and those who want Southend can stick it exactly where they like, for all I care."

"So you don't think I'll do much good in the public houses or hotels with my line?" I said.

"Wot? Workin' the tick-off?" he said. "You won't take chicken's food. I can lurk with this 'ere thing of mine—I 'ave to lurk. In fact I've bin on the move all the ruddy mornin'. But it's not worth a light for me, and it's just not on for the tick-off. You must 'ave a tent or something, and even then you'd catch a dead shice if you stalled round here. They 'aven't got it, son. They 'aven't got a coal.

"I'll tell you what 'appened to me today," he added, suddenly confiding. "I was stallin' by the entrance to the Kursaal there and was 'opin' to pull up a few couples as they went in. You know the old business . . . free of charge and all that. Get 'em to stand still and leave the rest to me. I bungs 'em a frame in their mitts and before they know what's 'appenin' they're reefing for their gelt and smilin' for the picture."

He paused and eyed me.

"Well, I was 'angin' round with me blinks open when suddenly a chara [charabanc] drives up. They look all right-un's to me. I always likes a chara load.

Just arrived and no chance to 'ave spent their gelt. There they were, sittin' there quiet-like, just as any one could wish for. I gave 'em the how-d'ye-do and a tick-tacking like, and I got the camera set."

He sighed.

"They all grinned and nodded and I thought I was going to 'ave a burster. I took over twenty smudges as quick as kiss yer 'and, and as I took 'em I bunged a frame in their mitts so as they wouldn't scarper before I got their dough. But none of them attempted to shift. They sat there in the chara and grinned 'appily away.

"You wouldn't think I could miss, would you?" he said, stopping for a moment in his story. "There they were, just arrived and all together. What a souvenir of their day's outin', I told them. I knew that as soon as I'd got the first one hooked they'd all naturally follow. I ought to be kicked right round this town."

He was silent while he took a long drink.

"You ought to kick me. Kick me right in the pants."

He spoke with such earnestness that I half wondered if he expected me to take him at his word. Finally he sighed and finished the story.

"It was not until I'd taken over twenty smudges that the driver thought it time to tell me that the whole bunch of 'em was a lot of barmies from some loony bin somewhere.

"'Ere, 'ave a drink," he added recklessly. "They say grafters end in the loony bin and I ain't sure if I ain't on the way there meself. Thirty years on the road with a mug faker and I come to Southend and graft to a bunch of grinnin' Lakes o' Killarney."

It was a pathetic tale, I thought; the sort of thing that might easily have happened to me. It cheered me up somehow.

When I left the public house and the little man, who mournfully assured me that he was "going stone-lakes" and that I really ought to kick him, I walked towards the sea.

I had no particular reason for doing this, and I was beginning to wonder if my best plan would be to start walking to London.

I reviewed the situation.

Here was I, clad in full evening kit, standing on the esplanade at Southend of all places in the height of a blazing summer's day. I had six and fourpence in the world, and I had not eaten. Something had to be done and done immediately. Fortunately at this point I had a happy idea.

My attention was attracted by a large man in a blue jersey, who made the observation to myself and any one else who might be in earshot that it was a lovely day for a sail.

As a matter of fact, it was a motor launch in which he was trying to interest us, but this did not seem to matter.

Quite a number of people were sitting in the boat, and, according to the man in the jersey, one of the finest trips on the east coast was about to take place.

There was a cabin-like arrangement in the middle of the boat which I supposed contained the motor, and around this was seating accommodation for about thirty people. They sat facing the sea, and at the moment they appeared to find this very interesting.

I discovered that the trip took about half an hour, and I felt that after they had once got out to sea there would not be much for them to do. I saw them all as prospective clients.

There were several men in blue jerseys about, but the one who had first attracted my attention appeared to be in charge.

I told him that I proposed to tell people's fortunes during the trip and offered him half my takings if he would permit me to do this.

"You won't do any good," he said. "I've had to reduce my price to a shilling from two bob, but you can have a try if you like."

This was good enough for me. There were far too many counter-attractions on the shore, I felt; but here, in an open boat with no possible chance of escape and with little to keep the punters' minds occupied, I decided I had a chance.

"Here's Lord Muck himself," shouted a young woman good-naturedly as I walked up the plank, only just preventing my silk topper from being carried into the sea by a gentle gust of wind.

"Be yourself," another woman told her, but, seeing that I was anxious to be matey, she laughed a little uneasily and called to me, "Are you going to play to us? Where's your instrument?"

A number of people laughed at this sally.

"Where d'you think he keeps his instrument?" said one.

They were a vulgar and good-natured crowd.

"Ladies," I said, beaming at them, "I have come at the special request of the Captain. I am here to tell your fortunes, and the ridiculous fee I charge is just one shilling."

I handed my cards to a number of them and returned their jokes in the best way I could.

"I'm here to help you," I said with the firmness and conviction of desperation, "and I want you to understand that I accept my fee after the reading and not before. Only satisfied clients need pay. Now I believe I can help *you*," I said to the most likely-looking woman among them.

She was a jovial, happy old soul with a bottle of Guinness in her lap.

I then seized her hand.

I made it an exceptionally long reading, and the others, who crowded round to listen, acted as useful prompters.

Fortunately she was satisfied when I had finished and paid over her bob quite happily.

She set an excellent example and others decided to follow.

When I told one woman that there was a man in her life who was not to be trusted, a curious expression came over her face, but I think she was only feeling a little seasick.

We were some distance from the shore now and the water was getting choppy. Swaying over my client, with my topper pulled well over my ears and my head bent down, I did not feel too good either. The tails of my jacket flapped in the breeze, and at times I had to rest on my client's shoulders to keep my balance.

Most of the women appeared to have a supply of alcohol, and one of them offered me a drink of beer out of her bottle, but although I did not wish to offend her I did not feel like it at all. I had not had much to eat that day and I am not a very good sailor.

They were good spenders, however, and I was certainly a great success. Quite apart from fortune-telling I think they enjoyed my company and laughed at me the whole time.

We were now heading towards the shore, but we had a long distance to go and I thought I would have time for two or three more readings.

"You are about to have a surprise," I told one woman, but I never explained what this was.

It was unfortunate that I was the only one who was seasick, for I could hardly expect any one to be sympathetic. It had only needed something like this to happen to make every one else thoroughly enjoy the outing, but it was not good publicity.

It is impossible to retain one's dignity when one is hanging over the side of a boat, and a top hat is apt to look ridiculous.

I did not tell any more fortunes on that trip, and when we landed I had taken eight shillings. I offered the man in charge half of this, but he told me to give one of his men a drink instead.

I had a talk with this man and we came to an arrangement. I was to give him two shillings every time I made a trip.

It worked very well, and I had over thirty shillings on me at the end of the day.

CHEAPJACK   43

Some of the trips were quite fruitless, however, and I decided that there was not much of a future for me at Southend.

My luggage was at the station. That night I bought a ticket for London.

The view from Pier Hill, Southend, late 1920s.
Southend Central Museum

The *Princess Maud*, an excursion vessel off Southend, *circa* 1930.
www.simplonpc.co.uk

CHAPTER 5

I return to London, where I observe some ladies of the town. I meet a man with a cat in his bonnet.

At about three o'clock on the following morning I sat in a café overlooking the stage door of a West End theater. Here one could get beans on toast, a mug of coffee and a decent-sized helping of apple pudding for a shilling.

Besides, it was a convenient resting-place.

Twelve customers made the room crowded, and at this time of the morning there were usually quite twenty people in the place.

You bought your food at the counter and paid for it when you got it.

People strolled in, exchanged a few words with some one they knew, and left without buying anything. No one hurried over his food and some sat for hours behind an empty cup while they argued and talked more or less amicably with those around them.

As long as there was no fighting the proprietor seemed perfectly happy.

At this hour most of the customers were women, and the men present comprised taxi-drivers and the peculiar kind of man you see standing at the corners of Lisle

Street and Shaftesbury Avenue. Every one appeared to know every one else.

Some of the women gave money to the men who were not taxi-drivers, paid for their food and told them not to spill anything on their clothes.

The steam on the window which overlooked the street prevented any one outside from seeing in, and the door was kept tightly closed. It was a warm, noisy little place, and the few women who had really expensive clothes and whose hair had been cared for with the utmost attention made a sharp contrast with the others, whose finery was tousled and whose faces and figures seemed to have grown frayed and untidy with their clothes.

Even here there was a little class distinction. However, the majority of the women were friendly enough among themselves, and it was mostly jealousy which caused the arguments.

As I sat there eating, a man whose body was twisted and who carried a large suitcase with the utmost difficulty, shuffled into the shop. He was stone deaf and could not talk very well either.

Every one glanced at the door as it opened and then turned away again.

The new arrival looked at me inquiringly, and presently sat down timidly at my table. But he sat there for only a moment, because one of the women in the opposite corner beckoned him and he went over eagerly, dragging his bag.

I was interested to see its contents, and when he opened it I saw he had silk stockings in it and a miscellaneous collection of ladies' underwear.

The women examined these carefully and handed them round.

"This is just what you were asking about the other night," he said very politely to a woman who was seated near him as he handed her some flimsy garment.

She turned it over.

"How much?"

The woman who had first beckoned him repeated the question in his ear, but he did not seem to hear her and handed her a pencil and a piece of paper.

Several women bought stockings, and one of the men gave him a cup of tea.

"Tell him I'll pay him early next week," one of the women shouted. "That'll be thirty-two bob I owe him."

"He can leave mine over till tomorrow," said another.

It was all rather like the Beggars' Opera.

As the little twisted figure shuffled towards the door he smiled at me. He seemed quite contented, and doubtless knew his customers.

After I had handed my card to the man behind the counter and explained my business to him, I approached a table, and before I left the café less than half an hour later I had told thirteen fortunes and taken thirteen shillings.

Those who had not the money borrowed it from their friends, and although one of them remarked casually that she was not going home until she had got her rent, she gave me a shilling readily.

I do not think it was because she particularly wanted

her fortune told, although the idea greatly appealed to them all. But she did not think in shillings.

I was convinced that their profession was only so extraordinarily unsatisfactory because they invariably got such poor value for their money. I told one of them this, but I don't think she knew what I was talking about. She wanted to know if there was any love in her hand, and she was very serious, poor woman.

I had previously booked my old room in New Compton Street for a few days, and as I was turning the corner from the Charing Cross Road a man stopped me. He asked me for a light, and, after I had given it to him, did not seem in a hurry to walk on.

I wondered if he was going to ask me for the price of a night's lodging, although there was not much of the down-and-out about him.

"Been on a spree?" he asked at length, looking at my clothes and smiling in a rather superior fashion.

I told him I had hardly been on a spree, and, having answered him so much, I thought I might as well inquire what he had been doing.

He smiled. "Oh, I've been to Jimmy's club," he said. "I work there."

But what his work was I never discovered.

"I don't like it," he continued. "I'm fed to the teeth with the game. Not married? Well, you're lucky. Women are all right so long as they're married to some one else. You're sorry for them until you know them, and when that happens it's usually too late and you're too darned busy being sorry for yourself."

I was tired, but it required a certain amount of

effort to walk away, so I remained listening to him. He seemed so anxious to talk.

"My wife's a bad woman gone to the good," he said. "That's what you'd call her. Has it occurred to you that if women weren't so damned changeable there wouldn't be half the trouble in the world? They don't know their own minds for two minutes together. D'you know what I've learnt about women?—and I've known a few of them in my time."

I told him I had no idea.

"Nothing," he said. "Absolutely nothing. No one can understand women, and they don't understand themselves. They don't want to."

I decided that there was not much to be gained by standing at the corner of the road hearing his views on women, and I made an effort to go. But he stopped me.

"D'you see that cat over there?" he said suddenly.

I did see a cat. It was hanging round the doorway of a house opposite, but there was nothing very unusual about it.

"She's always there when I leave the club," he explained. "This is about her time. Still looking for mugs, I suppose. What a life! I'm fed to the teeth, as I told you. She wasn't a bad kid when she was alive. I knew her well. The girls called her Dolly, and she was a decent enough woman in her own way. But she died quite young—T.B., you know."

I felt slightly uneasy and looked at him more carefully than I had done before. I had knocked into all sorts of cranks in this part of the world, but there was nothing very unusual in his appearance.

"Are you still talking about that cat?" I asked him.

"Yes," he replied casually. "That's Dolly, all right. There ought to be another of 'em around here somewhere."

He looked up and down the street.

"I wonder what's happened to her tonight?" he said. "There's usually a big sandy-colored cat who walks this beat. She was known as Big Bertha before she died. That was a few years ago. It's interesting to think I used to know most of the cats who walk around here now."

"What are you talking about?" I said as I gradually got his idea. "A sort of transmigration of souls?"

"That's right," he said. "When they die they turn into cats. Why, you've only got to look at a cat to see that. Look at Dolly over there. She's loitering, just like she always used to. You never see her going anywhere in particular."

He seemed completely in earnest.

"I ask you," he said reasonably, "have you ever seen a cat setting off on a walk like a dog or any other respectable animal? If you will keep a cat it likes to lie in front of a fire, and if you want any affection from it you've got to be fussing it the whole time. You can hit a dog and he'll still obey you; but try that on a cat. Feed them and fuss them and they'll purr at you. They'll let you fondle them, but only on sufferance. They know that you appreciate the privilege of stroking them without them scratching. But tread on their tail—quite accidentally, you understand—and they spit and hiss like a live woman. They're cunning, too, and they know how to look after themselves. Let a dog loose in London and in a couple of days he'll be the most wretched, ill-cared-for little blighter in the world. But a cat'll be all right."

He looked across the road.

"You'll always see them about at night," he said. "They often prowl about in pairs, and whenever you see them they're never going anywhere in particular. Look at Dolly now," he continued. "She'll come up to you and rub herself against your leg if you walk over to her, and she'll look up at you all friendly and inviting; but push her aside ever so gently and she'll spring away and call you all the names she can lay her tongue to. That's women all over. Thank God they're not just a little different or we'd never be able to do anything with 'em. I'll give them their due: they're dead clever. But if they had just a little something else they'd rule the whole damned world."

The idea of this seemed to make him shiver, and probably realizing for the first time that we were getting very cold standing there at that time of the morning, he showed signs of going.

"Let's have another light before I go," he said, and placed the end of his cigarette against mine. "Good night," he said. "You never know; we may share the same kennel one day."

CHAPTER 6

I spend August Bank Holiday at Hunslet Feast, where I find a friend in a bowler hat. I meet my first gypsies, and am led into a dissertation on my friend Ezra Boss, head of his tribe.

O<small>N AUGUST BANK HOLIDAY</small> I was in Leeds. I had arrived there a few days before, after spending a fortnight in London, where I had managed to save a few pounds earned in cafés and public houses while I gradually got together a complete rigout for the Road.

I was working at Hunslet Feast, which is held on the outskirts of Leeds. There were a number of fortune-tellers there, and we made a curious mixture. Some of them were gypsies working from their caravans. Others, sitting at the openings of their tents, fed their babies and called to the passers-by that they had lucky faces and that they had only to step inside to discover all that the future held.

Prince Bullayow was there also. He was a short, fat-faced, smiling man who wore a wide-brimmed Stetson which seemed far too big for him. He was colored, and in that part of the country this is an advantage.

I was not on the fair-ground itself, but had a small stand near the entrance. It was a good position.

Next to me was another male fortune-teller. I never knew his exact nationality, but thought it possible that it was a mixture of some of the finest races in the the world. His skin was dark and one of his eyes was permanently closed.

I was eager to get on with every one, and we made friends.

The name over his tent was "Professor Ali Singh," but he told me he was known as Sammy York. He did not speak English very well, and it surprised me that his clients knew at all what he was talking about. It is quite possible, of course, that they didn't, for I know that he spoke particularly badly if any one asked him a question which he found difficult.

He was not a very successful worker. Apart from a turban, which he wore while engaged in his business, he adopted no kind of uniform and his clothes were shabby and unclean. His linen was frankly dirty and there were holes in his shirt where the points of his collar rubbed against it.

When he was not working he wore a bowler hat.

"You know, you're rather conspicuous at the best of times," I said. "Why don't you always wear your turban? It would create a better impression on the people who recognize you in the street."

But he never saw this. I could never make him see that much of the success gained by Prince Bullayow, the tipster, was attributable to his habit of wearing his striking costume the whole time.

However, I wasn't going to fall out with a man over a bowler hat, and we got along pretty well for a time.

I took a great deal of trouble over my clothes. It

was my aim to look smarter than the people who patronized me, and the fact that I was working in a particularly mean neighborhood, among people who regarded clothes as coverings and little else, made me all the more fastidious about my own appearance.

I had great trouble in getting my boiled shirts properly laundered, but the trouble was worth it. My "clobber," as the grafters called it, was part of my show, and my immaculate evening clothes were something of an attraction at Hunslet Feast.

Some of the fortune-tellers were offering to read people's hands for sixpence, but I did not reduce my price. I did not take a lot of money. The majority of people who visited the fair seemed very poor. They were also far more simple and illiterate than my London clients had been.

It was a four-day affair, and I had plenty of time to look about me.

While their women were telling fortunes, the male members of the gypsy families appeared to have nothing to do. When the caravans arrived on the ground they had known at once where to build up their tents, for they visited this fair every year and occupied the same positions.

But if there were any arrangements to be made with the roundabouts proprietor in reference to the ground, the women saw to it.

Among the gypsies, the woman earns the money and she is very content. They seemed to me to have every right to perfect happiness, for whereas they are invariably quick-witted and talkative, the men are slow thinkers and very seldom mix in any company but their own.

A gypsy woman does not appear to expect much from her husband. He should be able to give her children and fight for her if necessary. Both these things he usually does very well.

While the fair was on, these men lounged about in groups, smoking whenever they were given a cigarette and adding a certain picturesqueness to the scene, for although their clothes were shabby most of them wore brightly colored mufflers, while a number wore earrings and had colored buttons sewed on their jackets.

I walked through the fair-ground during that slack interval when most people are having tea.

"Bit 'ard, aren't they?" said a woman who was standing at the entrance to her fortune-telling tent. She looked under thirty, and the whiteness of her teeth was accentuated by her dark skin. A brightly colored shawl covered her shoulders, and beneath this she wore a tightly fitting dress of some black material. Her figure was attractive and her eyes made you forget to notice any other part of her face. They were bold and really flashing, and they looked upon the world with confidence.

"They are a bit hard today," I agreed, and stopped to talk to her.

"Yes. There's not much money about this year," she said. "Dook reading isn't what it used to be. You've got to tell the tale for your money these days. Are you on your tod?"

I gathered that she was asking me if I was on my own.

"Yes, I'm working alone here," I told her, "and I'm not married, if that's what you mean."

I noticed that her manner had become slightly uneasy, and, glancing behind me, I saw a number of men watching us idly.

They were gypsies, and when they were only a few paces away they stood watching in silence. They made no attempt to disguise what they were doing, and remained perfectly silent and continued to watch, their faces expressionless.

"Funny you not being married," she said, ignoring the others. "And you working the tick-off too."

I had already decided not to pretend that I had been working the fairs long. I knew I should not be believed. I stuck to my original story that I had been a fortune-teller at a London night club.

I told her this, and it appeared to explain everything. Apparently I had been puzzling her before, but now there was no sign of bewilderment.

I guessed this information about myself would be rapidly passed round the fair-ground, and I was glad she had spoken to me.

"It's as much as I can do to keep myself, let alone any one else," I told her, expecting her not to believe me.

But she evidently knew more about my occupation than I did, and I think she took me at my word.

"You might find some one to help," she replied quickly, smiling and displaying her teeth. "You never know, you know."

I glanced at the name above her tent.

"I'll keep a lookout for one," I said politely.

But before she had time to reply I was suddenly reminded of the gypsies behind me. They had begun to talk rapidly in Romany, a language I could not understand. As they talked they looked at me and it was obvious that I was the subject of their conversation.

The feeling one has when people talk about one openly and yet go to the trouble of hiding from you what they are saying is unpleasant.

Bidding the lady good-by as casually as possible, I walked off, quickening my pace and resisting the temptation to look behind me, but later on in the day I made friends with the group and we got on very well together. Before the end of the fair they accepted me as a not unpleasant oddity and talked quite openly in my company.

The gypsies are a suspicious race, and although the majority of the womenfolk have been quick to adapt themselves to the habits and manners of the people with whom they mix, the men, being slower in everything they do, are still very simple and less quick to understand the changes which have taken place on the fair-ground during the past half-century. But once their confidence is gained they are very loyal, and far less ready to turn against a friend than are their wives.

"We don't take to every one and we ain't naturally mixers," Ezra, the head of the tribe, said to me one day. "But when we do take to any one we takes to 'em."

He was a small man, and he talked with great seriousness, his peculiarly dark brown eyes looking earnestly into mine.

"I've sort of took to you," he said simply.

Although I considered I knew him pretty well when this happened, I felt a little embarrassed. People do not talk like this on a fair-ground as a rule, and for a moment I wondered what his ulterior motive might be.

But it was impossible to doubt his genuineness for long, and although very serious, he, too, was a little embarrassed.

"You know, our people are spread all over the country," he continued with a touch of pride, "and I can always lay me hand on about a hundred people at short notice who'd do anything I tell 'em."

He paused for a moment, but never took his eyes off mine.

"We're simple people," he continued rather apologetically; and I hurriedly contradicted him.

"Well, we ain't exactly eddicated, to your way of thinking, I suppose," he said. "I can't read or write, and there's a lot of things I don't know. But—well, I'd always like to help you if I could. If ever you're in any bother or find yourself in a hole somewhere, just let me know and we'll all see as you're all right."

Any one who has traveled alone on the fair-grounds will realize what this meant. To be promised the support of a powerful family like the Bosses was something of which to be proud, and I was not slow to appreciate it.

"I shall keep you to your word, Mr. Boss," I said, shaking his hand solemnly. "And if ever I can be of any little service to you I know you'll approach me."

He was a happier man when it was over. His speech had probably been on his mind for some time, and his face now wrinkled into a smile and he breathed deeply, as a man who has just regained freedom.

"I think this calls for a bevvy," I said, and we walked off to the nearest pub together.

It was after several drinks that Ezra referred again to his family affairs.

"You know, we never bothered much about eddication," he said. "We never really needed it in them days. But I'm bringing up me chavvies all proper like. You know my little Sarah? She can read books and tell timepieces as quick as most eddicated people. I can't read meself, but I'm making them all move with the times as much as possible. It was all right when we only mixed along with ourselves," he went on a little wistfully. "But since we've gone among other people we're getting more civilized, as you might say."

He looked at me sharply.

"You know, I made my old people get married only t'other back end. We were at Hull, and I was having a bit of a barney with a man there, when he ups and calls me a bastard. Of course I chinned him—I couldn't help meself. But, as me brother David pointed out to me afterwards, this 'ere finger called me a bastard—and he was right.

"Of course he shouldn't have said it," said Ezra, looking at me for support. "But it didn't sort of put me in the right, exactly. So I put a stop to all that. We made all the old people get properly spliced, and I was hitched up meself, according to real religion, soon afterwards."

After this meeting I didn't see Ezra for several months, since I "jumped" to the south, but I was glad I had talked to him.

Ezra Boss was a man who kept his word.

CHAPTER 7

I go to Bradford with Sammy York. We visit Whitby. I meet the Little Major, Doncaster Jock and Sheeny Louie. Parny on the Tober. I am initiated into the mysteries of the R.O. and have leisure to observe the London Mob. I go to Sleights, where I find a different punter.

I LEFT LEEDS WITH SAMMY York and we followed the fair to Bradford. He told me that I had been paying too much for my lodgings, and for ten shillings we booked a room for a week.

We had to share a double bed, but the place was clean enough and the landlady cooked any food we cared to bring in without any extra charge.

We did not stay for our full week, however, as business was not too good at Bradford and Sammy said that we could not afford to waste time during August.

On the Sunday we caught an excursion to Whitby Bay. Whitby regatta took place on the following day, and Sammy thought it was well worth a visit. I was on for anything, and glad to get away from the sordidness of our surroundings.

In addition to my tent and personal luggage I now had a large canvas sign which, fastened to two poles twelve feet high, hung over my tent and informed people that I was Society's Leading Palmist and that I had been patronized by the nobility, and quite a lot of other things not strictly true.

Fortunately these poles were hinged, and folded together into six-foot lengths, but they were fairly heavy and, with my other belongings, I had as much as I could carry.

Sammy did not have much personal luggage, but his tent was much heavier and more bulky than mine and we were pretty well loaded.

By booking an excursion ticket we saved quite a lot of money on the single fare, and we could well afford not to use the return half, although Sammy tried very hard to sell his at the other end.

But with an excursion ticket one is not supposed to have any luggage, save that which one might reasonably require for the day.

"What do you think you've got there?" said the ticket-collector as Sammy staggered in front of me at Bradford station with his folded tent as big as a mattress balanced uneasily on his shoulder.

"My lunch," he whispered, and hurried on.

There were several other grafters with us, and in the general excitement I managed to get past the barrier without any trouble. I at least did have a ticket, which was more than some of them had, so I had really very little to worry about.

"Here we are, boys," cried Sheeny Louie, spotting an empty carriage. "We'll reserve this compartment. Who's on for a game of broads?"

But no one seemed eager to play cards with him, and when he realized that there was no possible chance of a game he started to show us card tricks.

He was really amazingly good at these. I never saw such a performance. I understood the others' reluctance to play with him.

There were five of us altogether. The others were the Little Major, a hunchback with a quiet voice and a precise manner, and Doncaster Jock, who worked the windbags.

A windbag worker, I found, is one who sells mystery packets. Usually he carries a number of envelopes in a suitcase and the name is probably derived from the fact that the envelopes seldom contain much more than air.

However, as a rule these envelopes contain a tiepin or other cheap scrap of jewelry worth at the most a penny or two.

The windbag worker inserts watches and one-pound notes into other envelopes in front of his audience. These he mixes in with his main stock.

His customers buy the packets, hoping to get a watch or a pound note for two shillings. Naturally, people who expect to get such astonishing bargains from a man in the street obtain just about what they deserve.

If the bidding is slow, the worker often tears open an envelope which he has been offering for sale and the impressed audience sees that it contains a pound note.

On these occasions the worker has a "rick," that is to say, a confederate, planted in the crowd whom he can always choose as the first bidder should an ordinary member of the public be so inconsiderate as to bid for the lucky packet.

I have known one or two clever workers in this line

who have actually let some one buy a watch and carry it off. When the right sort of person got a piece of luck like this he did a great deal to encourage other people to buy, and since the windbag worker can always choose his fortunate punter (sucker) this is obviously the intelligent way of running the business.

But Doncaster Jock belonged to a different school.

"Give 'em nothing!" he used to say savagely. "Some of the chumps tell their pals they've got a pound note from me so as not to look as though they've been caught. Besides, a man who did get something would probably keep his mouth shut and walk away. I don't want 'wide' people and I don't want sports. It's the greedy, half-baked lumps-and-bumps I'm after, and I'd take their bloomin' shirts off them if I could."

By "wide" people he meant intelligent, widely informed people.

The Little Major had not decided what he was going to work at Whitby. By the way he talked he seemed to have tried every line at some time or another. He spoke quietly, smiling to himself when the others started to lay down the law.

They did this pretty frequently: in fact, one or other of them argued about something the whole journey.

I liked the Little Major. He seemed to know every one, and, whatever the others talked about, he was always able to settle their arguments, although he never did this until he was invited to do so.

I discovered later that he spent a lot of his time making illusions for side-show proprietors, and that there was very little about the show business with which he was not familiar.

He was extremely well known, and, since he was the type who enjoys helping others more than attending to his own work, he was very popular.

If you got into trouble with the police, found yourself stranded somewhere, or required other help in any form whatever, the Little Major would at once make it his business to look after you. He would work like a demon in some other person's interest, but never seemed to be able to put himself on his feet properly, for the slightest effort seemed too much for him when his own affairs were concerned.

His linen was always spotless, and he took a great interest in his clothes. When I first met him, on the train to Whitby, he wore a very smart black jacket and striped trousers, and appeared to be extremely successful, although I discovered that he had less than three shillings in the world.

None of us had much money. Sammy and I had a terrible job to get digs that night, and at last we had to pay eight shillings between us for the use of a bedroom with only one bed, and this, since we were up at dawn, was, as Sammy said, poor value for our money.

There is no room for the usual type of amusement at Whitby regatta, but the corporation lets certain spaces on the promenade to fortune-tellers, market demonstrators, and any one who can conduct his business from a stall occupying only a few feet in depth.

Many people were about when we arrived, and we claimed our pitches.

I say we claimed them, although of course we could not be sure of getting in at all until the official from the corporation arrived, and he was not due until after nine o'clock.

Rain was falling, and the sea was rough, casting up huge waves over the promenade.

I had exactly sixpence in the world, and Sammy was broke. He wanted me to buy some tea, but I would not part with my sixpence, and he was really very reasonable about this.

I claimed a position opposite the bandstand, and Sammy selected a likely pitch some twenty yards away.

"They'll have to scratch some of the sailing events," predicted an old sailor as he looked out to sea. "It don't look too good to me."

It didn't look too good to us either. A steady rain was falling, and sheets of water splashed the promenade. There was no protection from the wind, which blew round the bandstand like a cyclone. The canvas of my tent was sodden with rain and sea water and the ropes which tied it in a bundle were covered with mud and dirt.

"Well, boys, I think we're all in for a dead shice," said Doncaster Jock cheerfully when he arrived about eight o'clock. I took it that he meant a wash-out, and agreed with him.

We had been hanging about in the rain for several hours, afraid to go far away from our pitches for long in case some one else moved our belongings and claimed the ground; for although the rule of the Road on occasions like this is first come, first served, it is the person who gets on to the position last who really holds it.

A piece of wood or a chalk-mark claims a position,

but should any one remove this and build up his stall on one's ground there is little hope of moving him. So the first job is to get a space and the second is to hold it.

"Yes, I'm afraid this is a day for the King," remarked Doncaster Jock happily. "Funny. We usually have parny at Whitby."

"Parny," I discovered, meant rain, and we certainly had plenty of it at Whitby that day.

"If you ask me, we can all go home," Jock continued.

"I never asked you anything," said Sammy, shaking out the water which had accumulated round the brim of his bowler and hurriedly replacing it on his head. "I suppose you're fixed up somewhere?"

"There's plenty of time for me," said Jock airily. "I'm not worrying. I'll get a few fly pitches if it clears up; and if it don't, none of you need bother about pitches."

This seemed true enough. I envied Doncaster Jock. He had no stall to build up, no preparations to make for the slight possibility of a day's work. By "fly pitches" he meant that he could open his portmanteau anywhere at a moment's notice, and after giving a demonstration in one place could walk off to another part of the promenade and begin again. He used to follow the crowd, selecting the best positions, places that no fixed demonstrator could possibly occupy. Besides, he seldom paid any toll. Sometimes in a town where there was no fair he would take a pitch on the pavement outside Woolworth's and if the police moved him before he had time to make any sales he lost nothing, but hurriedly got a crowd together somewhere else.

He could afford to be cheerful, but I wasn't feeling too good. I had had no breakfast and I was wet and cold. My evening shoes had had a lot of wear recently, and even when they were new they wouldn't keep out water.

But eventually we were granted our positions by the corporation official, and we started to build up.

It was a pretty hopeless task. The framework stood all right, but directly I tried to put on the canvas the wind caught it like a balloon and nearly lifted me off my feet.

Sammy managed to lash his tent to the railings which ran along the promenade opposite me, but there was nothing to act as a support where I stood.

Sammy's tent was a pretty crazy affair at the best of times, and it looked decidedly drunk that morning. But it stood up somehow, and once he had fixed it more or less securely he came over to give me a hand.

He brought with him a couple of iron pegs quite twelve inches long, but it was of course impossible to hammer these into the concrete, although we tried.

Eventually we weighted down the framework of my tent with lumps of concrete which Sammy helped me to carry from a garage not far away. They were amazingly heavy, and it took both of us to lift one of them.

We managed all right, though, because Sammy was clever with a rope. He knew how to tie knots that would not shake loose, and had had more experience with tents in windy weather than I.

He had been a ship's cook once, he said, and doubtless he learned a lot about knots then, although he may also have been a cowboy at some time or another, because as far as I could gather he had been everything during his travels round the world.

Anyhow, I was very glad he was at Whitby with me then.

Two of the wooden supports for my tent split and we had to lash these together with string.

Round about half-past nine the Little Major arrived and provided cigarettes and useful advice.

"If it was fine there'd be a pitch on now," he said, "but there won't be much doing until the afternoon unless it clears. The weather's always at the top of the bill. You can't beat the parny."

We could not afford breakfast, and it looked as if we weren't going to get any lunch, either.

Next to me was a stall selling toys and novelties. An old man was in charge, and with him were two Italian boys who were blowing up balloons and fixing them to the ends of wires which they stuck into a turnip bound to the end of a bamboo pole.

These boys were gazers, Sammy said. This meant they did not occupy a fixed position, but, using the toy stall as their headquarters, they walked about the promenade selling wherever they could.

It was about ten o'clock when the London Mob arrived. They drove up to the back of my stall in an old-fashioned Buick and clambered out, glad to stretch their legs.

There were four of them and they were all Jews.

They wore their hats at a rakish angle and their overcoats were waisted and flounced at the skirts.

One of them wore a velvet collar, while another had the side pockets of his overcoat cut on the slant. Their shoes were very pointed and one wore spats.

There was a space about six feet wide between my tent and the toy stall, and in this space they obviously intended to put their car.

"Well, well, if it isn't the Little Major!" said one of them, shaking his hand warmly. "I hope we haven't missed anything. Only just come up from the Smoke. Might just as well go back, I think."

"Stick around for a bit, kid," said the Major afterwards, as he quietly took me on one side. "Don't budge an inch, whatever they tell you. These boys are dear fellows really, but they're dead hot on the hustle. They're liberty takers. Do you get me? They're hot on the blarney, too. They'll talk their way in anywhere and they'll muck you about so much that before you know where you are they'll be in and you'll be out."

I could not follow every word of his advice, but I gathered what he meant and I soon realized that he knew what he was talking about.

"Now, let me see, this is our pitch, isn't it?" said one of the London Mob, standing back and looking at the six-foot space between the two stalls. "We'll have to get the car on the slant a bit."

He illustrated with his hands how this could be done.

"Yes, we'll have to get these two stalls moved for a few minutes, I'm afraid," said another, and approached me.

But I explained that I couldn't possibly move my tent, as it had taken me several hours to build it up and it wasn't too secure now.

They approached the toy stall. Some minutes later their car was driven on to the pathway and it occupied not only the space between my stall and the next, but also the space which had once been occupied by the toy seller.

He had moved his joint and it remained where he had moved it.

There was a row, of course, but it was a solid car and with it were four very solid-looking men. No one interfered with any of them.

The toy seller, threatening and calling them a lot of dirty snodders, eventually moved his stall, assisted by the Italian boys and the Little Major, to a less favorable position.

A fine drizzle fell all day, but the wind dropped a little, and by midday we were all able to do some business.

The London Mob were working the R.O. This is short for the "Run Out." Standing in his car above the people's heads, one of the men started to throw things at the passers-by, and had no difficulty in collecting a crowd.

"Does any one here write?" he shouted, and flung a few lead-pencils among them. "In order to advertise our new shop, which we are opening shortly in this town, we are giving things away today. Here, who wants a notebook?"

He gave a quantity of things away. He threw a

number of little paper books into the air and his audience scrambled to get them.

"Rough luck having the R.O. right on top of you, kid," said the Little Major to me. "They work mob-handed. As soon as one is finished another'll have a go."

"But surely they don't hold a crowd like that all day?" I said in consternation, for the people were crowding in front of my tent, practically hiding me; and my canvas sign, which I had put on the ground in front of me because of the wind, had been trampled on and was of no earthly use.

"Well, of course, they're only plundering at the moment," the Major explained. "The crowd is always eager to get something for nothing. But when he 'comes to his bat' a lot of them will scarper. But the Mob will be at it all day."

The man in the car suddenly took a pair of field-glasses and raised his hand as though he were going to throw them at the audience.

"Just a moment!" he shouted. "If I throw these they'll probably get smashed or hurt some one. Wait a minute. In order to keep them out of the hands of children I'll see if I can adopt a different method of giving them to you."

He placed the glasses on one side and produced a handful of pipes.

"Now, who smokes?" he inquired, smiling broadly.

Quite twenty hands went up, and several of these belonged to women.

"That's the trouble," he said. "I can't let you all have a pipe, although I have a number of other things to give you. Who will give me a penny for this pipe? A gentleman over there? Here you are, sir. Have it for nothing."

He threw the pipe to a man in the crowd who was a stranger. But when he did the same thing with a rather nice-looking silver cigarette-case the man to whom he threw it was one of the Mob who had arrived in the car.

All this, I supposed, was to get the people's confidence, but even then I could not see where he was going to get his money.

However, later on this was not quite such a mystery. He got several people to bid him a shilling for a box containing a glass butter-dish.

Even with my slight knowledge of showmen's swag, it did not look as if they had obtained much of a bargain.

But this was only the beginning.

One of his party collected the shillings and, arranging twelve butter dishes in a row on a board across the car, he placed a shilling on the top of each.

"It won't be so bad now," murmured the Major to me. "He's got his nailers out, and as soon as he blows out the others the happier he'll be."

I inquired what he meant by "nailers."

The Little Major looked at me in surprise.

"Well, you see," he explained, "he's got their shillings and he hasn't given them anything yet. So he's sort of nailed them down. They can't walk away. He can hold them as long as he likes. Now he's only interested in the twelve people who've already paid good money, and the others he'll try to blow out, or get rid òf, as soon as he can. One or two of the twelve have probably got a bit of gelt on them, and he'll be satisfied with one good punter out of this pitch."

I watched the man in the car.

"Now I'm going to make the people who've spent a shilling with me say thank you before I've finished with them," he said.

Several people in the crowd realized that by not being one of the chosen twelve they had missed their chance, and they walked away, while others stopped to see what was going on.

But I managed to persuade a couple of girls who were watching idly to enter my tent.

We stood while I read their hands, as I had to hold the cross-bar of my tent to prevent it from blowing over. The front curtain waved in the breeze, giving the crowd outside a clear view of my activities, and it was very difficult to create anything approaching a mystic atmosphere.

But my clients seemed satisfied.

When I had finished, the man in the car had still a few people in front of him, but most of his crowd had dwindled away.

"Bid me a pound! Bid me a pound because I ask you!" he was shouting, holding a watch and a number of other things to a youth in the crowd. "Have you got a pound?" asked the man at last.

"No, I ain't," came the reply sullenly.

"Well, of course, if you haven't any socks you can't pull 'em up, can you?" said the Yiddisher boisterously. "Here, Harry, give the gentleman his butter-dish.

You bid me a shilling for that, didn't you? Now you've got what you asked for and you're satisfied? That's right."

He dismissed the whole matter with a wave of the hand.

One of the Mob handed the youth his butter-dish, slapped him on the back and told him to advertise his bargain to his friends.

"Now what have we here?" continued the Jew in the car, turning his attention to the row of butter-dishes before him, which had grown, I noticed, considerably shorter.

He took up one of the boxes, which contained, I saw, a butter-dish, a shilling, a watch and a pound note.

"Now, who gave me a pound for this watch?" he asked, and a man in the crowd put up his hand.

"I'm going to make you say thank you before I've finished," the salesman assured him. "First of all, you gave me a shilling for this butter-dish, didn't you? So this shilling belongs to me and this box belongs to you."

The man nodded his head.

"Then you bid me a pound for this watch, so the pound belongs to me and the watch belongs to you. That's right, isn't it?"

Again the man nodded.

"Well, I'll tell you what I'll do," said the man in the car magnanimously. "I told you I'd make you say thank you and I'm going to prove that I keep my word. You were sporty enough to bid me a pound for this watch. I'm going to show every one what I do with sports.

"Here, Harry," he murmured to his assistant, "hand me up a bit of plunder."

Then he began to bellow again.

"Here's a solid synthetic gold chain to go with the watch, a pair of gentleman's cuff-links in a case, and if you smoke a pipe I'll put one of these 'ere English briars on the top. Advertise—tell your friends—that's all I want you to do."

In addition to the articles he had just added there were, of course, the butter-dish and the watch.

He held up the box that contained them, and then placed the pound note on the top.

"Will you give me two pounds for the lot?" he asked.

The man hesitated.

"Two pounds and you take the lot," insisted the Jew in the car. "There's a pound here, isn't there? Bid me two pounds and take the lot. Here, I'll tell you what I'll do, as you've been sporty. Here's the shilling on top as well. Bid me two pounds and you get more than half of what you bid back right away in cash."

The man in the crowd drew out his wallet and the man in the car drew a deep breath.

"Funny how they still fall for that," said the Major, who was standing by my tent watching the scene, a faint smile on his birdlike face. "Not one in a hundred realizes that he's buying back his own guinea."

I saw now, at any rate, where the man in the car got his money.

The London Mob worked in turns unceasingly all day, and they must have done pretty well.

Sammy and I were among the last to pack up, and in the evening, when the excitement had died down, we were both kept fairly busy.

When I ushered my last client out of my tent and counted up, I discovered I had taken three pounds seventeen shillings. Ten shillings of this I had to pay for my pitch.

Sammy had taken just over fifty shillings. We decided to have something to eat.

Although we felt comparatively rich, neither of us wanted to waste money on lodgings. Sammy brightly suggested that we should sleep out in one of the shelters on the front, and this we did.

It was a large shelter near the bandstand, and stood back some way off the promenade. It sheltered us from the wind, but it was wretchedly cold in the night and I did not sleep much. No one objected, and two other grafters shared our sleeping quarters. They lit a fire with some old newspapers, but this really wasn't a good idea. It gave little heat, and the burnt ashes smothered our clothes in the morning.

Although cold, the following morning was bright, and after I had had a wash and changed into some ordinary clothes I did not feel too bad.

I did not see Sammy for some time after this, as he decided to go back to Bradford.

I heard about a day's show at Sleights, only a few miles away, on Wednesday, and I decided to try it.

It was a horticultural show, and by paying three shillings only I obtained permission from the secretary to build up my tent by the entrance to the field in which the marquee stood.

Some gypsies, who had sole rights for amusements regularly every year, and whose wagons were drawn up at the far end of the field, were naturally not at all friendly, but I had my permit from the officials and I was not going to move for any one.

I took the precaution, however, to sleep in my tent that night in case some one should smash it up while I was away, and I think it was worth it, because I made over a fiver the following day.

Telling fortunes at Sleights was easy. The people who patronized my tent were a type I knew and in whom I had always been vaguely interested, so that telling them the things they wanted to hear was quite good fun.

Young men in riding breeches and thick tweeds, but whose hands were soft and manicured, told me hurriedly before I started that "they didn't believe in this sort of thing," and then offered me an extra shilling if I could describe their future wives.

Elderly men approached me to pay for the whole party of their women-folk and told me in a whisper not to tell them anything that they wouldn't like.

"You're a gypsy, aren't you?" asked one girl calmly as I was reading her hand. "I've always wanted to talk to a real gypsy."

As it was my ambition to please, I told her that I had a lot of gypsy blood in me.

"I knew it," she said, looking me over in the casual yet inquisitive manner that is characteristic of the young woman with a considerable income of her own. "Mother would have it that you were a gentleman."

Obviously she did not consider that she had said anything unusual, and before I had finished her fortune she did her utmost to flirt with me in a rather childish fashion.

I quite enjoyed myself at Sleights.

'I bought an immense bookmaker's umbrella which, in addition to being a very fine flash, made it possible for me to work when there was a slight drizzle.'

CHAPTER 8

I meet the Church Militant.

In the third week in August I went to the fair at Ashton-under-Lyne. It was Wakes Week, and roundabouts and side-shows had taken possession of the market square which stands right in the center of the town.

I was becoming accustomed to my new life, and the more I got to know about it the more I liked it. For the past few weeks I had been working at small shows and regattas, and it was good to be with a big fair again.

I liked Ashton-under-Lyne. Although many of the townsfolk go to Blackpool for their holidays, those who stay behind enjoy the fair thoroughly. For a whole week the holiday spirit invades the town.

The mill girls discard their clogs and, dressed in their best clothes, adopt as best they can the language and airs of their favorite film star.

Every one goes about feverishly hunting for a good time. There is only one holiday, and it only lasts a week.

On Sunday I went out to inspect the layout. Canvas coverings were drawn across the entrances to the side-shows, and, save for an occasional group of show-people, the place was practically deserted.

The townsfolk were waiting for the holiday to begin on the morrow.

Since it was Sunday, I had discarded my perpetual topper and was wearing ordinary clothes, and I wandered about hoping something would happen.

The whole atmosphere was expectant, like the moment just before the guests arrive at a party.

In the middle of the afternoon I noticed a crowd collecting in the very center of the fair-ground, and, for want of anything better to do, I went to join it.

I found to my astonishment that it was a sort of anti-fair prayer-meeting, organized, as far as I could see, by a pink clergyman who was doing a spot of publicity for his church.

Hand-bills were given out among us inviting us to visit a special series of evening services at the church during the coming week.

The subject of the addresses as set down on the bills seemed to be mainly warnings against the evils of attending the fair. I thought this was rather bad form, since he was on our ground; bad form and cheap advertising.

With the pink clergyman, whom I should not have liked personally even had his publicity methods been less tasteless, were several earnest young men and three or four elderly people who stood apart in a little group by themselves and appeared to be there only with the intention of "dressing the house."

We started off by singing a hymn, and then one of the young men suddenly climbed up on the steps leading to the steam-yachts and, without any preamble, told us how wonderful it was to look into the face of Jesus.

It was rather disgusting.

However, after he had told us that the Lord was his friend, in rather the same manner in which some people boast that they are on speaking terms with Lloyd George or Gladys Cooper, we had another hymn, and this attracted quite a number of people who were hanging about the streets waiting for the holiday to begin on the morrow.

The rest of the audience was composed entirely of show-people, who were tolerant but slightly irritated.

The clergyman was middle-aged, plump and comfortable-looking. He wore gold-rimmed spectacles, and held a hymnbook in one hand and an umbrella in the other; and whereas these things in themselves were inoffensive enough, it is difficult to describe the pompous, smug condescension which oozed from every pore in his body and hung about him like a sickly pink cloud.

He, too, climbed on the steam-yachts, grasping the newly polished brass rails with his damp hands. I don't think he actually kicked the paint, but I felt he might.

Peering at the show-people with his wet, near-sighted eyes, he smiled as though at some superior and secret joke, and said in a loud voice, with hardly any expression in it at all:

"Will any young man come forward, and, kneeling at my feet, offer his soul to Jesus?"

There was an awkward silence. I think the gypsies and show-people were as acutely embarrassed as I was. The audience shuffled uneasily.

"Make a joyful noise unto the Lord, all the earth!

Make a loud noise, and rejoice, and sing praise!" he continued, and went on to explain, quite without foundation, I thought, that the passage referred to hymn-singing only and not to the steam organs on the roundabouts or the laughter round the dart stall.

He then appealed once again to some sinner in the audience to step out and open his heart to the Lord and the other sinners around him. But he hurried over this part and still spoke with the same small, secret amusement which had from the beginning so irritated me.

Although he actually requested some one to do this appalling thing, he used the words as though they were part of a set-piece and had no real meaning. I wondered vaguely what could happen if some one did step up. In my mind I saw him stooping to pat them on the head, overbalancing and slipping off the steam-yachts. Looking at him, I thought he would not risk this fiasco, but would leave it to the Lord to show His appreciation in His own way.

Had the God of the Old Testament sent a thunder-bolt, or even a miraculously flowering shrub, I felt he would have taken to his heels without more ado, and as I looked at him I thought he was quite horribly irreligious.

Presently he climbed down. While he had been talking he had looked up towards the sky most of the time, and I suspected that this was in an attempt to keep his balance rather than in an earnest desire to find the Lord there. It was all rather condescending, and sounded much less sincere than Sheeny Louie's insistence that "You couldn't lose" on the rings.

When he was firmly on the ground again the clergyman peered into the faces of the showmen nearest him.

"Will any young man take my place for a few minutes?" he said. "I would appreciate it very much if some ordinary person with us today would get up and say a few words."

When no one accepted his invitation his secret amusement increased.

"Come along, somebody. Come along, some sinner. Don't be frightened. The Lord will be with you."

I don't know why I stepped forward. I think it was because he had annoyed me so, and I felt that in all justice he ought to get some little of that for which he had been asking.

He gaped at me.

"Would you really like to say a few words?" he said in astonishment.

That astonishment settled it. I climbed up the steps of the steam-yachts and looked at the crowd. I had never addressed any sort of gathering before, and I had not realized that the group was quite so large or that it contained quite so many of my companions of the road.

It dawned upon me that the first thing to do was to say something. I have never considered myself deeply religious; I have never liked going to church; but I firmly believe in a Deity, an omnipotent Being from whom nothing is hidden.

"First of all," I said firmly, "I shall tell you a story."

I knew an anecdote which was perfectly true and which seemed to fit the bill.

"When I was a very small boy," I said, "I lived with my family in a large white house in the country. In front of this house was a big lawn upon which my father used to play clock-golf. When he lost a ball, as he often did, for he was short-sighted, he used to offer me a penny if I could find it."

The crowd seemed interested, or at least they did not move away, and the clergyman still wore his perpetual condescending smile. His smug conviction that he was not as other men irritated me beyond reason.

However, I had no time to think about him just them, and I went on with my story. My voice, I noticed, was beginning to sound more natural and I felt the crowd were my friends.

"One day I had spent over an hour looking for one of these balls," I continued, "but I could not find it. I was a very little boy, and suddenly the obvious way out of my difficulty occurred to me. I knelt down on the edge of the lawn, put my hands together, shut my eyes, and asked the Lord to help me to find the ball.

"Of course," I went on, "you may think this was only a coincidence, but when I opened my eyes, there in a flower-bed in front of me I saw the golf-ball for which I had been looking so long."

My story, which, after all, was true and rather odd, went down quite well, and I had another look at the clergyman. He was laughing, but I felt that his amusement was directed more against my simplicity than in sympathy with any graceful act of the Deity.

Having told my story, I had to think of something else to say. As far as I could remember, the construction of a sermon was the statement of a text, followed by a series of more or less pertinent reflections and deductions arising out of the example.

"Well, I've just told you a story," I said, "which, although admittedly very simple, impressed me greatly at the time. Ever since then, whenever I have wanted something I have always asked God for it. It does not always work, but it's worth trying."

My enemy, the pink clergyman, looked shocked, but the showmen had the kind of minds that appreciated the rather simple logic of my statement.

As I looked at the clergyman I thought I might as well say something about his address.

"In my opinion," I said, "the reverend gentleman who has just addressed us asked too much when he invited some one to come forward and kneel before him in the dust. I take it that most of us say our prayers, and I don't see why he should have suggested that we did not. Saying one's personal prayers, after all, has one thing in common with taking a bath: it is a thing to be done in private, and the majority of us do not see any reason to go through life bathing or praying in public.

"However, since we are discussing prayer, if there *is* any one in this audience who does not make a practice of asking God for advice and guidance I would respectfully suggest that it is worth a trial. If you want anything, ask for it. On the irrefutable evidence of honest people, both in the past and present, it does sometimes work."

My congregation appeared to be most interested, and, although I had said all I had to say on the subject of prayer, I had always found it difficult to stop talking once I got going, and I thought that while I had them listening to me I might continue. It had occurred to me from the very beginning that the whole meeting was a publicity stunt for the pink clergyman's church, and I did not see why it should not continue to have its advertising flavor.

"Our friend," I said, indicating the clergyman, "has compared this ground to Vanity Fair. As you know, that is a derogatory term. This is a place of amusement, the kind of amusement of which he does not appear to approve. In this, I think our friend is wrong. Quite obviously he does not appreciate the work which the showmen are doing in bringing this fair to your town.

"We are Christians, and the only direct evidence we have of our God's desires for our conduct is contained in the New Testament, and I assure you there is nothing there to show that the Lord does not want us to be happy. A fair makes us happy. After all," I said, warming up to my subject, "what other ancient institution produces more healthy gaiety than the fairs of England? As I say, our friend does not appreciate this, but I do, because I belong to the fair.

"You see, ladies and gentlemen, I am a palmist, and my tent is over there."

This announcement caused quite a lot of excitement, and I was glad to see that some of the pink clergyman's smugness had vanished.

"I honestly consider that I do as much good by traveling round the fair-grounds of England as our friend does in his parish," I continued. "After all, we both set up as prophets. He tells you what will happen to you after you die, and I tell you what will happen to you in the near future. He advises you, and so do I. People seek my advice on matters which they would not discuss with a clergyman, and I honestly feel that I have been able to help them.

"True, I charge a fee—we all have to live—but I will not be impertinent and inquire into any financial arrangements which our friend may have. I accept my fees after I have given advice, and never before. People pay voluntarily for the help I give them."

My speech was going down well, and I went on.

"My greatest desire in life is to be of real help to my clients," I insisted. "If ever you want my help, you know my name. It is painted above my tent over there. And if you haven't a shilling to spare, don't let that bother you. I won't turn you away. Remember, I'm only a fair-ground palmist, so you won't have to put on your best clothes to see me."

I climbed off the steam-yachts and that was that. I had finished, and very nearly finished the meeting.

The pink clergyman shook hands with me as if he were doing a fine thing.

"I must thank this young man for his few words," he said hurriedly to the crowd, and had the impudence to add that he hoped I would soon see the Light.

Then he scuttled off to his retreating followers.

In the back of the crowd I saw Sheeny Louie laughing so much that he had to be supported by his wife. I was sorry about that. I did not feel that I had done anything funny or disgraceful. The meeting had begun as an advertising stunt, with one's immortal soul for the "flash," and as an advertising stunt it had ended.

I don't know whether I got more publicity out of it than the clergyman did for his week-day services, but it certainly did me a bit of good, and I was kept pretty busy in the tent on the following Monday.

A few of my clients made direct references to the previous day's meeting.

On the whole, I think I got more out of it than the clergyman, because it gave me my second idea. It surprised me to find how interested my audience had become and how easy it seemed to talk to a crowd.

I remembered Doncaster Jock and the quack doctors I had seen, and I wondered. Instead of talking to only one person at a time, I thought, it surely must be more profitable to talk to a hundred.

Whatever other effect it may have had, the prayer-meeting made me think that one day I might become a "pitcher," and of course in the end I did.

CHAPTER 9

I experience my first big fair. I come to grips with the law. The truant policeman. Madame Clarissa advises me to go to Llandudno.

From ASHTON-UNDER-LYNE I went to Oldham. It was the last week in August, and it was Wakes Week.

Oldham Wakes Fair is one of the biggest in Lancashire. It is held on several acres of ground called Pennyfields, where in ordinary times the market takes place every Monday, Friday and Saturday.

But during Wakes Week Oldham forgets the market. The long avenues of stalls, of which the corporation is justly proud, are stored away somewhere, and the hundreds of market-folk either take a holiday or find some other place to work.

When I arrived, massive roundabouts, Pat Collins' Diving Whales, and Green's Gondolas, occupied prominent positions, while towering up amid the long rows of shooting-galleries and coconut sheets were the gaily colored canopies over the steam-yachts and helter-skelters.

At every turn one came across a set of dodge-'ems or chairoplanes.

There were long rows of round stalls, every one more or less the same, and at these people could wheel pennies on to squares and sometimes win a lot of money.

There were over fifty stalls, all next to one another, at which you could buy a postcard for twopence, and if the number penciled upon it was the lucky one you went off with a prize worth several shillings. These were called giant spinners.

All these attractions had to be fixed up before the market superintendent would devote any of his time to tick-off workers. The ground allotted to the big shows had been mapped out and booked long before, but there was always some discussion. Some one was occupying too much space, and some one else wasn't in his right place.

I had no difficulty in finding the superintendent. He was walking about most of the time with a tape-measure in one hand and a large notebook in the other, and followed by a considerable crowd, each member of which wanted to talk to him at once.

Several palmists had regular positions, which they occupied every year, and many had written several weeks before.

But once all these had been fixed up I saw it would be the first man to apply who would stand a chance of getting any odd pitch which might be going. I only wanted about six feet, so I was not discouraged.

Although I knew it was useless to get in that day, I joined the crowd, hoping to speak to him so that he would remember me later.

I followed him for a couple of hours and then managed to get a word with him.

"Palmist? I don't think there'll be any room. But I can't see any of you people until tomorrow."

This was good enough for me. I had applied before the last rush had arrived, and I had every hope of getting in eventually.

The following day I was on the ground early. Most of the amusements were built up in readiness for opening that night, and there were over a dozen palmists already at work. These were mostly gypsies, for they find there is always a chance of getting a customer from among the people who stroll round the fairground before the show begins, and gypsies seldom miss anything.

Gazers and hawkers of all kinds were also crowding into their places in the street.

Entering a refreshment room by the main market hall, since it advertised hot pies with peas for fourpence, I noticed a man sitting with his back to the door. His bowler hat looked familiar, and I was not mistaken.

It was Sammy.

He seemed pleased to see me and I was glad to meet any one.

"Not fixed up yet?" he said. "Take my advice and see if you can spot a likely pitch. Don't build up, but leave your joint there. If no one moves it by tonight, build up and take notice of no one."

This was not at all a bad idea, and as it happened it worked successfully. I found a pitch in one of the main gangways, opposite the gondolas and backing on to a set of steam-yachts. I placed my belongings on the ground here and spent the rest of the day trying to catch the eye of the superintendent.

When I did catch his eye I did not tell him that I had selected my own ground, but inquired if he could fix me up anywhere.

It was evening and the fair had begun. I followed him into his office. He seemed tired and I thought probably thirsty.

"I know you're too busy to have a drink with me now," I suggested, "but if you'd have one with me later—"

I offered him a ten-shilling note.

He looked at the money and then looked at me, and I knew I had made a mistake.

"I don't drink," he said, and I knew that this was not true. "I've already told you that there isn't any room, and you'd better get out before I throw you out."

I went away regretfully.

I told Sammy, whose tent was built up near the side-shows.

"Funny," he said. "I always thought he took the dropsy. If you'd made it half a dollar he might have taken it. But there, you never know. You'd better stall around for a bit, and if no one claims your pitch, build up. A different chap comes round for the toll. Pay him in silver, giving him an extra two-bob. If he gives you the two-ender back, take it and say nothing. But he'll probably cop."

He did.

I built up on the following day and remained till the end of the fair. I never saw the superintendent again, and when the toll-collector came round he asked no questions.

What with the organ on the steam-yachts directly behind me and the music of the gondolas in front, it was rather a noisy position, but apart from this it was not considered a good position for a tick-off, because in addition to the noise it was too much in the thick of things for a palmist.

People were naturally unsettled right in the midst of the fair, and those people who might have consulted me were pushed on by the crowd before they could make up their minds about it.

The best place for a palmist is considered to be near the entrance, or in some corner where there is little attraction and room for people to stand about.

But, curiously enough, I did quite well. There was plenty of light, and my evening kit seemed to be an attraction. I got quite worked up. I used to go outside my tent and persuade people to come inside. Had I not been in this particular spot this method of advertising would have been resented, but here every one had the carnival spirit. The music made them feel like dancing, and I had to bellow to make myself heard.

You can shout all sorts of things into a woman's ear which you couldn't possibly say to her quietly. This is curious, but it is true, I find.

I had just finished a reading, and was showing my client out, when two men practically forced their way in. They were both over six feet, and they wore their clothes as if they were not used to them.

"You want your hands read?" I asked dubiously.

One of the men grinned. "Yes. That's what you do here, isn't it?"

"Yes. Quite. Sit down, will you?"

I had two stools, one on either side of my little table, which was an orange-box covered with some cloth. The stools were only about a foot and a half from the ground.

The men balanced themselves unsteadily on them, their knees nearly touching their chins. The tent was crowded.

"Do you mind if we smoke?" asked one of them, taking a pipe from his pocket and nearly upsetting the table.

"Certainly not. Fire ahead," I told him. I wished he'd burn.

Even with my small experience I knew they were policemen.

I suppose the show people would have called them "splits" or "rozzers." I could have called them practically anything.

I am not a fatalist, but I knew that if they were here to "book" me it would not make much difference what I told them, for I should not be charged with that but with something I had told some one else before. A woman, probably one of their wives, had no doubt had her hand read by me, and, having collected all the evidence she wanted, the two men had come to charge me.

It would be foolish, therefore, to stick only to characteristics as a safeguard, I decided, and I thought I might just as well give them their full money's worth of the future.

If there was going to be a case, I could make my defense that I had powers to tell people about themselves, as of course I have up to a point.

Optimistically I thought I might even get a bit of publicity for my fine.

But I was not feeling too sure of myself, and I took one of the great paws guardedly.

They both decided to have a half-crown reading to start with, and I did not like the look of this. They could afford to spend freely if they were going to charge up expenses.

"I must explain to you," I said. "A palmist's greatest value is not as a prophet but as an adviser. There are people, I believe, who claim to be able to tell you if your future wife will be blonde or brunette, knock-kneed or bow-legged. But this is, of course, absurd. I cannot tell you what you *will* do, but I can tell you what you *should* do."

I held the massive hand in mine and studied the lines upon it through a magnifying-glass while I tried desperately to collect my scattered wits.

"In the same way as by looking at a railway map one can trace a train journey, so I can trace your life's journey as it should be run by looking at the map of your hand," I explained. "But in the same way as a train is held up in a fog or delayed at a station, so can your life's journey be brought to a standstill if you remain too long in one position or make some sort of mistake."

I was talking rapidly, keeping my eyes fixed on his hand and wondering if it had been his or the other man's wife who had visited me earlier to collect evidence. I had probably told her that she had married the wrong man, or that her line of life was longer than her line of matrimony and that she would marry again.

As I thought about these things I felt very uncomfortable and my face became flushed, although I was feeling slightly cold.

"You should find success in some position of authority," I continued hurriedly. "But a certain amount of secrecy should be exercised. You have many enemies, and those who pretend to be your friends may possibly turn against you. You cannot afford to have too many friends, and although I see promotion of some kind indicated in the near future, anxiety and opposition are also written here."

I took my eyes off his hand for a moment and glanced up at his face. I was relieved to see that he appeared unusually interested, and, feeling a little encouraged, it occurred to me that his face would probably be a better guide to me than his hand.

I went on to tell him a lot of his characteristics while I thought out something else of importance that I might tell him.

In a roundabout way I told him that he was a damned fine fellow with a forceful personality and the courage of a lion. I thought this might sound rather good in court.

His friend found my remarks amusing, but my client was not only amused. He prompted me by a series of grunts, and I decided it was about time to bring things to a head.

"I see a uniform in your hand," I said. "A uniform and some sort of official position."

I hesitated, and then suddenly decided to discover the worst.

"As a matter of fact," I blurted out rather awkwardly, "your hand clearly indicates that you're a detective or something to do with the police."

It was his feet that had indicated this more than his hand, but I saw no point in mentioning this.

"You're correct," he said, grinning. "As a matter of fact, we're both policemen. But how you can tell it beats me."

There was no point in beating about the bush any further.

"Are you here professionally?" I inquired.

They both laughed, and I thought we were going to have the tent over.

"We're just here for a bit of fun," said one of them. "We've got the missuses outside and they made us come in. They've been in to you already. I don't know what you told 'em, but whatever it was they seemed mighty pleased about it. Said you were real good, although I've never thought much of this sort of thing myself, you know."

"Naturally. You're men of the world," I assured him, feeling rather an ass. "There's such a lot of humbug about this sort of thing that the average man very wisely keeps away from it. But although, unfortunately, there are many humbugs pretending to tell fortunes today, there is a lot which a genuine palmist can tell from looking at the lines on a man's hand. It is a recognized science, you know, and I have devoted a great deal of my time to it. Of course, the trouble is that so many people expect magic. That's why I appreciate some one like yourselves. Realizing the limitations of palmistry, you also appreciate its values."

I again looked at his hand. I thought they must be telling the truth, and I felt much happier.

"For example," I continued, "it would be absurd for me to suggest that you were going to lose your job. I suppose it would be very difficult for a policeman to do that. But I will suggest that there is a very slight danger in the near future. You should guard against those with whom you work, for there is jealousy here, and trouble in connection with your work is to be avoided."

They were a couple of bobbies out for a bit of fun with their wives, and I felt rather a fool for getting the wind-up. But the way they had walked into my tent had made me suspicious. I did not see that they had come half-defiantly, since their wives had been persuading them to come in all the time I had been engaged with another client.

When they had discovered that I was disengaged they had suddenly made up their minds, and their official manner had only been a cloak for their embarrassment.

I finished reading the other man's hand, and both seemed perfectly satisfied. They were happy punters.

"I say, about my job," whispered one of them, hanging behind his companion as they were leaving. "I don't belong to this town. I'm the officer at a little village near here, and if anything happened in my absence it might be awkward. I shouldn't really be here. You see, there's no one there now, and if the

Inspector 'phoned or anything like that it might lead to a lot of inquiries."

I had meant to give him something to think about, but of course I had no idea that he had run away to the fair, and I didn't want to spoil his fun.

I assured him there was nothing to worry about, and he thanked me warmly.

I felt so relieved myself that I felt kindly disposed towards the whole world, even policemen. He reminded me of an overgrown schoolboy as he hurried off to join his companion.

Linking arms, they walked towards the Diving Whales, and I knew by the way the women listened that they were discussing all that I had told them. The men were doing the talking, but I knew that whatever the women said about their readings would only be the things that they wanted their husbands to hear.

So we were all happy.

I liked the Oldham people and they seemed to like me. They seemed not to have seen any one quite like me before and I got on very well with them. Most of my clients were women, who seemed more interested in the future than men.

I tried to cheer them up, of course, and when my client looked as though she found her life monotonous I told her that the future held much that was unexpected and that good times were in store.

To others who seemed to possess the ability to enjoy themselves I gave more practical advice. In fact, it occurred to me that I talked to them rather like a Salvationist, but because they were paying for my advice they listened to it.

I also spoke very simply and in less difficult terms than the Salvationists use.

"You have a very generous temperament," I told one girl, "but this is a quality which is also a danger. There is nothing you would not give to the man you love, but—well, you don't want to love too many people."

"Can you see that in my hand?" she asked, and her eyes were open very wide.

"I can see a lot more," I told her.

She drew her hand away from me hurriedly. She seemed to think that I was really psychic.

One girl wanted to know if she would ever go on the films, and I told her truthfully that she wouldn't. She was a pathetic little thing with moist hands, and teeth that damned whatever looks she possessed.

"Your real happiness comes in marriage," I told her. "There is some one in whom you can place your entire trust. You may think him a somewhat ordinary person, but he is some one who can give you true love. He should be in your life round about this time, and I should advise you to accept his proposal."

"That would be Alf," she said quietly, more to herself than to me. "Alf's the only lad that loves me."

As she left she looked to me like one who had reached a decision.

Of course there was no way of warning Alf, but probably I had done him a good turn.

I was convinced all the time that the advice I gave

most of my clients was of some use to them. There were so many people who wanted to tell their troubles to some one, and the majority of my clients appreciated the most obvious counsel. They wanted their own views confirmed and a few of their doubts dispelled. They wanted encouragement and the promise of better times ahead. And as so much depends on one's mental outlook, it is more than likely that where they expected to find happiness they often discovered it.

Anyway, a number of my clients left their inferiority complexes behind them with their half-dollars. It suited me, and I thought it was a fair arrangement.

I wondered at one time if it would be possible to be a professional adviser without being a palmist. I felt that I understood people, and that, being an outsider and genuinely interested, I could really advise them far better than the average friend.

However, I realized that without the popular appeal of fortune-telling few people would want to seek my advice. Hardly any one attaches much value to advice, and it was only by professing to tell fortunes that I persuaded people to listen to what I told them.

So I decided to continue in my present way, using my powers of observation and deduction to gain their confidence and interest, and then to tell them the obvious practical things. It seemed to me that I could not do much harm that way, and there was always a chance that I might do some one a little good.

I was, at any rate, quite as genuine as any one on the fair.

On one occasion I was at Macclesfield and the palmists were placed in one long line in the road leading to the fair ground. Our joints were so close together that it was impossible not to hear some of the things that were said in the tents next door.

A gypsy was on my right, and every now and again throughout the day I heard her say when she raised her voice in a certain stage of one of her recitations: "And when you get home there's a big surprise for you."

Of course there are one or two tick-off workers who are more or less confidence tricksters. These people have been known to get several hundreds of pounds from one client, and it is these people, of course, who attract the attention of the police.

Sometimes, if a complaint is made to the police about some palmist on the fair, every one professing to tell fortunes is charged, but apart from those who have obtained big money the fines are usually small.

I am fortunate never to have been "booked," for the majority of fortune-tellers look on a summons as something all in the day's work.

It was while I was at Oldham that I met Madame Clarissa. She wanted to know if I could drive a car, and I discovered that she had a motor caravan. She was not a gypsy, but the man with whom she was living had adopted the ways of that race; in fact, the majority of men connected with lady palmists appear sooner or later to retire and live on the earnings of their wives. For this reason, of course, they are often called very unpleasant names.

But I think the women are really to blame for it. They like their men about them and do not encourage them to work.

However, I was afraid Madame Clarissa was looking for a new husband. But whatever prompted her to confide in me, she certainly did me a very good turn, for it was she who advised me to go to Llandudno.

"George Dell opens there tomorrow," she told me, "and it's worth pounds to you. I can't go myself—in fact, he wouldn't have me—but if you can get in there's work around Wales for months."

Palmists do not as a rule help their fellow-workers, and naturally information about a good fair is very closely guarded. When there are so many fortune-tellers on the road no one can afford to shout about places where money is to be made.

"I had it on my tod last year," she told me, "and even if there's a bit of opposition it'll be worth your while. But don't tell any one or there'll be a mob there."

If I had been more experienced I might have doubted her. There are people who delight in sending some one else miles to a place that is useless, but I felt that she was speaking the truth.

I did not wait for the last day of Oldham Fair, but set off for Llandudno. It was a long journey, and the train was late.

It was raining when I arrived.

CHAPTER 10

I meet Mr. Dell and his family. I join his Fair and learn Mary Ann Bevan's story.

A FEW HUNDRED YARDS from the General Post-office at Llandudno, on the road that leads to Conway, there is a field. It is this field which separates the football ground from the road, and it was here that I found a number of living-wagons and the skeleton of a fair.

I knew that there was often as much money to be made at a small show-ground as at a large fair, or at least I had heard so; but my first impression was not a good one.

There were no more than a dozen wagons, and not many more side-shows.

As I drew nearer, one thing in particular attracted my attention. This was a large tent about twelve feet square with a most elaborate front curtain and a huge sign over the top on which was painted in gold the inscription: "The Original Royal Gypsy. Palmist."

Next door there was another fortune-telling tent, less ornate, but nevertheless much more impressive than mine. They stood near the entrance, and the fair itself consisted of several side-shows forming a circle round a set of roundabouts.

It was about four o'clock in the afternoon, but there was no sign of activity. The roundabout was only partly built and the other stalls, too, were in various stages of erection.

"Yes, I'm Dell," said a tall man with a ragged sandy mustache and very pale blue eyes, whom I found on the ground. "You be a-wanting me?"

I explained my business. He looked depressed. The weather was bad and I think it had got on his nerves.

"Seeing as you've come all that way," he said at last, "I expect we'll have to fix you up somewhere. But to tell you the truth, I don't want you."

I was sorry to hear this, and I told him so.

"I've had a lot of bother with such as you, and I ought not really to have had them others here at all," he said, jerking his head towards the Royal Gypsy's tents. "But now as you are here we may as well make the best of it."

This seemed a very good idea, and I thanked him for his consideration. We walked along together.

"We ain't opening tonight," he told me sadly. "The weather's bad and we had a lot of trouble a-getting here. But we'll open tomorrow if it ain't too bad."

The whole thing seemed a bit happy-go-lucky. I could not even discover how long he intended the fair to last.

"Probably be 'ere about a coupla weeks or more," he said. "Can't say any nearer than that."

He showed me where I could build up my tent. It seemed a very good pitch to me. My tent was the first inside the gate, so every one who came to the fair at all would have to pass me.

My rivals, the gypsies, were some way away on the other side of the entrance.

"It'll cost you a pound a week," said Mr. Dell gloomily, and I paid him a pound before he could change his mind about letting me stay.

I liked Mr. Dell very much when I got to know him, but he was not a man with whom one made friends quickly. His fair was a family concern, and no doubt he realized that any money I took would otherwise be spent at one of the other attractions, in all of which he had an interest.

He had spent his entire life in a wagon, traveling round north Wales, and he was like a gypsy in many ways. Small gold rings decorated his ears, and he thought and spoke slowly. He could read only very simple sentences, and these with difficulty, but he enjoyed looking at comic papers.

He had a wireless set in his wagon, though, and he was very proud of it. I don't think it was ever turned off. He would listen to Fat Stock Prices and talks on gardening with the utmost interest, or at least the utmost concentration.

His wife was a motherly little person with dark skin and very brown eyes. He told me that she enjoyed a glass of Guinness, but that he seldom drank.

They sometimes went to the pictures together and she would read the captions to him.

They, and the rest of the show at Llandudno, were slightly suspicious of me at first. I am afraid they did not like the look of me, and anyway they were of the type that does not take readily to strangers.

However, I enjoyed the time I spent with George Dell and his family. I have said that he was the head of the entire fair; and because he owned the roundabouts he was known rather curiously as the Riding Master.

His brother-in-law, Dick, had a set of swings, and Dick's wife was in charge of the coconut sheet. Bill, who was some sort of relation to Dell, had the rifle-range, and Bill's wife looked after this most of the time while her husband attended to the steam-engine on the roundabout.

Mrs. Dell had a sister called Mrs. Parsons, who lived with a daughter in a wagon on the far side of the ground. No one ever talked about Mr. Parsons; no doubt he was dead; in fact, all men were dead, as far as Mrs. Parsons was concerned. Everybody called her Jack, and she had no use for men.

She and her daughter Susie had a dart stall, and they looked after this and themselves with amazing competence. Susie was about sixteen. The first time I saw her she was carrying an enormous bucket of water towards her wagon, but I realized that it would be resented if I offered to help her. It was their pride that no work was too heavy for the Parsons.

The main attraction in the fair, apart from the roundabouts, was a giant spinner. A peacock, with its large tail studded with electric lights, spun round in a circle and the point at which it stopped decided a lucky number whose holder received a prize.

This joint was owned by Charlie Wigton, who lived

in the most up-to-date trailer on the ground. He probably rented his space from Dell, although it is possible that the Riding Master had some sort of share in the business.

At the far end of the fair stood two side-shows. They were both managed by the same man, and Dell had a share in the takings. One was a freak and the other a posing show.

Mary Ann Bevan, the Ugliest Woman in the World, was the freak. She lived in a wagon at the back of the show tent with her daughter Mary. As people paid to look at Mrs. Bevan, she seldom left the wagon, and it was only when it was dark that she sometimes took a little walk in the town.

Mary, her seventeen-year-old daughter, was not unattractive, but few people would look at her twice. Certainly, no one would pay to look at her, so she lived a more or less normal life. On most days she passed my tent several times during the evening with a jug of beer; this was when business justified the expenditure. We usually exchanged a few words.

"Y'know, Mum's a fool to herself," she told me once. "She got a real lot of money when she started, and when she went over to Coney Island she was taking a hundred pounds a week. But she's never done nothing with it. As soon as we get finished with the run and get back to the Smoke she gets a lot of her chinners round her and they just sit in the 'ouse and talk and bevvy till all the money's gone and we 'ave to start again. Y'know, we could 'ave a lovely living-wagon and run our own show if only Mum would take an interest in the business."

I felt sorry for Mary Ann Bevan. When your business is being the ugliest woman in the world it seemed to me that it might easily be hard to sustain an interest in it.

I visited her show a few nights after my arrival in Llandudno, and I preferred Mrs. Bevan to most of her audience.

"How'd you like to wake up with that next to you, Charlie?" said one particularly hideous woman to her husband; and a man who was standing next to me suddenly exclaimed: "Gawd, ain't she terrible!"

But Mrs. Bevan appeared to take no notice of the remarks. I think she was so inured that she hardly heard them. Smiling mechanically, she offered picture postcards of herself for sale.

"If any lady or gentleman would care to possess one of these cards," she said briskly, "the price is only twopence this evening. At one time they were sold at sixpence. I might add that the proceeds from the sale of these cards are for my own private use."

Mary was standing by the platform with a bundle of these photographs of her mother, looking eagerly for a buyer, for it was the sale of these cards that would decide whether she made another journey with her jug before closing time.

It is pathetic when any one loses his popularity and is forced to carry on to earn a living. It is always sad when a woman loses her beauty. But Mary Ann Bevan's case, although different, was even more pathetic, I thought, because the Ugliest Woman in the World was becoming more ugly every year.

Doctors had explained to her that this would be so. A malady which had been turned into an asset was lasting longer than its public appeal. Few people wished to see Mary Ann Bevan more than once, and since her first triumphant entry to the fair-grounds the Ugliest Woman in the World had traveled far.

I liked her. She was very polite, almost gentle, when we met, and she was very fond of her daughter.

Fakes are common in the freak business, and when Mary Ann Bevan first joined Dell's fair a number of the show people were convinced that she was a man disguised as a woman. The show people do not make up their minds quickly, but once they have formed an opinion it takes a lot of shifting.

However, Mrs. Bevan fell ill and the doctor who attended her convinced the Riding Master that she was perfectly genuine.

Her story, which Mary told me, was very sad. She was not born in the show business and she had not always been ugly. As a young woman she used to work in the fields, beginning about five o'clock in the morning. One day she was late, and the farmer who employed her lost his temper. That was at the time that a daily paper offered a hundred pound prize for the ugliest woman in the world.

Mrs. Bevan was not well. She had a disease which was incurable. Her features were growing out of all proportion, and her feet and hands had become twice their normal size.

But probably the farmer did not realize all this.

"You're no good to me," he said. "All you're fit for is the ugly woman competition."

Mrs. Bevan did not read much, but she read the daily paper, and that night she took the farmer's advice. She won the prize and afterwards went on the fairs.

The posing show next to Mrs. Bevan's stall was very much the same as any other of its type on any fair-ground. The spieler outside did most of the work. He is sometimes called a "barker," and his job is to interest the public sufficiently to get them to pay threepence to see the show. He talked for about ten minutes, and when he had finished his spiel Mademoiselle Yvette joined him outside.

She was his wife, and was always called Betty. She wore a bit of tinsel tied round her head and an ancient red velvet opera cloak.

When you went in she took off the cloak. In a pair of tights she posed in various attitudes and was supposed to represent famous art studies.

Mademoiselle Yvette proved to be a great attraction. She was not good-looking, and her figure was suitable only for studies in very modern art. Often people made the same sort of remark about her show as they had done on visiting Mary Ann Bevan next door.

But Betty did not mind. She sold quite a lot of postcards, and business was always good in Wales, she said.

The other fortune-tellers, myself, and Clarry Kidd, who had a spot-joint, comprised the rest of the fair. Clarry and I were the only two who had no living-wagons, so naturally we made friends.

He had big ideas, he said. He wanted to make a lot of money and start a retail fish-shop, but he never did this, as far as I know.

CHAPTER 11

My friend Clarry introduces me to his future mother-in-law's extraordinary ménage. I become a part of it. I fall in love with a gypsy queen and Clarry acquires a pair of boots.

It was Clarry who introduced me to Mrs. Dandi, and I stayed with him at her house all the time I was at Llandudno. This was one of those new council houses with all the latest conveniences and oldest discomforts.

Mrs. Dandi was an Irishwoman, and her husband was an Italian. They had seven children.

Polly, the eldest girl, was sixteen, and looked much older. She was very pretty, with jet-black hair, long eyelashes and a face that stood the enormous quantity of make-up she used. She looked Italian, and bright colors suited her.

Directly I saw her it occurred to me that she would make a good fortune-teller, but Clarry, I found, had already thought of this.

I got on well with Mrs. Dandi. She was very fat and very jolly, and she knew all there was to know about the show business. She made money out of various things. She had no shop, but she carried on a second-hand clothes business in her house and she had most of her horde of children employed at one thing or another. One of her sons sold newspapers, and two of her daughters worked in an amusement arcade during the season. They seemed to do extraordinarily well, but their employer, I heard, was losing money.

Mrs. Dandi also owned two ice-cream barrows. She used to make the ice-cream in the back scullery every evening, and she employed a couple of men to sell it.

Her husband was on the dole. Occasionally he made money at racing, and he collected bets for a bookmaker in the town. They were a weird family.

I slept in a double bed with Clarry, and we had a room to ourselves. All sorts of things were stored in the small space surrounding the bed, but the mattress was comfortable and it seemed fairly clean.

Mrs. Dandi was a free-and-easy landlady.

"I won't rob you, my boy," she said when I first approached her about terms. "Pay me what you think fair when you've been here a week and we won't fall out about it."

She seemed delighted to have us stay with her, although without us the house was pretty crowded. Clarry, of course, was a prospective son-in-law, and she may have thought I was a sort of second string.

A few nights after my arrival Clarry kicked me in bed.

"Did you hear that?" he whispered. "Now we're in for a bit of fun."

I had heard something. We had been in bed for about half an hour, and I was just dozing off to sleep. We had had a busy day, and Mrs. Dandi had arrived home late from a drinking party, but we had helped her make her ice-cream, since she needed help if the ice-cream was to be even as palatable as usual.

"The old girl's having a barney with the 'pot and pan,'" said Clarry. "She can't half let fly when she gets going."

There was a terrific noise from the room opposite ours, which was occupied by Mr. and Mrs. Dandi and a few of the younger children.

Clarry was wide awake and enjoying himself.

"What a woman!" he said. "I wouldn't be in that old boy's shoes for anything."

From the room across the passage, and above the general hubbub, there suddenly echoed an appalling scream. Clarry sprang out of bed.

"Better see what's happening. We don't want murder," he remarked casually, and I agreed with him heartily.

From our door I could look right into the bedroom opposite.

Seated on the bed, and in full view of the open door, was Mr. Dandi, clad only in a shirt, and he was holding his head, which was splashed with blood.

Mrs. Dandi was standing over him. She was covered by a large nightgown which touched the floor and made her look a bit taller than she was really. She looked just as fat, though, and made a rather terrifying figure, I thought.

In her right hand she clutched a pottery handle, but this was attached to only a part of the original vessel, and pieces of china scattered the floor at Mr. Dandi's feet.

His wife was very excited. Still clutching her strange weapon, she shook it menacingly at her husband.

"Now say you're sorry you married me, you good-for-nothing layabout!" she shouted.

I went back to bed, since Clarry seemed to think the affair was not as serious as he had supposed.

Words had long failed Mr. Dandi, and we heard no more of him that night.

But this sort of thing was quite a common occurrence in the Dandi household, and the children, and certainly Clarry, enjoyed the fun. I mention the incident since it was typical of the life of the household, which was unlike anything I had met before.

Although Mrs. Dandi was quick-tempered at times, she was a very good-hearted woman, and I think she liked her husband. She had grown used to him, at any rate, and would have missed him had he died or gone away.

Once when he was ill she nursed him most devotedly, and in spite of the fact that she used to blackguard him herself she never allowed any one else to say anything against him.

I spent nearly three weeks in Mrs. Dandi's house, and I became one of the family.

Business was good on the fair and work was amazingly easy. We did not start until the evening, and then there was little business until after seven o'clock. The fair was over by ten, but every night I took about three pounds, and I was averaging a steady eighteen pounds a week.

I made my lowest charge eighteen-pence, and I

never asked more than half-a-crown. People waited to see me, and business was brisk while it lasted.

My clients were different people from the Lancashire crowd. Most of the Llandudno folk regarded half-a-crown as a modest fee. The majority of the people who came to see me were visitors, but there were also dozens of local youngsters who had been employed in the town during the season. They had all been busy during August, and this was one of their first opportunities to spend the money they had made.

The fair visited Llandudno just at the right time. The holiday rush was over, and it was too soon for the people who had made money out of the holiday folk to feel the pinch of winter.

Boarding-house proprietors and landladies were in the mood for a little relaxation, and they were all, it seemed, astonishingly curious about the future.

One good lady visited me four times during my first week, and when I had begun to think that if I probed any further into her future it would have to concern her after life, she told me she wintered in the south of France and suggested that I should accompany her. I did not go, of course.

I fell in love at Llandudno.

I fell in love with Susannah, the niece of the Royal Gypsy, who was my rival on the ground. Susannah was practically pure Romany, and she was very pretty. We were wonderfully happy. There was plenty of time, the weather was ideal, and there was little to do during the day save enjoy ourselves.

I was making money for the first time in my life, and that was pleasant, too.

I think I should have married Susannah, but I didn't.

I bought a lot of new clothes at Llandudno. It was pleasant to go into a shop to buy a shirt and then suddenly decide to buy two. I had only bought things singly before, or had things bought for me by my mother.

I dressed carefully, because people recognized me in the street after I had been in the town a week and I believed in publicity.

Susannah and I often walked through the big shops before going to the fair in the evening, in case the people who worked there and who had already visited us would remember and tell their friends and customers.

We did the same sort of thing everywhere, and whenever I took Susannah to one of the big hotels for lunch everybody knew that we were from the fair, for although I was in love with her, and would probably have thought so anyway, Susannah really did look like a gypsy queen with her bright black hair and bright eyes and bright shawl.

Llandudno was a good place.

Clarry found business only fair. He did not do so well as I did. He wanted chumps, he explained. He was working on the "spot," which is one of the best-known spieling lines on the fairs.

I am afraid it was because it was so well known at Llandudno that Clarry did not do so well. The sign at the back of his joint, which he called his "flash," explained that covering the spot was "the latest American mathematical problem," which was good in itself, I thought. It also explained that it was a game of skill. However, the police did not always agree with him on this latter point.

Clarry gave the punter five circular discs about the size of a saucer, and with these the man had to cover a red spot about the size of a tea-plate, which was painted on a piece of white oilcloth. This round spot had to be completely covered, of course, and when he came to try to do this he found it most difficult: in fact, unless he knew the "ready," as Clarry called it, it was quite impossible.

Everything depended on how the punter placed his first disc, but, even if he hit on this by some miracle, he would most certainly fall down on the others unless he knew the full strength of the game.

Clarry made his own spot cloths, and he made them very difficult to cover. In fact, sometimes he couldn't even cover them himself in demonstration. But on these occasions he always managed to smother the odd red spot with his thumb, he told me.

Once a punter started to gamble Clarry had to win, but his difficulty lay in finding any one foolish enough to begin.

One night it rained, and, as I had made just under three pounds, I packed up a little earlier than usual. There were only a few people on the ground, and a number of the other side stalls had started to close down.

I walked over to Clarry's joint, which was next to the dart stall.

"One of the best nights I've had," he told me cheerfully. "I got a man for thirty holes just after I'd opened up, and then, not long ago, some chump down from the hills rolled up and dropped three nicker. I got him trying for denars to start with, and then I doubled him up to quids. Nanty!" he said. "Here's the man back!"

A bull-necked fellow, probably a young farmer, approached us. He stood for a while watching Clarry pack up, and I recognized him at once. He had been in the tent when I had watched Mary Ann Bevan some nights before, and I remembered that I had disliked him intensely. He was a noisy, uncouth soul, who had argued at most of the stalls and had made a general nuisance of himself.

At last he made up his mind and stepped forward.

"I haven't got my 'bus fare home," he said, and there was a hint of a threat in his tone.

At first Clarry appeared not to have heard, but suddenly he turned on him.

"Well, what about it? What do you expect me to do? You've got a good pair of boots, haven't you?" he demanded.

As he spoke he glanced down at the man's feet.

The young farmer looked sullen, but said nothing.

"They *do* look a good pair of boots," remarked Clarry thoughtfully. "I'll tell you what I'll do. I'll give you ten bob for 'em and you can have mine."

Clarry was wearing a pair of very pointed shoes. I happened to know they let the water in, and they looked as if they did, too. But the young farmer did not seem to mind. He unlaced his boots by the side of the stall without saying anything.

When Clarry had put on the boots he gave the

farmer a ten-shilling note. It seemed a fair price to me.

However, Clarry had not finished.

"Want to win some of your money back?" he asked.

The other hesitated only for a moment. He was soon playing. Covering the spot is a most fascinating game.

I knew Clarry was sensitive about an audience, and when Susannah wandered over to join me we stood back talking a few yards from the stall.

In less than ten minutes Clarry called us over. He was alone.

"I'm afraid he'll find it a long walk home in my daisies," was all he said. "Come on. I'm going to scarper before he decides to come back."

"Good Lord, I couldn't have done that," I said, feeling ashamed of him.

"Oh, I know how to deal with a real chump," he said. "He'd never have given me anything. I've been on the floor often enough to know that. If you get a 'wide finger' it's different, but chumps will always be chumps, and he was a right 'un if ever there was one."

It is only fair to Clarry to say that he was always the first to help a grafter who had come to grief.

"You can't refuse 'em," he used to say. "I've been skint so often myself."

It was really very difficult to help liking Clarry.

CHAPTER 12

I go to Llanfairfechan and visit No Name, where I am tempted by my anger to become dishonest. I return to Mold, where I part from my love and meet a Napoleon. The apple with a shilling in it. I spend a strange night, and in the morning, on hearing of the fruits of my dishonesty, become dissatisfied with Wales and decide to follow love to Hull.

Business on a fairground depends on the weather to an extraordinary extent. My luck was in during September, and when I followed Dell's fair to Llanfairfechan I had about thirty pounds, in spite of many rank extravagances.

There was nearly a week between the closing day at Llandudno and the opening of the next fair, so I thought I would try some of the markets round about.

Most of these were held in the main street of the village, and the people who came to them were farmers and their families.

The majority, I discovered, were ashamed to be seen entering my tent, and therefore the most favorable position for me was somewhere out of the way; so that which was popularly supposed to be the worst pitch in the market usually suited me best, and once I realized this I found little difficulty in getting a space.

I did not make much money, as expenses were high. It was not the tolls: these were reasonable enough. At Mold I was charged five shillings for the day, and at Ruthin and Corwen the ground rent was only half-a-crown. But railway fares were large, and I had to stop at a different place every night.

I knew nothing about markets, and relied upon a list of market days in a railway guide, and upon gossip among the stall holders.

After working at Mold on a Wednesday I decided to stay the night there. I tried to get lodgings, but it was not easy, and eventually I booked a room at the Red Dog, which seemed to be the best hotel.

It was run by several sisters, the youngest of whom was very charming and affable.

They charged me nine-and-sixpence for bed and breakfast. But several people who were staying there wanted to have their hands read, and I made my expenses.

On the following day I wanted to work somewhere, and the only place I could find in the railway guide within reasonable distance was called No Name.

The weather looked good and I made an early start. The station at No Name seemed a long way from the town. It stood by itself in the middle of the country and I was the only passenger to alight. The man who took my ticket told me that he could not leave the station and there was no one else about who might have acted as an outside porter.

I had left my skip, in which I had all my personal things, at Mold, as I meant to go back there, but in addition to my tent I had a large framed picture of the

Prince of Wales, quite two feet square. This had been Sammy's idea, and it had "Your Prince has had his hand read. Why not You?" painted on the mount. It always seemed to me to be a silly "flash," but Sammy seemed to know the game.

I had also a couple of folding-chairs and a bundle of iron stakes.

I decided to leave the chairs and the stakes at the station and set off for the town with the remainder of my tackle.

It was a long way. I had gone over a mile when I came to a small green, round which a few houses were scattered, and a large inn.

A man who was leading a horse looked at me as though he expected me to say something, and so I asked him how far I was from No Name. I suppose I must have been an unexpected apparition in full tails and laden like a camel wandering about on the side of a Welsh mountain.

"This is No Name," he said. "Who is it you'd be wanting?"

I decided it was a drink I really wanted, and I tried the public house.

A few farmers were in the bar, but there was nothing to suggest market day.

"It's a bit early yet," explained the publican, "but there'll be a few farmers in in the afternoon. There's a bit of a sale on in my yard, but there ain't much of a market hereabouts."

"But aren't there any people selling groceries or clothes?" I asked him.

He looked puzzled. "No," he said. "There ain't nothing like that here."

"I suppose these farmers bring their families with them?" I asked hopefully.

"No, they don't bring their wives with 'em," he replied. "That wouldn't do, would it, Bill?"

Bill, who was standing next to me and who smelt abominably of cowsheds, made a gurgling noise in his throat and grinned foolishly.

The others in the bar laughed.

"You've got enough cattle as it is, ain't you, Bill?" said some one, and again they all laughed.

Bill, I think, had a reputation for being simple. None of them looked bright to me, and I did not fancy my chances as a psychic adviser that day.

I had a look in the yard, which was only large enough to hold a few people. The smell was pretty bad too, so I decided to build up my tent on the grass opposite the main door of the public house.

From my point of view No Name was a God-forsaken hole. A couple of children watched me, and by the time I had finished they had been joined by a few more.

"What you doing, mister?"

"He's taking photographs in there."

"Go on! Where's his camera?"

"Why is 'e wearing that 'at?"

" 'E's going to do tricks."

"Look! 'E's got a white tie."

The children were interested enough, but there was not a sign of a likely-looking client. I got everything ready and then I went back to the bar.

"What're you having?"

It was a good greeting, and I looked at the man with interest. He was dressed like a farmer, but his clothes looked new and his hands were soft compared with the majority of hands I had seen in No Name. He was probably a little drunk, but his smile was genuine and he was friendly.

"You don't know me," he said.

"I'm sorry, but I can't say I do," I replied as I studied him more carefully.

"No, I don't suppose you do," he said. "But I've seen you before. I saw you last market day at Corwen. You tell fortunes, don't you?"

"Yes. That's my profession," I said.

He grinned and nudged me in the ribs. Unfortunately he nudged with the arm that was holding his pot of beer, and some of it splashed. I was glad he was friendly, but I wished he would not do this.

"D'you call it a profession?" he asked. "I've heard it called a crime."

He had dropped his voice to say this, and he was still grinning.

"Good luck to yer, son," he said. "That's what I say. Good luck to the man that can get owt from a Welshman. Here, you 'aven't said what you're going to 'ave." And he called to the man behind the bar.

A few drinks later I discovered that this man had something to do with a firm that called itself the Farmer's Friend. He visited all the markets round north Wales and canvassed orders for farm implements and animal food. He seemed to know every one and took life pretty easily.

"I'll get you some customers," he told me. "You see that old boy over there? He's a big farmer in these parts. Dead jealous of his wife. He's got an illegitimate child, too. In fact, they've nearly all got bastards round here. Dirty lot of devils, these farmers."

He paused for a moment to take a drink from his pot.

"You see that bloke that's just come in? 'Im with the fancy waistcoat?" he whispered. "His old woman snuffed it three years gone, and he's looking for another. Got stacks of dough and fancies his self a bit. But don't say nothing about a servant girl he had. He's a bit sensitive."

In spite of myself I obtained a lot of information from my new friend, but I saw great difficulties in persuading any clients to come into my tent. A Welsh farmer was the last person I would have chosen as a punter.

I could not gather what most of the people in the bar were talking about. They spoke half their sentences in Welsh and half in English, and the English half was almost impossible to follow.

Now and again one of them would look straight at me and intone something in Welsh, and his companion would then turn to regard me and reply in the same sing-song language. It was all most disconcerting.

"You get out to your doings. It's just on closing time," said the representative of the Farmer's Friend. "Leave it to me. I'll get the b—'s to come in."

He kept his word. When the bar emptied some twenty farmers staggered out of various rooms in the public house and stood regarding my tent with amusement.

My friend seized one man by the arm and led him towards me.

But when they were only a few feet away the farmer shook himself free and hurried back to the others. My friend bellowed something at him which I could not understand, and everybody began to laugh and shout.

No one liked the idea of being the first to come forward, and so my friend entered the tent.

"You needn't bother to read my hand," he said when we were inside. "You told my fortune at Corwen. But I'll wait in here a few minutes and then go back and tell 'em all about it. I particularly want you to tell one old b— something. Give him something to think about. They're a cunning lot of clods, these Welshmen."

"I wish I could speak their language," I said. "You seem to manage it pretty well."

"Why, of course I can," he said. "I'm a Welshman. I was born and bred in these parts. I know 'em inside out."

I was very glad he was on my side. He certainly worked hard for me, but I was among foreigners.

I remained in my tent when he left me, and a few minutes later a farmer entered warily.

A Welsh farmer is without exception the most difficult person with whom I have ever had to deal.

This man expected magic. Characteristics did not interest him. He took it for granted that I could tell him Everything about himself, his family and the people he knew, but if he could not find out something useful about them he did not think he was getting his money's worth.

There was nothing he wanted to know particularly, but he wanted me to find something exciting in his future and make it happen.

I did my best. My friend acted as doorman, and he was a very useful prompter.

"Ah, Mr. Jones, you're the next child to be led to the slaughter," he said, laughing.

But by the way he glanced at me when he said "child," I could not help knowing exactly what he meant.

"Now, come along, Mr. Davies," he said to another man. "If the Professor can't find you a good wife I don't know who can."

I certainly needed help. Every man who visited me that afternoon tried to beat me down in price, and they all grumbled. Also, when the subject of money came up I had the greatest difficulty in making myself understood.

Realizing that there were only a few prospective clients, I made my lowest charge two-and-sixpence, and I went out to get as much as I could. I felt that it was fair enough. They were certainly not likely to pay more than they could afford: besides, I felt an outcast, anyway, in this land of queer, sharp-eyed, tight-fisted foreigners.

I had just finished one man's reading when he took out a little leather bag from a pocket in the lining of his trousers, and this was a feat in itself. He hesitated before opening it.

"How much did you say, young man?"

I repeated that my fee was half-a-crown. I had made this quite clear before starting.

"Di-ow! I'll give you one-and-six," he suggested.

"You'll give me two-and-six," I said.

He pretended that he did not understand, and said something in Welsh.

"Good heavens, you're satisfied, aren't you?" I said.

"Satisfied?"

"Yes, satisfied. I've told you the truth, haven't I?"

"Yes, yes. Of course, young man, else you would be a swindler."

But the neck of his little leather bag was still securely tied, and he did not show any signs of undoing it.

Most of them behaved like this. If I had charged sixpence they would have tried to get me to take threepence.

I stuck to my price, however. I knew that if I reduced it he would boast to the others outside. Some of them did pretend that they had made me take a reduction, for they liked to appear clever bargainers.

However, I got my money, and when some of them suggested that I had taken less previously I denied it with truth and, I think, conviction.

I grew to hate Welsh farmers that afternoon.

"You'll take a shilling, won't you?" one man said. "I can tell you a lot of things about the others."

I was very insulted at this.

"Yes, and I could tell them a lot about you," I said involuntarily, and for a moment he looked alarmed.

I had been most polite to them all before this, and had spoken quietly and very precisely, but I now raised my voice a little and decided to appear as tough as possible. The sudden change was most effective.

"Why, my dear man," I said, "I can read you like an open book. I can read you all like books. And, mark this, I'm a very quick and extensive reader. Nothing is hidden from me. I could tell you things that would be worth fortunes to you all. I can see your wives and the women you've wanted and the women you've had. I can see your enemies: people with whom you drink, but who would do you out of your fortune if they could. But I'm not going to discuss all these things with you for a paltry piece of silver. Why should I help a wretched man who refuses to pay the fee that has been agreed upon? I don't know why I'm wasting my time with you."

He sat opposite me, his mouth partly open and a vague expression on his face. I was afraid he had not understood what I had been saying, and wondered if I could remember it if I had to repeat it.

"Here, give me your hand," I said.

I had made up my mind to talk quickly and to keep on talking, for I had found that I usually said something sensational when I did.

I told him about his farm, his wife, and a fair woman who was in his life. I told him that he ought to have been in jail at some time or another, but that he had been amazingly lucky. I enjoyed telling him this, and he did not interrupt me. None of the farmers seemed to have any ordinary morals, I had discovered, and anyway I was so angry with him for his meanness that I was most imprudent.

"There's a very young girl in your hand," I told

him. "There's love there, but I strongly advise you to avoid this person if you wish to escape criminal proceedings."

He grunted. He appreciated my advice, but seemed a little disappointed that the fates were to be against him.

"And now you owe me five shillings," I said, and held out my hand.

"But I haven't got five shillings," he protested. "By the dear Lord above, I haven't."

"Do you realize I've probably saved you from jail?" I demanded. "What have you got?"

"Holy Jesus, I can only give you two shillings. Man alive, you do not talk reason?"

"But you agreed to pay me two-and-sixpence before I started," I said, "and that's my fee. Now come on. I don't want to have to appeal to the people outside. It would take too long repeating everything I've told you."

He was silent for a moment. "I will have to get the money outside," he said.

But I was convinced that he had it with him and I did not like the idea of letting him get out.

At last very reluctantly he produced a pound note.

"I have no change withal," he said.

I do not approve of tick-offs who take large money, and I did not quite know what to do next. But I took the pound: that seemed the first thing to do.

"I am afraid this is very unlucky money," I said, examining the note carefully. I then folded it slowly and put it in my pocket. "Money has come quickly to you but it will also go quickly away. Do you understand?" I asked.

He nodded his head, but he looked very puzzled. I was not quite sure what I was talking about either. I was trying desperately to think of something that was worth fifteen shillings to him.

"You have gained much success," I continued, "by your own unassisted efforts. You have made money and your keen business brain has outwitted all with whom you mix."

Again he nodded and looked quite intelligent.

"But unless you take care your possessions will suddenly vanish like this"—and I pretended I was blowing out a candle. "Like snow in the blazing sun your wealth will dwindle, dwindle, dwindle."

His eyes were fixed on my hand, and his head followed it as it descended gradually until it nearly touched the ground at our feet. I had a dog once that used to do the same thing with exactly the same apprehensive expression.

"But why should I help you?" I persisted. "Why for twenty rotten pieces of silver should I assist you again to outwit your friends? I've a good mind to let you fight your battles alone."

He looked at me in terror, and I realized suddenly that he believed in black magic. Mean and cunning and anxious to get the better of any bargain, he was really very simple. I had obviously hit upon a few of his activities that were not generally known, and he was prepared to believe everything I said.

I was half disgusted with him, and very nearly told him to get out and take his pound with him, but he had tried to cheat me at the beginning and I certainly felt he was getting his money's worth in sensation. Besides, I wanted the money. So I carried on.

"My God, it'll be a big fight this time!" I said, looking at his hand. "I'm afraid you haven't an earthly chance without my advice."

This suggestion that his wealth was in danger worried him much more than any of my previous revelations, the jailing included.

"Tell me everything you can see," he said.

This I did, and more, of course.

"Yes, it's a disease. Some sort of illness. I don't understand these things," I said breathlessly, "but your cattle will be in danger. I see death, but I do not see them dying. They will have to be destroyed."

I felt a little puzzled by this myself, because I had no idea why I had said it. He urged me to continue.

"You must realize," I said, "that Destiny does not cut out a definite path for you. It does not force you to travel in a certain direction, giving you no opportunity of using your brains. Danger is threatening, but being warned is being armed. Possibly you can avert this tragedy."

Before he left me he was quite satisfied; in fact, he seemed quite pleased. The terrible events which I had predicted, hardly realizing what I had been saying, actually appeared to cheer him up, and when I had pointed out that being warned was being armed he had chuckled and agreed with me readily.

I had quite a good day at No Name in the end.

Of course I had been most dishonest. In the bar that evening I realized this, but I stood my good friend a number of drinks and argued with my conscience all the way home.

Business was very poor at the fair at Llanfairfechan, so I only worked there during the week-ends. A couple of weeks later I was again at Mold, on a Wednesday. It was quite an eventful day.

I was in the middle of reading a youth's hand when Susannah put her head into my tent. I left my client and went out to her.

The husband of the Royal Gypsy had had a barney with some of the show people at Llanfairfechan, and the whole caravan was off to Hull Fair.

"I saw your joint as I was passing through," said Susannah, "so I had to make them stop just to say good-by."

It was good-by, as a matter of fact. It was over two years later when I saw Susannah again. We met at Henley Regatta. She was married, and had a baby too.

"I wish you'd been at the fair," she said, standing outside my joint in Mold High Street. "There was the devil of a barney, and we decided to clear off first thing the next morning."

I was sorry I hadn't been there, too. I walked over to where their caravan was parked some way down the street. It was an old single-decker bus that had been converted into a living-room and had chintz curtains over the windows which ran the whole of the van on either side.

"We're scarpering to Yorkshire," said Freddie, the Royal Gypsy's husband. "I'll be glad to get out of this monkery. They're a lot of uneducated savages."

"Monkery" was a new word to me, and I discovered afterwards that it meant "district."

"We'll be meeting again," his wife told me. "Hope you have a bit of luck. But Wales is no place for the back end. These are summer gaffs, you know."

I was sorry to lose Susannah, but somehow I couldn't decide to ask her to join me.

It had all happened very suddenly, of course, and I had not then been in the game long enough to want to tie myself to it, so I found myself waving good-by as the old red bus lurched forward and, following the bend of the road, was eventually lost to sight.

Susannah leaned from the door at the back, waving to me, until she was out of sight. Her blouse looked very white against her dark skin, and a vivid red handkerchief floated from her hand.

She was always fond of bright colors.

I returned to my tent and discovered my client still waiting for me. I had been away for over twenty minutes and had forgotten all about him.

He worked in a grocer's shop, and wanted me to advise him about marriage. His girl was employed in some tin works at Denbigh, and she wanted him to marry her, although he was not yet in a very good job.

I did not blame her. I had seen girls working in a tin works once.

I was just in the mood to advise him.

He probably had the banns put up that week.

Later, when business slacked off in the market, I called in at the Red Dog to book a room for the night. Here I was disappointed. The night before I had sent Dorothea, the youngest sister of the house, a box of chocolates, and these were returned to me and I was told that there was no room. I was rather startled. My offering had been a rather foolish gesture made because I had had a good day.

It was a pity. I gave the chocolates to my next client. I told her that I always presented a box of chocolates to the most attractive lady who visited me at every town. I could not think of any other possible excuse on the spur of the moment.

However, this was not a bad idea. She talked about the gift a good deal, and recommended a number of her friends.

Business was a little better than when I had been at Mold before, and it was not until five o'clock, when the market was practically over, that I had a look round.

There were the usual regular stall-holders: people selling clothes, silk by the yard, and groceries by auction. There were a number of fruit and vegetable stalls and a man who sold sweets.

He boiled toffee on the stall, and was known as a "candy slinger." He used to mix up butter and sugar into a thick mass until it looked like several pounds of dough. This he hung on a hook which was fixed to the side of his joint, and pulled it out.

After a certain amount of this treatment it looked like a skein of silver wool and he used to take strands of it and throw them over the hook just as they were falling.

It looked very difficult and attracted quite a crowd.

His name was Sammy Horner, and people said that he was the best candy puller on the gaffs.

But farther down the street, practically outside the market hall, was some one new to Mold market, and he was holding the biggest crowd.

There was not room for a really big crowd, but people blocked the pavement and I had some difficulty to see what was happening.

In the center of the group stood a tall African nigger. He wore no hat, and his closely clipped head rose to a dome, so that it looked rather like a coconut. He had a bright red jacket heavily embroidered with gold, and a pair of very loosely fitting trousers of bright blue material which were gathered at the ankles and looked like a pair of plus fours which had slipped.

He was well over six feet high, and had exceptionally long arms.

". . . life is a game of chance," he was saying as I arrived. "Everything is chance. Can you tell me one thing, ladies and gentlemen? How is it that I was born black and you were born white? How is it that some are born into a life of luxury and others into poverty and the slums? It is just a matter of chance, ladies and gentlemen. Just a matter of chance."

Towering above those around him, he talked with enthusiasm. His long arms trembled above his head one moment and shot out in a dramatic gesture the next. His eyes bulged and swiveled and his teeth looked very white.

"Some of you will turn away, perhaps," he continued. "Some of you will say it is nothing to do with chance, but is the will of God. I do not know your God. I am a black man, a heathen. The God I worship is the God of Chance, the God whose images I carry with me here."

He held up a little tray on which were a number of lucky charms such as gypsies sell on race courses and buy by the gross in Houndsditch.

He paused for a moment while he placed aside the tray he had been holding.

"Have I not been told that your God is a just God, a gentle God? Is it His will that children are born without limbs, damned to suffer till the day of their death? Is it God's will that your sons were made targets for enemy bullets and young men were crippled before they had begun to live? Can you tell me that it is only God's chosen who ride about in motor-cars today while thousands of men walk the streets looking for the work they will never find? No, ladies and gentlemen. It is just a matter of chance."

The people around him were interested. They listened in silence and watched his every movement.

"I am going to prove to you that life is just a game of chance by a simple illustration," he continued, arranging a small table in front of him, on which were three apples. "I bought these apples this morning from one of your market salesmen here," he explained, "and I have reason to believe that there is a shilling inside one of them. I am going to show you that unless the God of Chance smiles upon you you cannot choose the right apple. Now, who will select an apple?"

There was silence for a moment.

"It's quite simple. There is one in the middle, one

on the right and one on the left. Just call out which one you would like."

"The one in the middle," said a man standing near the front.

"Very good, sir," said the nigger, throwing it to him. "You have made your choice. You might easily have selected the apple on the right, or the apple on the left, but you have decided on the middle apple. It is just a matter of chance. Chance decided that you should not get the shilling. Have you a knife? Good. Cut open the apple and look for yourself."

"Now, ladies and gentlemen," he went on, "I have but two apples left. Which is it to be? The one on the right or the one on the left?"

"The one on the left," shouted some one at once.

The nigger picked up the apple on his left and threw it to him.

"Cut it open for yourself," he said. "It is just a matter of chance. Some one here might easily have chosen the right. But no. Chance was not with them. Chance has decided that I shall have the shilling."

He picked up the last apple carefully and held it so that all might see it. Then, cutting it open, he dramatically disclosed a shilling embedded near the core.

A very large crowd had collected by this time, and it was quite a quarter of an hour later when he finally reached the articles that he had come to sell. They were the little lucky charms, and he claimed that they would bring luck to whosoever should possess one. He charged sixpence for them and told the people that if they failed to bring them luck within ten days they were to return them, and not only would he refund their money but he would give them five times that amount. He held up half-a-crown to impress them.

Where exactly they were to return them he did not say, but the crowd was convinced, and he sold over a score in that demonstration.

As he served each customer he placed the lucky charm against his forehead and muttered some sort of magic formula. The words which he repeated, I noticed, were "Parny on the tober, parny on the tober." Since, as I have said, this meant that it was raining on the fair-ground, I was surprised, for it was a beautiful day.

I suppose it sounded as good as anything else.

He did not have another pitch after this. Most of the stalls had already packed up, and, seeing me watching, he came over.

"What sort of day?" he asked.

I told him business had not been bad.

"Good. I can't grumble," he said. "Of course, markets aren't much bottle for me. I work the flip and muzzel. They're together."

I discovered that "flip" meant racing tip, and "muzzel" was a Jewish word for luck.

A muzzel worker was a man who sold lucky charms.

"I won't be a minute," he said. "I've only to put these things in my peter and then we'll have a bevvy. I want to talk to you."

His peter was obviously his suitcase, in which he carried everything he required. I envied him for this. Windy weather didn't worry him much, and there was none of the bother that is connected with a tent.

I was glad to meet him and I felt like a drink. We went together to the Black Lion.

"You ought to join me—we'd be the strongest workers on the road," he told me after a few drinks. "I took to that clobber of yours directly I spotted you. You know the value of a flash and you can talk. You could say such a lot of things about a darkie which I dare not say myself. We'd knock 'em all cold."

After a few more drinks I rather liked the idea myself, but I had never been keen on partnerships. But I was attracted to the idea of the muzzel, especially in Wales.

"How did you work that apple trick?" I inquired.

Napoleon Jackson, for he had told me that was his name, smiled, and I noticed his eyes were a little bloodshot.

"It's not much of a trick," he said, "but a little business like that keeps the crowd interested. Of course I put the shilling there beforehand. It's easy to work a coin into an apple without leaving a mark. I never have the one with the denar in it in the middle. So long as it's in one of the outside ones I can make 'em take which I like. If a chap says he wants the left one I give it to him, if it isn't the one I've readied. And if it is, I give him the one on *my* left. It's very simple. Their left side is my right side.

"I used to work the Mystic Table once," he went on. "That's another good pitch getter. It always attracts a crowd. I used to wear a ring all the time I worked that trick. You do the stunt with a light card-table. You place your hands flat on the top, with your fingers stretched out in front of you, and after a bit of moody you raise your hands in line with your head and the table moves with them. I used to have a bit of a fanny about table rapping in those days."

"Moody" meant a bit of humbug. It is a very common word among the grafters. They would say, "We'd better moody the landlady a bit," when they meant that they would pay her a few compliments; and when they did not believe something you were saying they would tell you to "cut out the moody."

"Of course I used to catch my ring in a nail I'd had specially fixed in the table," Napoleon continued. "If you get this fixed on the slant in the right position it's dead easy, but it looks good."

I gradually realized we were getting very drunk. The pubs were busy on market day at Mold and the bar was crowded. It was after eight o'clock, and we had been drinking for nearly three solid hours.

"This isn't a bad trick," said Napoleon, dropping a penny into a glass of beer.

After he had said a few magic words to it, it righted itself and rose mysteriously up the side of the glass.

"It's easy," he explained. "I've got a hair fixed on to a button on my waistcoat. You can't see it unless it's pointed out to you. It's also fixed to the penny by a little piece of candlegrease. You can use chewing gum if you like. I've only got to sway slightly backwards and naturally it pulls the penny up. You want to do it very slowly and it puzzles every one. Of course you want to use your own chewing gum or some one else's beer," he added seriously.

We had a pleasant evening. About nine o'clock the

market superintendent found us and told me that I had to get my tent out of the roadway.

Napoleon realized at the same time that he had only a few minutes to catch the last train to Manchester, so we both left the Black Lion.

I found some children with whom I arranged that they should pull down my tent for me, and they helped me to carry it to the station.

"Where can I stop tonight?" I asked. "I don't want a hotel."

I was very dazed, and remembered little of what happened afterwards, but I know they took me after a lot of discussion to a part of Mold which I had not before seen.

The streets were narrow and ill-lit, and people sat on their doorsteps and talked across the road to their neighbors opposite.

The house to which the children took me was a large one. It was a lodging-house, the first real doss house I had experienced.

I remember walking into a large room not very well lit, with a well-worn brick floor. It was of an unusual shape, very long and yet seeming full of corners. The ceiling was lower in some parts than in others, and some of the plaster had fallen, showing the rafters underneath.

I remember the place smelt a little, but it was a warm smell and I decided that it was an attractive room on the whole.

A number of people sat about. Most of them were grouped round the fire, which burned in a large open grate in the furthermost wall.

There were several wooden forms set round the fireplace, and I particularly noticed a wretched woman who lay on one of these. Her bare foot was showing through the sole of one of her boots and her hair hung in wisps about her face.

In spite of the warmth the atmosphere was gloomy. I know I felt very happy, and I decided that every one needed cheering up. So I asked where I could get some beer.

I was still wearing tails and a topper, of course, for all my stuff was at the station. However, as far as I remember, no one minded about this. It was still comparatively early and one man told me that he knew some one who would serve me with beer at the back door. I welcomed him like a brother, although he was not a pleasant type. He was far too obliging.

I had met people like him before: people who, when I had inquired the way of them, had insisted on personally conducting me to my destination. It is curious that these people never seem to expect a tip. They are content to be seen walking with a stranger and, no doubt, to find out something about his business.

I remember we got the beer and we made merry in the doss house that night. What happened afterwards, though, I have never been able to remember.

I woke early the next morning. My mouth was dry and my forehead was wet. I had an appalling headache and it was a few moments before I remembered where I was.

There was no covering over the floor, and there did not seem to be much on the bed. Mine was an iron affair and was near the wall. This was whitewashed, but wanted re-doing, I noticed.

I sat up suddenly as I remembered my money. There were six beds in the room, and all were occupied except one. This had been slept in, but its occupant had already risen.

I looked about me cautiously, but no one seemed to be awake. I discovered that I was clad only in my shirt and underlinen, while my evening jacket and trousers lay on the floor at the foot of my bed. I examined my pockets. I could not find a penny.

I was feeling pretty sick with life, and furious with myself, when I experienced a great wave of relief. Lying in the bed in which I had been sleeping I saw my wad of notes. I had probably gone to sleep holding them, but had unfastened my grip while waking.

I had taken nearly four pounds in silver the previous day, but whether I had spent it or lost it I never knew. At any rate, I saw no point in letting it worry me.

Dressing as quickly as I could, I found my way downstairs. The large room was less attractive by daylight, and it was cold, although quite a number of people was gathered there.

I recognized no one. There were no women about, and a man was boiling water in a can on the fire.

I wanted to get a drink of water, and I exchanged a few words with a man who was shaving at a sink. I felt that my costume required some explanation, and I thought I ought to say that I was a grafter.

"I've had a bit of a thick night, I'm afraid," I said. "I've been working on the market."

"I know you have," he said. "You'd had a good day, hadn't you?"

"Not too good," I replied cautiously. "I'm a fortune-teller, you know."

" 'Course I know," the man replied. "Wasn't you telling all our fortunes last night?"

I suppose I must have looked a little astonished.

"Surely you remember telling old Bill's hand?" said a little rat-faced man who had just joined us.

"Yes, you must remember that," butted in the man with the razor. "You remember Bill? A big man with a red face, and sort of angry-looking. You told him that he weren't married but ought to be. Told 'im straight out in front of all of us that he was living with a woman that weren't 'is missus. And you told 'im the bloody truth, son. That did you credit."

"That's right. 'E's been wanting some one to tell him that for some time," remarked the other man. "You must remember Bill," he continued, glancing round him a little nervously, I thought. " 'E ain't down yet, but 'e ought to be 'ere any minute."

But I had no desire to meet Bill at the moment. I wanted a bath.

It was very early morning and the shops were not yet open. I got into the railway station, though, and, since it was deserted, I persuaded the man in charge to let me change my clothes in the luggage office.

Later I got something to eat and I managed to get a bath at the Swan.

I was still feeling a little shaky, and I had a double brandy and a Gaymer's cider at the Black Lion while I tried to think out where I should go next.

I was still thinking when some one slapped me on the back and I turned to find the representative of the Farmer's Friend at my elbow. He looked disgustingly fit, and seemed overjoyed with himself.

"Fancy seeing you!" he said. "What you 'aving?"

When I told him how well he looked he told me that I looked like death warmed up. He wasted no time in small talk.

"I say," he said slyly, "what did you tell that farmer the other week?"

"I don't know who you mean," I said honestly. "What farmer?"

"Oh, come on, you remember," he said. "You'd have recognized him, all right, if you'd been at No Name a couple of weeks back. It's a most extraordinary thing, but he sold all his cattle. Sold the whole b— outfit. It's the talk of the countryside. There's never been a sale like that in these parts for years, and I said to myself at once, I said, 'That there Professor's at the bottom of this, I'll lay odds.'"

I was appalled.

"I believe I do remember him," I confessed.

My friend chuckled. "And I'll bet he remembers you," he said. "I bet you told him a pretty tale, and I'll lay odds that he's looking for you in a week or two. He's a shrewd man, but he practically gave his stuff away. Seemed quite happy about getting rid of 'em, too. Gave 'em away to 'is pals."

I did not know what to say. The man had certainly annoyed me at the time, but I had not contemplated this sort of mischief. It seemed to me to be a very

CHEAPJACK 147

dangerous thing to annoy a magician; more dangerous than even the magician knew.

I looked at my friend dubiously. Although I had had a bath I still felt as though I had slept out all night, and it was difficult to keep up with his good humor.

I returned to the contemplation of my future. Business with George Dell's fair was poor now, and it was not worth while following him through the winter. Moreover, I decided that I was tired of Wales. Wales, I thought, should have a rest.

So I took the first train to Hull. I had heard a great deal about Hull Fair, and the Royal Gypsy had said her caravan would be there.

Endpapers drawn by 'Grog' (A. J. Gregory) for the first UK edition, 1934.

CHAPTER 13

I take part in Hull Fair and meet many strange and interesting people, including Mad Jack, Peter the Whistler, and Madame Sixpence. I am invited to become an orthodox Jew, but decline and leave Hull.

Hot pies and peas and silken candy, nougat and fish and chips. There's something for everybody at Hull Fair.

There were nearly a hundred fortune-tellers' tents set up when I arrived. Thin-faced gypsies; fat, red-cheeked women who looked like publicans' wives; niggers in dusty eastern robes; and unshaven "professors" complete with caps and gowns were there to tell the tale.

Over a dozen smudge workers were there, too, with their cameras, while gazers selling balloons or little celluloid dolls with fuzzy hair presented women visitors with their goods and blagged the money from their escorts.

R.O. boys plundered the people as they passed, and windbag workers gave pound notes away to the ricks in their audiences.

Jews in tightly fitting clothes auctioned chocolates, and men with long noses and pointed boots sold rock and a sweet that looked like cotton-wool and was called "sea-foam candy."

Grafters sold "gold" rings at sixpence each and engraved two sets of initials on them free of charge.

There were tea joints, coffee stalls and a crowd of odd little refreshment tents which proffered plates of mussels, winkles or jellied eels for their patrons' delight.

All this was in Walton Street, a road about half a mile long which leads to the main fair-ground.

The stalls stood close to one another along the entire length of this road, on both sides, and my tent was about halfway up on the right as one approached the fair. I was lucky and was on corporation ground, so that my toll was only a pound for the whole week. But the pitchers on the opposite side of the road paid anything from three to ten pounds for their space to the householders, whose frontage was let to the highest bidder.

Higher up towards the fair-ground the houses had gardens in front of them. Fortune-tellers filled these, and the rents were very high. But a whole family of gypsies would work from one big tent and thus all possible space was occupied.

When I settled down I discovered that I had on one side of me Madame Cavendish, palmist, and on the other a Jew auctioning boxes of chocolate. Directly opposite was "Professor" Desmond, another fortune-teller, but on his left was an entrance to some barracks, which had to be kept open.

The roadway was packed with people. They were

a noisy crowd and laughed and shouted at the top of their voices, so that the uproar was terrific.

Among the gazers and the holiday makers and the fly pitchers wandered a single man with a large placard on his back. On this was painted in large white letters the somewhat bald statement, "The Wages of Sin is Death." He was quite the traditional specter at the feast.

It puzzled me how we were all going to get a living. I had heard Hull Fair called "the tick-offs' gaff," and I realized that there was something in the name. Walton Street was a road of fortune-tellers.

This is the last big fair of the season, and practically all the grafters meet here before scattering over the country for the winter. I calculated that about two thousand pounds must be spent on fortune-telling during the week.

But thinking it over, I imagine I underestimated the amount. Business was good at Hull Fair. I took over thirty pounds.

But when we were standing outside our tents watching the crowd make their way towards the fair, Madame Cavendish sighed.

"There's not the money about that there used to be," she said as she tried to attract the attention of the passers-by. "This used to be the best gaff in the country for dook reading. Just after the war my old man used to carry the takings back to the wagon at night in a bucket—a great big slop-pail full of silver. We used to be too tired to count it. I couldn't take money fast enough. I didn't bother after big money. Tosheroon and sometimes a caser, that were good enough. In and out they come as fast as I could spiel to 'em. Them *were* days."

She was a tall, not unattractive-looking woman, with untidy hair and a frock which suggested that she had once been fatter. It hung loosely about her and was rather dirty.

She had a number of children who hung about quite happily, and her husband told me that he did a bit of horse dealing and hawking.

"I reckon the game's about beat," she said. "There ain't the money about, for one thing, and the public's getting a lot too wise. It don't give you a chance, you know. The girls today think more about their silk stockings than they do about marriage, and they know just how many chavvies they're going to have better'n you or me could tell them."

"Chavvies," I knew, was the gypsy word for "children."

Madame Cavendish was very down on birth control. It spoilt business, she said.

"Gawd knows what they'll be up to next," she observed. "It don't give you a chance to get an honest livin'. Yes, lady. Step inside, my dear."

The final part of her conversation was addressed to a girl who was hovering in front of our tents. Although my neighbor enjoyed a chat she kept a keen eye open for business.

"Step inside, my dear," she repeated, and, wandering over to the girl, she whispered something.

The young woman was timid, though, and eventually walked away.

"There you are. 'Tain't what it used to be," said

Madame Cavendish, returning to her tent and resuming her conversation.

She had only one subject, though, and I found it a usual one among the fair-people. Every one complained to me at some time or another that the game was not what it used to be.

But I did not think it was too bad.

Of course, whenever I got any money something happened to prevent me from keeping it; but I have always experienced that difficulty. Here, of course, it was impossible to save much, as a bad period usually followed a good fair.

However, I was far from being broke at the time and life seemed pretty good.

The space next to "Professor" Desmond, which was the open way to the barracks, was a favorite resting-place for the gazers who walked up and down Walton Street. Each of these men had a ticket pinned to his lapel which showed that he had paid his toll. They obtained their tickets daily and they cost two-and-sixpence each. For that fee they obtained a permit to sell things as they walked about the fair, but they were supposed to keep on the move the whole time.

One of the best gazers I ever saw was Mad Jack. Although I stayed in the same house that he did at Hull I never learned his real name. Everybody knew him as Mad Jack and it was the name he called himself. He seemed pleased with it. He was Jewish, but this was not very noticeable. His face was like a red-nosed comedian's and rather on the fat side; he looked like a chubby schoolboy, although he must have been somewhere between thirty-five and forty. His face was always very red and his nose was big. Unlike the thin, sensitive nose of the Jew, it was a soft, fat nose. It looked comic and as if it were false. He was always smiling, and his energy was amazing. He really enjoyed his work.

Mad Jack sold Harold Lloyd hats and goggles. They are the sort of things that are given away at carnival dances. The goggles had no glass in them and the hats were made out of cardboard, fitting on the head by means of a piece of elastic under the chin. These were about as big as the lid of a milk saucepan.

Directly Mad Jack arrived on the fair every one knew it. He used to get about a dozen small boys to follow him about, the cheekiest he could find. He gave them a set of goggles and hats, and, wearing these, they marched about the place with Mad Jack as their leader, shouting for all they were worth.

If there was no carnival spirit about, Mad Jack seemed to create it. I have seen him stop people in the street, place one of his hats on their heads and insist on dancing with them. No one ever seemed to be annoyed with him.

He was always working—on railway stations, in the train, or in the streets. I think it was a habit which had grown upon him and that he probably grafted at home.

"He's stone-crackers," some of the grafters said. But he certainly made money.

He did not drink, and what exactly he did with his gains no one ever knew, for he was nearly always broke.

Eating was his greatest pleasure, I think, but he

could not possibly have spent all his money on food.

Peter the Whistler was another gazer who interested me. This was the first fair at which I had seen him. Dirty, unshaven and dressed like a tramp, he is often to be seen, particularly in the winter, in London. He is a tall, lanky person who has a peculiar habit of grimacing while he talks.

How he manages to get to all the important fairs is rather a mystery. Usually he, too, has a number of children following him, but I think they make fun at him rather than with him.

He usually works for pennies, and children are his customers.

As he walked through the fair he made a curious birdlike noise. He had only one little tune, and he made this with a bit of tin that looked something like a button. He carried these in his pocket and sold them to the children. But I think he could probably make the noise without any assistance, for he could imitate the call of most birds, but he used to stick to his little tune most of the time.

Like Mad Jack, he used to work the whole time.

When I walked up Walton Street on the morning of the first day of the fair I saw Peter sitting up on some one's empty stall. No one had bothered to open yet, for, apart from grafters, there were few people about. He was whistling his tune, which consisted of less than half a dozen notes. A number of barefooted children stood round him, and it was obvious that not one of them had a penny.

As I noticed him he stopped whistling and suddenly

shouted at the top of his voice, making the most terrifying grimaces.

"They say 'Good old Peter.' Peter the Whistler, that's my name! People say I'm mad, up the pole, Lakes of Killarney, crackers!"

The children who knew him regarded him stolidly, but one or two of them stepped back hurriedly. There was something frightening about him when he was in this mood.

"Well, my children, I'll tell you something," he continued, thrusting out his head towards them and grinning so that the tip of his nose nearly touched his lower lip. "I am mad. Mad as a coot."

He then continued to whistle his tune, which grew monotonous after a while. He ignored every one and made no effort to sell anything.

Where he sleeps or how he gets about the country no one knows. Most of the grafters shouted, "Oi, oi, Peter!" as he passed, but apart from just recognizing him no one seemed to know anything about him. But I think he would be missed very much if he did not turn up. Like the man with the "Wages of Sin is Death" placard, he has grown to be a part of the fair.

A number of grafters stopped to exchange a few words with me as I stood at my tent. I did not recognize some of them, but my eternal dress-suit was conspicuous and they had seen me before somewhere.

"It's about time I got down to graft," said one man, pausing to speak to me, "but it doesn't seem to be much bottle for the screechers 'ere, does it?"

He glanced across the road and was obviously referring to a couple of street singers who had commandeered the pitch in the opening opposite me for a few minutes.

We had been talking for a while when he asked suddenly: "Have you got a jam jar?"

"No, I haven't one," I said, looking vaguely about me, "but you'll probably be able to get one from one of those little grocery joints up the street. There's a shop there where I get my paraffin."

I am afraid he must have thought that I was trying to be funny. He looked at me doubtfully for a moment and then explained himself.

"What's the idea?" he asked, grinning. "You know what I mean. Have you got a jam jar—a car?"

I understood what he meant at last. Even then I was not always prepared for slang.

I told him that I had no car, but that I traveled by rattler. I was rather proud of the word, for I had only recently discovered that all the grafters gave a train this name.

"Oh, you ought'a have a jam for this game," he told me emphatically. "Why, it must cost you a pile getting about the country, and rattlers are always a nuisance. I got a jam jar. You can't beat 'em. If you'd only told me when I seen you last I would 'ave given you a lift. That was at the Hiring Fair at Abber, wasn't it?"

I had worked at the Hiring Fair at Abber. It was only a few miles from Llanfairfechan. But I did not remember my companion.

"Gawd, you must remember me," he said. "We had a cup o' rosy together. I met you in the coffee whack there. Don't you remember?"

I looked at him more carefully. He was a thickset man, about forty. His bowler hat was superior to the variety usually worn by grafters, and, although his shirt needed washing and looked the worse for wear, his blue serge suit was practically new and of a good material. His face looked familiar, but I could not place him.

" 'Struth, I thought you nobbled me," he said, grinning. "But you've never seen me with me scotchies on before. You get me now, don't you? Remember the little titfer on the side of me 'ead and the placard on me back?"

In spite of myself I glanced at his legs. I did remember him, but when I had seen him last he had had no legs below the knee. He was perfectly frank, and appeared to see nothing unusual about the situation.

"These legs cost me a whole lot of gelt," he explained. "I leave 'em in the jam jar when I'm grafting. I'm all right on me pins as far as walking goes, but of course I can't handle the jam. Bit of a nuisance, but I've got a kid wot drives me about. It's the only way to do it. You ought to get a jam jar."

When he walked away I noticed that he was slightly lame. I remembered him perfectly. I had seen him walking among the people at Abber. He had been begging. His legs, which he referred to indiscriminately as his "scotch pegs" or his "pins," were missing, and he had been wearing a brightly colored tam-o'shanter. In his hand he held a well-worn cap, and this he thrust into the faces of the passers-by.

Few people could resist his appeal, for he looked very pitiful.

He was always amazingly cheerful, though, and demanded money from the punters with a broad smile.

On his back was a placard on which was scrawled in pencil: "From Glasgow to London."

After our meeting in Hull I was always knocking into him at most unlikely places. He believed in travel, he said.

He used to wear an old jacket while he was grafting, and this explained why his shirt was ragged while his off-duty suit was in perfect condition. He used to change his jacket in the car, and he left his legs in the same place until he needed them again.

Of course, when he was grafting in the south he used to have "From London to Glasgow" penciled on the card on his back. But otherwise he always seemed the same.

All the Yorkshire showmen and grafters from all parts of the country were collected on the main ground at Hull, but I had little to do with these, although I explored the fair carefully because I wanted to find Susannah and the Royal Gypsy.

But they were not there. Freddie had probably altered his plans on the way down.

They seemed to be the only absentees, however. Most of the showmen I had ever met were there, but Hull Fair is an exception. Generally speaking, showmen do not travel from one end of England to the other. As a rule they keep to their own district and, hindered by their very heavy shows, more often than not restrict their journeys to one county.

They are a people apart. Living in caravans and marrying among themselves, they are a very respect-

CHEAPJACK

able crowd who mind their own business and mind it pretty well.

They are not to be confused with grafters. The grafters are the true wanderers. Although they may make a center in a district, or "monkery," they only stay there for a time and sooner or later they are on the move again.

Grafters comprise fortune-tellers, demonstrators, crocuses, gazers, and those knocker workers who also graft at fairs and markets; in fact, every kind of person who sells things in the open or in tents and stalls and who pretends to give things away.

The word "crocus" is a general term for miracle workers, herbalists, and any variety of quack doctor. It is also the slang for a real doctor.

A "knocker worker" is one who sells things at people's front doors. He may claim to represent a well-known firm or he may simply attempt to sell a packet of lavender on the doorstep.

R.O. boys and windbag workers are, of course, grafters, though any one who holds a big crowd and does a good deal of shouting is usually called a "pitcher."

The quieter workers, who talk to only a few people at one time, are called "demonstrators," and these usually show some sort of labor-saving device or teach people how they may make woolen rugs or silver-plate their bronze.

There are many Jews among the grafters, but they usually stick to the chocolate "lark," or auction, the windbags or the R.O.

The colored men seem to be attracted to the "mystery" side of the business, although there are a number of very successful colored crocuses.

An enormous number of crockery sellers are Lancashire men, and their great stalls, where they sell all kinds of china by mock auction, are usually called "pot joints."

Outside a public house, about thirty yards up on the other side of the road from my tent at Hull, was Madame Suzie's joint. One side of her living-wagon opened out and made a platform on which she stood. She held a huge crowd all day, and drew up horoscopes for people while they waited.

These horoscopes were two large sheets of roneo'd paper, and she only charged sixpence a time for them. But she must have taken a lot of money. She paid ten pounds for her pitch.

"Suzie," like "sprasey," is the slang for sixpence, and she called herself Madame Suzie because she always worked for this amount.

"I'm a flarty too," she told me in confidence. "I don't really belong to the fair. My old man used to keep a photographer's shop at Bolton. That's my home, and I met him when I went to have my photo took."

Her husband, I discovered, had been the original Suzie, but he had died nearly three years before.

"He took me out of the mill," she told me, "and we was married. He was much older than me, but he was very good. Yes, I must say he was very good. They gave him a wonderful notice in the *World's Fair*. He used to do all the spieling, you know. You don't remember 'im, do you? He was dead clever. I never thought I'd be able to carry on by myself."

Madame Suzie was the strongest worker in Walton Street. She talked as only people from Bolton do talk, and she had personality.

The only other grafter in her line who could come anywhere near her was Florian. He worked with his wife and two sons. To get a pitch together they used to do the second sight act. The two boys were blindfolded and used to describe different things held up by the audience.

This was done with the aid of a very simple code, but they did very well with it and had arranged it so that it looked very impressive.

During Hull Fair I stayed in lodgings with eight other grafters. They referred to these digs as their "lettary," which is a usual term.

We stayed in the house of a Jewish baker and we ate orthodox Jewish food. I found the cold fish most appetizing, but the sweet soup and some of the other dishes were more than I could stomach.

All the grafters were terrific eaters. Mad Jack, in particular, had the time of his life. I disgraced myself at my first meal by asking for milk in my tea while we were eating meat. Every one was very shocked at this, but I was forgiven eventually.

Our landlady was a tall Jewess. Her hair was raven black and she spoke very broken English.

Some of the grafters had mistaken me for a Jew, but she was not deceived for a moment. She had great ideas of making me one, though.

"Vat? You not married?" she said. " 'Tis pity you're a goy."

This was at our first meeting, and for several days after this I noticed that she looked at me with more than common thoughtfulness.

"Vat is the use of traveling about all your life, my dear boy?" she said, pouncing on me one evening near the end of the fair. "Vy not settle down? Get yourself a business. You vould do vell. How vould you like a nice cleaning business? Or there is a beautiful flower shop you could have."

I was mystified, but at last she made me understand that I had only to become an orthodox Jew and I should be able to choose any kind of business I liked, the price I should have to pay for it being marriage.

With a wife of her choosing I would get a business thrown in.

But although she delighted in discussing the various advantages of a florist's compared with a cleaning business, or a half share in a second-hand furnishing establishment, the various ladies attached to these concerns did not interest her at all. Moreover, they were not supposed to interest me or any other of her prospective clients.

She was very persistent, however, and one young Jew who was selling nougat on the fair went into the matter seriously with her. He wanted a tailoring business, and she thought she could find him one.

But I saw no reason why I should become an orthodox Jew, and when the fair came to an end I left Hull and matrimony behind me.

CHAPTER 14

I have fifty pounds and decide to go to London. London has a bad effect upon me. I meet my conscience in very strange disguise and part with my fortune to two men in gloves.

From Hull I went to Ilkeston, and the first person I met on the showground there was Clarry. He had Polly, Mrs. Dandi's eldest daughter, with him.

They had been staying in the district, they told me, since Nottingham Goose Fair, which had closed just before Hull Fair opened.

"I bought a jam jar from a scrap dealer for eight quid just after you left," Clarry explained, "and if it hadn't let me down I'd have been at Hull."

He had got it mended, though, and when he showed it to me I was tempted to buy it. But fortunately I thought better of the idea. Clarry understood cars and I did not.

I had no fixed plans, but I had fifty pounds and I wanted to see London again. I did not want to go fortune-telling there, of course, so I offered to lend Clarry my tent. He was returning to Wales and intended to start Polly as a palmist.

I was going to catch the excursion from Nottingham on Sunday, and I did not want any unnecessary luggage. So it was decided that I should return to Llandudno when I took to the road again, and Clarry took charge of my tick-off outfit until we should meet.

Just before I left for London I was having a drink after my last reading when I noticed that the man next to me was Pat Collins.

"You look smart," he said, looking at my clothes.

"I wish I were as smart as you, Mr. Collins," I replied politely.

He smiled and ordered a drink.

"How do you know me?" he asked. "On at the theater, aren't you?"

I explained that I was telling fortunes at the fair, and he looked disappointed.

"Tick-off," he repeated with contempt. "What are you doing that for? You don't look scruffy enough for that game. A smart boy like you could do something better. Go and see one of my shows. I'll give you a job on the front any time you like."

I sometimes wished that I had taken him at his word, although he could not have paid a barker much and probably I should have had to sleep in one of the wagons.

I was rather proud of the tick-off at that time, however, and when I made him have a drink with me I could not resist letting him see my wad of notes when I paid, which was rather childish, now I come to think of it.

I caught my train to Nottingham and then to London.

By the time the train arrived at King's Cross I had practically forgotten all about grafters. For three weeks I had a complete holiday. I had meant to remain in London for only a few days, but once I had looked round I could see no reason for hurrying off again.

I visited all my old haunts and did the usual round of night clubs.

Nothing had altered much, I found, although many of the old crowd had vanished.

Unfortunately I arrived on a Sunday, and, since I could not find a soul I knew, I must have celebrated unwisely, for I woke up in the most luxurious police station I had ever known.

It was much more comfortable than most of my lodgings in the north, and a kind policeman took care of my money and cigarette-case and brought me blankets and in the morning a cup of tea.

I remember he asked if I would like to be bailed out, but even had I known any one this would have seemed a foolish idea.

I was fined the usual pound and I was very grateful to the police, who had looked after me and my money.

After this regrettable escapade I was more fortunate in finding people I knew. I acquired a bed-sitting-room in New Oxford Street, which cost me thirty shillings a week.

Apart from a new suit of tails, I did not buy much in London that was afterwards useful. I did purchase a book on palmistry, but it did not tell me much, and seemed very complicated.

After I had been in London just on three weeks I found myself walking along Tottenham Court Road with exactly a shilling in my pocket. It was long after midnight, and the streets were not crowded.

I seemed to think better when I was walking, and I felt that now was an ideal moment for me to plan out something for the future. Something, I realized, would have to be done pretty quickly.

I had spent the evening with Phyllis. I had known her for some time. She was more unusual-looking than pretty, and was the sort of girl who, at the first meeting, gives one the impression that she is cleverer than she really is.

I liked this peculiarity of hers, because when I discovered that I was nearly as clever as she was I felt I was cleverer than I had thought I was before.

I had enjoyed myself that evening. We had been to a show and had finished up at the Piccadilly Grill for some food. Now I was on my way back to my room, after dropping her at her flat in Baker Street.

I had had a good time in London, but I was now anxious to get out of the city as quickly as possible. A lot of people seemed to make money in London, but I knew it was a bad "monkery" for me. I felt it was a fine place for a good time, but I decided that when one has exactly a shilling in one's pockets it is a city that loses its appeal.

This shilling of mine started my mind working in a direction that I usually avoid after I have made a few hurried resolutions. As I wandered on I thought how exactly this resembled the occasions when I used to walk home after my nights out before I had become a grafter. This evening I had experienced the same anxiety over the final taxi trip, one eye on the meter and one eye on my companion.

The inside knowledge of the West End which I thought I now possessed, the true opinion of waiters about people who overtip, the probable thoughts of taximen and ladies of the town, had all availed me nothing. I wondered what Clarry would have thought of me. Probably he would have singled me out as a punter and would have taken my last bob off me.

Of course, I reflected, I did not altogether agree with Clarry's ideas. He seemed to think that every one who spent money must be a mug. I remember laughing at him when he pointed out a Rolls-Royce that stopped at the entrance of the fair at Llandudno.

"Take sight at that Rolls," he said. "There'll be some right mugs turn up in a minute."

We, who were using all our wits to make a few bob, he supposed to be the "wide" people.

This recollection was a little comforting, but then I had to admit that I had no Rolls and Clarry was probably a lot better off than I was on this particular night.

This brought me back to my shilling, and my shilling reminded me of one extravagance of the evening that only a mug would have committed. It was so small that it was hardly an extravagance, but it was because it was the exact amount that I now possessed that it bothered me.

Earlier in the evening it had been raining. A magnificent-looking fellow in a uniform that echoed the splendor of pre-war Russia had hailed a cab for me as we left the theater. He opened the cab door with a flourish, and a spotless white glove touched the peak of his gold-braided cap high above my head.

I had no gloves myself and was feeling rather silly without them. As we were ushered in, another white glove was very much in evidence. It twitched nervously, as some hands do just before an introduction.

It was raining. I was on the step, my head seemed to be in line with the double row of flashing medals spread across a vast cushion of blue.

My smallest change was a shilling. Dare I ask for sixpence back? Dare I wait while sixteen brass buttons were unfastened, while a spotless glove was removed and a massive hand was thrust into a trouser pocket, probably to emerge with nothing smaller than notes?

It was sheer cowardice on my part. He had "come to his bat" with a rush and I had meekly punted. The door had slammed, the white glove had flashed past the window as it vanished to touch the peak of a gold-braided cap.

And here I was but a few hours later with exactly half the fortune which I might have possessed had I not been singled out from that large audience as a soft-looking "punter."

If I had had only eightpence probably I should have given the matter little thought; but a shilling. My entire fortune.

My lost shilling, I thought bitterly, was probably buying beer at some little club for a man who looked upon me as a chump, a man who had blagged money from me as easily as a gypsy from a newly married woman.

More people were about as I neared the Oxford Street end of Tottenham Court Road. A woman asked me if I was lonely and then for a cigarette. It was about all I had, and I offered her my case.

"You're married, aren't you, dear?" she said as I lit the cigarette for her. "You don't want to let that get you down. It's not worth it, kid. No one's worth it. You're lonely. Come home with me."

Why married men were supposed to get more lonely than bachelors I did not know. I was not married, but I did not bother to explain that it was a shilling and not a wife which was giving me such serious thought.

I said good-by to her and walked on. She called after me that her name was not Josephine, and that even if it was she did not allow strangers to call her by her Christian name.

She spoke so good-naturedly and so glibly that it occurred to me that she had probably heard my farewell remark so often that her reply was like, "Quite well, thank you," to "How are you?"

I walked on, almost forgetting the man with white gloves who had taken half my fortune.

As I passed a small open-all-night café, a man who was looking into the window approached me. He was rather short, and his face was the shape of an egg. He wore a gray felt hat, but instead of being dented on top it remained exactly as it had come out of the hatbox, so that it resembled an unusually wide-brimmed, high-crowned bowler. His loosely fitting overcoat was buttoned up to his chin, and he carried an unfastened umbrella.

"I beg your pardon, but what is that on that ticket?" he asked politely, peering into the shop window.

I stepped up beside him, and, reading a ticket speared into a plate of dried sprats, I told him that it said "One-and-threepence."

Speaking with a slight foreign accent, he explained that he could not see without his glasses. He expressed his pleasure at my information by a little grunt. Then, wrinkling his forehead, he said:

"Let me see, how much do I pay for those?"

He gazed towards heaven as though he expected the voice of God to answer him. He had very bright blue eyes which now twinkled with peculiar enthusiasm.

"Yes, that's it, I get them for elevenpence. That's fourpence in my pocket. And why not? Why shouldn't I have that fourpence as much as the restaurant-keeper? Fourpence saved is fourpence in my pocket. A penny saved here and a penny saved there. That's strength. I buy all my things like that."

This information, volunteered in a very windy Tottenham Court Road at about two o'clock in the morning, made me wonder if my conscience had suddenly taken a very definite but somewhat extraordinary shape, so I did not hurry.

I was not quite sure at first if he were not "on the tap," and I wondered if he would ask me for something towards a cup of tea and a night's lodging.

A man had once stopped me at about this time of the morning some years previously. He had asked me for a light outside the London Pavilion in Piccadilly Circus, and had then inquired if he was on the right road for Birmingham. This method of attack had seemed so crude to me that I had told him to keep on walking until he met a policeman and then to inquire again.

But my friend with the peculiar hat was either rather clever or slightly mad, and for some reason I wanted to discover which it was.

I offered him a cigarette.

"Cigarettes and drink?" He shook his head. "They don't do you any good. Sap your energy. Cost money. I like a cigarette. I like a drink. But I deprive myself of these things. That's strength. I make sacrifices. I don't like it. But it's worth it. I travel."

He then mentioned the names of some twenty countries he had visited. He seemed to have been all over the world.

"Could I do this if I spent my money in cafés?" he demanded. "What does smoking cost one? Does one get anything out of it? Could I travel if I smoked? Could I travel if I was married?"

He paused, only for a moment.

"Penny saved here and there. That's the secret. I make my own lemon water. Three lemons last me three months. Now, here's a tip. Get three lemons. Don't cut them up. That's no good. Peel them. That's a bit awkward at first, but you'll soon get used to it. I put them in a bowl of water with just a touch of demerara sugar. Ah! and then there's prunes. Get a pound of prunes. Cost you eightpence. Put them in as well. That'll last you over three months. As you drink you add water. I drink all day."

At this point he chuckled and illustrated in dumb show how he dipped the cup into the bowl.

"At the end of three months," he said, "add three more lemons. How much does that cost you?" He shrugged his shoulders.

"And here's another tip. Tomatoes. They're so cheap. You can buy them in the market for next to nothing. You can eat them raw. You can cook them in so many different ways. It's simple. You're young," he said. "Under forty. The young always spend. They all do. Are you married? No? That's right. As a rule that's all young people think about. I think about travel."

I could not sum him up at all, and it occurred to me that if he was my embodied conscience it was making fun of me. I smiled openly at him.

He chuckled the whole time. Passers-by must have thought that we were sharing some particularly subtle joke. If he was my conscience, we were.

Presently he leaned forward and spoke as if he were confiding some great secret to me.

"What I'm telling you is worth sovereigns," he said. "I used to like to go to dances, but I deprive myself of these things now. I'm comfortable. I live on a pound a week. I'm not married. Got a little room to myself. Do my own cooking. Look after myself. Don't like domestic drudgery, but what of it? I've got a little brush. Some one had thrown it away, but I found it. I just sweep the dust into a piece of newspaper and, wrapping it up—" in dumb show he illustrated how this was done—"I put it in the dustbin.

The bed . . . so easy to make. Just pull over the sheet."

He showed me how this was done.

"But you must be a very lonely old man," I suggested. It was the first chance I had had to say anything.

"Not at all," he said. "I have my recreations. We must have our social life or we get stodgy. You know what I mean? I've been to Lyons Corner House tonight. Listened to the band. But I know the ropes. I only had a pot of tea . . . threepence. I make sacrifices, but I get what I want. I travel. I learnt it from my mother. A remarkable woman. We were a big family and had very little money. But we lived in comfort. Almost luxury. There were many of us. My mother studied the pennies. I said to myself, if my mother can do this with so many of us surely I can do it by myself. I do do it. I travel."

The wind was cold and I decided that it was my turn to travel now, and eventually we parted. He placed a fat gloved hand in mine and chuckled.

"That's how I do it," he said, and walked off in the opposite direction.

I was cold, and I suddenly realized that I was dead tired. A taxi slowed up inquiringly, as they do at that time of the morning. It stopped.

Hardly a minute later, when I had paid the taxi-driver for an absurdly short fare, I suddenly remembered the beginning of my walk home. I realized painfully that the old boy in the peculiar hat, whoever he was, had cost me my last bob.

One half of my fortune had gone to a man who

was probably happily asleep and dreaming of retirement, and the other indirectly to a man to whom I had supplied a certain amount of his required "recreation."

What really annoyed me was that both men had gloves.

Punters at Nottingham Goose Fair, *circa* 1930.
National Fairground Archive

CHAPTER 15

I return to the grafters and discover that the sun does not always shine. I meet London Joe, who persuades me to join him and his strange friend. I sell the "cockernen" and find Cross-eyed Charlie a difficult colleague.

As THE TRAIN GATHERED speed and the platform at Euston was left farther and farther behind me, I grew more optimistic. I had pawned everything I possessed that was pawnable, and I had borrowed a fiver from my sister Margery, who happened to have some money at the time and did not want repaying until the summer.

Even during the short time I had been in London I had got into a rut, and I felt now that there was nothing so invigorating as this making of a fresh start. I felt a new person. I was on the right side of the counter again, and once more I looked at the world through the eyes of a grafter. It looked good.

Porters became my fellow-workers and got only what they deserved. Every one I saw was a possible punter, and I was no longer the mug.

I was on my way to Llandudno, back to the tick-off tent and back to the fairs. I was full of confidence and as we passed the stations this confidence grew.

Had I known at that moment exactly what it is like

to spend a winter on the road, I think, although I should have gone on, I should not have been quite so cheerful about it. November is hardly the month any grafter would choose to set out on a new venture.

Apart from my new suit of tails, I had acquired nothing in London that might possibly be of any use to me.

I found Clarry at Llandudno, but with the ending of the summer the town seemed to have gone dead.

I went on to Pwthelli, where George Dell's fair was being held, and at first business was not too bad. But at the end of the month the weather was impossible and my tent was smashed in a gale.

I built myself another, with Clarry's help. This proved to be a bit of an undertaking, and after I had had it up but a few days I found it one stormy morning hanging from the top of the roundabouts.

The fair moved into a field at Bangor for the winter, and here the ground was often under several feet of water, and only very occasionally did some of the side-shows open for a few hours at a week-end.

I went to Rhyl.

As I sat in the train rain splashed against the carriage windows and the country looked inexpressibly bleak and sodden. I wondered why it was impossible to think about this sort of weather in the summer. After all, there had been enough rain that season in all conscience to remind us of days like this one. Yet the winter always found the grafters unprepared. I had not enough money to get a good pitch under cover, and even if I had, I realized by this time that there is never much of a living for the grafter, wherever he is.

People have less money to spend, it is a more expensive time for everybody, people require more food, and light and heat have to be bought.

I reflected upon these things as the train carried me through the hills, and by the time I arrived at Rhyl I was convinced that all grafters were slightly mad.

The following Saturday I worked at Carnarvon market, where I was charged ten shillings for my day's pitch. There were only half a dozen stalls, a fact for which the heavy toll probably accounted.

The market square at Carnarvon is in the center of the town. It lies in the shadow of the castle, and, since it is on a hill, it is a windy spot at the best of times.

This particular Saturday was not one of these. I expected my tent to go up like a balloon. However, I managed to take just over three pounds and I was very satisfied.

At the end of the day I had no plans at all for the future, but the first thing to do seemed to be to get a night's lodging, and from a woman who sold fruit and vegetables in the market I discovered the address of some digs where some grafters were staying. I went there intending to remain a night.

Actually I stopped several weeks, for at these lodgings I met London Joe. I had seen him before at various fairs, and I knew him comparatively well.

With him was an extraordinary person whose only name, as far as I knew, was Cross-eyed Charlie.

We three shared a bedroom, and I was glad of their company.

In the same house Madame Eve stayed. She had a palmistry joint in the pavilion in the town. There were also a couple of strangers to me who had a wheel-'em-in at the same place.

"The knocker's the only game in the winter," said London Joe as we were all having supper in the back kitchen. "You needn't bother about the weather then. The harder the parny the better the chance of finding some one at home."

He was a talkative little man, with very sharp gray eyes, and I looked at him with interest. I had last seen him on a fair in the north where he had been working "the cobbler." This is the same sort of game as "the spot," which was Clarry's racket.

The cobbler is even more simple. It is a ball game—"cobbler" is the slang for ball—and London Joe's joint is probably known by the majority of suckers as "the swinging ball game."

All the player is asked to do is to swing a ball that hangs from the top of the stall by a piece of string. If he can knock down a small skittle with the ball on its backward swing he wins a prize.

It is simplicity itself, and it is practically impossible for him not to win at the first attempt.

But when the grafter decides that it is time for him to get the fellow's money, he leans casually against the stall, placing his elbow on the shelf on which the skittle stands.

After that, of course, it is not nearly so simple; in fact, it is very often quite impossible.

The police stopped London Joe at Hull Fair on one occasion and gave him an hour to pack up and get out of the town. He was very upset about it.

The sight of me seemed to remind him of this occasion, and he mentioned it.

"It's these ruddy diddlum machines wot's done it," he said. "They're putting the bar up to every form of gambling game everywhere. The whole lark's not worth having, these days. First you have to wonder if you'll get in, and then when you're there you wonder how long they'll let you reign. It don't give you a chance to get an honest living. They want another war, that's what they want. Only t'other day at a one-eyed little gaff right off the map, a couple o' splits rolled up just as I was getting going nicely. They told me to pack up right away, and stood there while I did it. Wouldn't have it that mine was a game of skill. Said it was a game o' chance. 'Ow d'yer like that? The cobbler a game o' chance!"

He snorted indignantly, and crammed an enormous piece of bread into his mouth.

"Gawd blimey!" he said when he could breathe again. "The cobbler a game o' chance! Why, they haven't a bloody dog's chance if they punt to the cobbler."

London Joe liked talking, and, since the others at the table were too tired to interrupt him, he was in his element.

Madame Eve had been talking in her tent all day, and the two men who had been grafting on the wheel-'em-in seemed weary.

Business was not too good at the pavilion, and I knew from bitter experience that graft seems twice as hard when one is not taking money.

"I remember working the cough slum on the knocker

around Manchester a few stretch ago," Joe continued conversationally. "Manchester. That's the monkery for you! We were getting a steady deuce of nickers apiece every day, and no ruddy tober to pay either. You can't beat it in the winter."

By the "cough slum" he meant cough candy or any sort of throat lozenge, and when he had said "a few stretch ago" he had been referring to years. "A deuce of nickers," of course, was two pounds.

"As soon as I can lay me 'ands on a bit of gelt," he went on, "I'm goin' to lay it out in some good knocker gear. You can't beat gear. If you come unstuck anywhere you can always get a night's feather by slogging a bit of it."

"Speakin' about feather," interrupted Cross-eyed Charlie, "wot about it? I'm tired."

It was evident that he found great difficulty in keeping his crossed eyes open while Joe was discussing his future plans.

" 'E'll keep you gassing all the blinkin' night if you let 'im," he said to me. "What about slippin' up the apple and pears and gettin' in feather? I'm just about charvered."

"Apple and pears" is rhyming slang for "stairs."

"Charvered" is not a very nice expression, and no doubt Charlie would not have used it had he realized that Madame Eve was present. But on this particular occasion he used it to convey that he was tired out. It is a common enough expression among grafters, and often used when one worker "charvers" another, or in other words spoils his pitch.

Rhyming slang has always struck me as being particularly banal, but grafters speak a language comprised of every possible type of slang. Some of the words they use come from the Romany, others are Italian, and quite a number of words are Yiddish. These include "gezumph," which means to cheat or to overcharge; "snodders" for people who don't spend; and "yocks" for chumps.

Although it is all very childish, I suppose, I have known times when it has been very useful to be able to speak a language that is universally known by the grafters and seldom comprehensible to any one else.

There are times when earwigs—that is to say, people who listen to one's conversation—can be very dangerous.

It also works the other way. I remember once traveling in a train with two other palmists, one of whom was a successful gypsy woman whose hands were covered with diamonds, and the carriage also contained five very tough customers.

When one of them remarked, "Take sights. Screw the donah's groinies," we knew at once that he had suggested to his friends that they should watch the lady's rings, and, since they were a larger party than we, we changed our compartment at the next station.

Most grafters only sprinkle their conversation with slang, but Cross-eyed Charlie understood it better than any other language. It came naturally to him, and it was impossible for him to open his mouth without using it.

"Joe can keep 'is trap open longer than 'is blinks," he said. "It's time we all got some bo-peep."

It certainly did look as though Joe would keep his

mouth open long after his eyes were closed, and I was as anxious to sleep as any one. It had been a tiring day, and was now long past midnight.

However, I had not heard the last of Joe. He continued to talk when we got to our room, and finally succeeded in interesting me in the knocker.

I did not say much then, but I reasoned that it would cost me very little to have a cut at this somewhat ignominious form of graft, and the experience, I felt, would be useful.

Moreover, I liked the idea of joining up with Joe and Cross-eyed Charlie. At least they would be company, and it was loneliness that I particularly disliked.

I had a serious talk with Joe in the morning. I offered to get some gear on the understanding that the cost of this would be paid back to me before any of us had a cut-up of the takings.

We fixed on this, and I sent away to a firm in Blackpool for a gross of pads and pens. Why exactly we decided on pads and pens I do not know. It was Joe's idea. He said practically everything else had been worked too frequently in North Wales.

Cross-eyed Charlie was rather skeptical about the whole thing, and I, though keen, was a novice.

"The cough slum has been tanned round this monkery," Joe explained, "but they 'aven't 'ad the cockernens for years."

The word "cockernen," I found, meant a tenner or a pen, according to context.

Our stock arrived by return, and I liked the look of it. The important thing about the fountain-pens, Joe said, was that they had nine-carat gold-plated nibs. Afterwards we pointed this out to our customers.

I am afraid they had been manufactured to sell rather than to be used. They looked very fine, though, and quite impressive in a box marked "10/6*d*." which came with each one.

I discovered that they did not write very well, but Joe got over this trouble by leaving them to the customers to fill. They cost us fourpence each when we bought them by the gross.

The writing-pads were better value. They were very well made writing compactums, nicely fitted with paper and envelopes. These, also, cost us fourpence each.

It was quite fun working with Joe and Charlie for a change. Charlie and I were new to the game, but Joe took us in hand.

We used to go straight down a street: Joe first, then myself and then Charlie, each man taking every third house, and so on throughout the day.

Joe was a very good canvasser. Once he persuaded a householder to open his door he never let them get away. He enjoyed talking, and nothing discouraged him. If a woman tried to slam her door in his face she usually found that his foot was resting casually on the step. If she threatened to produce her husband he would welcome the idea and probably sell them both a pad and pen.

Charlie did not altogether take to the job. He had worked most lines in his life, before, but I don't think any of them interested him very much. Graft was graft to him, and there was no longer any novelty left in any kind of work to make it anything but unpleasant.

He got exasperated very easily, and I overheard one of his sales talks with a certain amount of apprehension.

"No, thank you. I'm not interested in anything today," said one woman practically as soon as she had opened the door to him, and instead of the soft answer which turns away suspicion Charlie adjusted his hat on the side of his head and picked up his portmanteau.

"Gawd blimey," he said, "I don't doubt you that this is one of your orf days. But you don't look as if you've got the brains to be interested much at any time. Ever tried to write?"

He then stalked away to a house three doors up and hammered upon it as if he were trying to smash it in.

Working together like this no doubt gave us a lot of courage which we should hardly have had on our own. But Charlie did not need courage. He needed a little restraint, and I was afraid he would get it.

One day he was working the house next to me and only an iron railing separated us. Unfortunately his householder was longer in answering the door than mine.

"I represent the Palace Mills Printing Company," I explained, sticking to our agreed story. "In order to advertise our new writing compactum, which you will shortly see on sale in the shops, I have been instructed to present you with our special half-guinea fountain-pen. This is absolutely free of charge, you understand."

My prospective customer was a middle-aged, frail little person, and she took the fountain-pen timidly.

"Well, well, that's very nice of them," she said quietly, and I was encouraged.

"It's just part of our free gift scheme," I explained, and went on to point out the few advantages which the pen possessed. "Of course, you haven't had your writing compactum yet," I went on when I had succeeded in getting her interested in my free gift scheme.

"A writing compactum? Dear me, what will they be giving away next!"

"This is a special advance stock," I explained. "They are not obtainable in your shops yet, but in order to create a demand for this really beautiful compactum we are selling them at exactly the same price as they will be offered by your retailer. And as an inducement to buy we are presenting to every customer this special presentation half-guinea pen.

"Of course you realize," I continued hurriedly, "that we have to charge you the full price for the writing compactum, since to make any sort of reduction would be unfair to the retailers. But we get over that difficulty by giving you this really magnificent pen."

I had reached the critical point of my story and was just about to mention the price of the pad, which was half-a-crown, when the door of the house next to me shut in Charlie's face. It shut with a crash, and my timid little punter started violently.

"I've seen better manners in a ruddy cowshed," shouted Charlie at the closed door. "Call yourself a lot of Christians? Why, I'd rather sell 'ymnbooks to a bunch of savages! We might 'ave known it with these Welsh b——s," he shouted, addressing me across the railings. "They're the sort of people to ask for a night's doss. They're right generous. They're the sort of blokes wot chucks their money about like people with no arms."

"Er—the price is only one-and-six," I said hurriedly to the lady.

But I knew it was useless now. She had been completely startled, and she looked at Charlie with a sort of terrified fascination. I do not think she had seen anything quite like him before. Quite apart from his verbal outburst, he did not look the sort of person a timid little lady would have liked to have had anywhere near her front door.

Charlie was a tall man, but he stooped slightly. His mouth was thick-lipped, and it usually hung open when he was thinking. Both his eyes stared at his nose, and it was not much of a nose either, since it was long and crooked and very highly colored. His jacket was too small for him and the sleeves ended several inches above the great bones in his wrists. This made his arms look unusually long, and his hands were rough and knotted.

I made one desperate effort to save the situation, and incidentally to save one-and-sixpence. I realized it was no longer possible to ignore Charlie. He was not the sort of blemish any salesman could overlook. He was holding several writing-pads in one massive hand, and my timid customer must have realized he had something to do with me.

"Get back to the motor-van at once, Charles," I said. "You know you have no business here. Your job is to drive the van, and if this sort of thing

CHEAPJACK

happens again I'll have to report you to the Head Office."

Handing back the fountain-pen, the lady hurriedly agreed to buy.

"Just wait here a minute," she said, "while I go and find my money."

She turned into the house, closing the door behind her. I considered I had earned my one-and-sixpence. But a second later I heard the bolt being fastened in the door.

Cross-eyed Charlie was a difficult man with whom to work.

'The biggest fair in Great Britain was going to be held on the Town Moor' Newcastle, early 1930s.
National Fairground Archive

CHAPTER 16

*I make three new friends and we are all faced
with a pressing problem. We solve this problem
and rid the City of Manchester of a pest.*

As THE WEEKS WENT ON
we got the impression that the people of Carnarvon
had got to know us and familiarity was not breeding
contempt so much as irritation.

So we tried the villages of the district.

This extraordinary optimism reaped its own reward.
Pads and pens are not the things to try to sell in that
part of Wales. Many of the people were unable to
read, let alone write, and in some of the villages where
Welsh was practically universally spoken few of the
people knew what we were talking about.

However, we managed to get a living and I enjoyed the experience. I had a certain amount of beginner's luck, and, since I was a novice, I naturally
worked harder than Charlie did.

It was quite impossible to beat Joe, as far as enthusiasm went. I think it was enthusiasm that had kept
him alive. He was always ready to work late into the
evening, and was the first to get up in the morning.

He seldom worked on Saturday, as this is a bad day
for the knocker, since people are usually out doing
their week's shopping.

I found it more profitable to work a market on Saturday with the tick-off, but in comparatively small places like Carnarvon I discovered that a number of people recognized me and they seemed to think it strange that a representative of the Palace Mills should also be a fortune-teller.

However, this never bothered me, nor them very much, and Saturday was too valuable a day to be missed.

Fridays and Mondays were our best days on the knocker, and of course Saturday is always the best day of the week for a market grafter.

After several weeks around Carnarvon, we found ourselves at Manchester a few days before Christmas. Here, until after Christmas, at any rate, we decided to represent the Beau Brummell and Pompadour Perfumery Company.

"There's nothing like funkum at Christmas time," said Joe. "They're present-mad for the next few days, and we must get 'em something fancy. There wouldn't be a cat's chance in hell with the pads."

By "funkum" he meant perfume, and it was arranged that we should get some fancy boxes of soap and some small bottles of perfume and tell the same sort of tale about them as we had done with the pads and the pens.

"Gawd! I never thought I should 'ave to be a ruddy perfume salesman," said Charlie; and Joe and I, looking at him, agreed that we would not have thought so either.

However, the funkum seemed a good idea and

showed a slightly bigger profit than the pads and pens.

"If you ask me, everybody thinks about nothing but munjary at Christmas time," Charlie went on, "and if we got loaded with a lot of gear on our 'ands we could always make a meal of it."

We were sitting in the kitchen of our new lodgings at Manchester on the first day of our arrival. It was a house in Devonshire Street, Ardwick, and the landlady was a plump, cheerful old party who understood our type of lodger.

This was fortunate, because Charlie needed a little understanding. He did not like women, and he said he did not hold with putting himself out for a bit of skirt, not even a landlady. With Charlie, "putting himself out" was an elastic term. He believed in taking off his boots just whenever he wanted to and he liked to put his feet on the stove.

As I said, it was fortunate that the landlady at Devonshire Street understood him.

By "munjary" he meant food, and his idea was that we should buy a stock of fancy biscuits or sweets; but he was a fiend for food and we did not cotton onto the idea.

There are many swag shops in Manchester, and the following day Charlie and the rest of us became representatives of the Beau Brummell and Pompadour Perfumery Company.

I had more doors slammed in my face here than ever I did in Wales, and those people to whom I managed to talk seemed to have had the world's representatives of most things at their doors in the past few months.

But we did fairly well, considering.

It was after Christmas that we felt the pinch. People had no money to spend and every day it became more and more apparent that the knocker workers had been busy since Joe was last in Manchester. Householders were thoroughly tired of answering their bells, and some of them peered at us timidly through their windows as if afraid to open the door. I felt we were a menace; but we had to pay the landlady.

The city was full of knocker workers: legitimate canvassers for newspapers, down-at-heel and trying desperately to get the required number of orders a day necessary to keep their job; young girls selling bath salts, who worked in a team from a motor-van at the corner of the street; and numberless people who were working on their own, selling everything from stain removers to patent medicine.

There were men trying to sell vacuum cleaners and others traveling in hosiery and women's and children's clothes. Everybody seemed to be at it.

When we returned to our lodgings one night after a rather disheartening day we discovered that three other knocker workers had rolled in. Joe and Charlie knew them all, but they were strangers to me. Like ourselves, they were market grafters who had fallen back upon the knocker for the winter.

When the usual greetings had been made we were all seated round the table eating fish and chips. Joe inquired what they were working. One of the men looked anxiously around him to see that the landlady was not within hearing.

"Well, to tell you the truth," he said, "we're about on the floor. The only gear we've got is a few ropes of pearls and three or four dozen dummy kettles. But the whole blinkin' lot will only bring in about a deuce of nicker. I haven't chatted the old girl about the bat of this joint, but I don't suppose it matters much. Luckily she hasn't asked us to drop anything yet, and we're just lying low."

Joe was very cheerful. The lodgings, he said, were very reasonable. It was not likely that the landlady would require any money for a few days, and by then something should turn up.

"Kettle" is the slang for "watch," and by "dummy kettles" the man had meant toy watches. These are well made little things on expanding wristbands. They look like gold, but they have no insides and cost about three ha'pence each. They are often sold in mystery packets by gazers.

"We rolled in here from Newcastle this afternoon," explained the man who had spoken before, "and apart from a bit of silver we're about skint."

The others called him Barney, and he seemed to be the spokesman of the party.

The other two were a curious pair. One was a dark-complexioned, fat-faced Jewish fellow of about thirty-five. He had black curly hair and very dark brown eyes. His name was Alfie, and he spoke quietly and with a certain amount of culture.

The other was introduced to me as Three-fingered Billy. He was probably about forty-seven or forty-eight, although it was difficult to tell his age. His face was deeply furrowed, and there were wrinkles at the corners of his eyes. All the same, when he smiled there was something almost childlike about him. His eyes were ridiculously blue and looked incongruous in his pug-like face.

When I first saw him he impressed me as a tough, but as I watched him it suddenly occurred to me that he was shy. He did not talk much, but left the explanations to the others.

"Well, I don't know about you blokes," said Joe, addressing Charlie and me, "but I think these boys had better row in with us. I don't suppose the game will be much bottle for any of us, but we may as well stick together."

I was ready for anything and Charlie was eating. He never talked much during meals.

"Well, that's that. What about it, boys?"

Joe was delighted.

"We've got a bit of funkum and some soap, which can be worked in with your pearls, and we'll probably be able to make up a few lots with your kettles and what pads and pens we've got left."

"Well, let me work the cockernens. I feel like a bloody pansy lumbering a lot of funkum around with me," said Charlie, trying to edge a chip into his mouth, which was already too full. "I'd rather 'andle a man any day than a lot of these silly palones."

I already knew that Charlie was not a lady's man, and by "palone" he meant girls. The other words he used to describe them were "molls," "skirts," and "brassnails," although this last word is only used as a rule in reference to ladies of a certain definite profession.

So it was arranged that we should all work together, and for the next few weeks we had a pretty thin time of it. Barney was used to a well-worked territory, and he was prepared for Manchester. He actually carried a little wooden wedge with him, and directly the door was opened he fixed this so that it prevented any one from shutting it again. He was a good salesman, though, and once he got some one to listen to him he was a persuasive talker.

His party was undoubtedly an asset to us, and they pulled their weight.

Alfie was a pleasant, quiet worker, and although Three-fingered Billy obviously shared Charlie's opinion about the whole business he was undoubtedly a trier.

We all shared a certain loyalty to each other which I have seldom experienced before. Being up against it, as we were, we got on extraordinarily well together, although Charlie and Billy did not look like being friends at first.

They were very much alike in some ways, and this probably accounted for the friction between them.

Alfie had once been a singer of some sort on the stage, and Barney, who was also Jewish, took an intelligent interest in the morning newspaper and seemed very human. Both these men took care of their clothes and went about the business in an intelligent fashion.

Charlie, of course, was interested in nothing but his immediate comforts, and Billy, although he was anxious to pull his weight when working, appeared to have no real interest in anything except beer.

He talked about beer as some men discuss art treasures, lovingly and with knowledge. It was only on this one topic that he showed any sort of enthusiasm. With Billy, beer was not merely a drink: it was a life study. He knew everything there was to know about it and there was not a brand you could mention that he had not sampled and upon which he could not offer an intelligent, well-thought-out criticism.

Barney and I were satisfied with any kind of beer if the inn was a pleasant one, and we usually hunted out a public house where there was music or a pretty barmaid.

But Billy preferred to go off on his own to some miserable little hovel in a side street where he had discovered the best beer in the neighborhood. Like Charlie, he had no use for women. He had a wife in Nottingham, he said, and offered no other explanation.

"Whatever we take today, boys, must go for more gear," said Barney one morning, "or we'll find ourselves on the floor with no gelt and no gear. Things are not too good, you know."

This seemed sound enough, and we agreed to go out to get enough money for a fresh stock. But what this should be we could not decide. Every conceivable line had been worked to death all round Manchester, and it was difficult to think of anything new.

Things were looking really bad. We were in debt with the landlady, and Joe and I had decided that none of us should be allowed to sneak out of the lodgings without paying. The good lady might have to wait for her money—that was obvious—but we were stuck in Manchester until we could pay and get enough together to take us to a fresh district.

"I'm taking a tip from you, Barney," said Joe, taking a lump of wood from his pocket as we were leaving the house. "You need a wedge for the doors around this monkery. But what with the weather we've been 'avin' my daisies ain't too firm. A woman slammed the door yesterday and I thought she'd crippled me for life."

We were all getting a bit desperate. I found out that I was in this state when, on finding a door open, I walked boldly inside.

At the end of a passage I found a man in his shirt-sleeves, having his dinner at the kitchen table. He was so surprised when he saw me that when I canvassed him he bought from me. But this was one of the few sales I made that day.

"Boys, I've got a great idea," said Barney suddenly after supper that night. He was standing on the hearth, and he looked round at us all before continuing. "It's just come to me right out of the air," he said, and he looked pleased with himself. "Right out of the air. And believe me, boys, it's a winner! This time next week and we'll be holding a bundle."

We were all glad to hear this, and the landlady listened with as much interest as any one.

"Now, this is a real stunt," he continued, "and it must be worked out carefully. There mustn't be a hitch, and we must work right through the town and then scarper. Now you," he said, addressing me, "and Alfie and I, and I think you, too, Joe—we'll have to be the salesmen. You two can be the mechanics," he added, glancing at Charlie and Bill.

"Mechanics!" interrupted Charlie. "What the 'ell

am I goin' to be next? I don't know nothin' about mechanics."

Barney ignored him. He was too interested in his scheme to bother about any unnecessary explanations.

"There's a darned sight too many knocker workers round here," he continued, "and the public's getting real fed-up with 'em. I haven't got this 'ere idea too clear in me own mind, but I'll give you a rough notion of it and when I've finished you'll see it's a winner, all right."

When he had finished even Charlie had to agree that it certainly was a good idea.

We made a tour of the swag shops the following day and got exactly what we wanted for eight shillings a gross.

"This is the sort of bunce I like," said Joe. "What about working them at a denar a time and making it quick?"

The profit certainly did seem good enough, but Barney pointed out that we were to work on the better-class houses and he thought we ought to stick to one-and-six. This we agreed to do, and in just over a week we had taken over fifty pounds between us and were able to pay our debts and get as far away from Manchester as we desired.

Three-fingered Billy and Cross-eyed Charlie were our mechanics, and they had nothing to do with the interviewing, which was a very good thing. Joe, Alfie, Barney and I did the actual selling.

"I'm a representative from the Shopkeepers' Protection Association," I explained as soon as a door opened. "It has come to our ears that this district has been infested by a number of cheapjack salesmen. In fact, some of these people, we understand, pretend, entirely without authority, to be representatives of well-known firms in this city. We are anxious to take preventive measures against these imposters, and we ask you to assist us by your cooperation."

The majority of people were more than ready to hear more. They agreed with everything we said. Occasionally, of course, we ran into some one who remembered us when we had been selling something else, but this did not hurt the scheme. Manchester is a big place.

"It is not only in the interest of trade in this city, but also in the interest of every householder," we explained, "that this sort of thing should be stamped out. All we ask is your cooperation. By assisting us in this matter you will be doing a great service to the whole community."

Most people said, "Of course," and we went on.

"We have our mechanics outside," we continued, "and there is just the nominal charge of one-and-sixpence to cover the bare expense—the cost of fixing, you understand."

Charlie and Billy hung about in the background. Both of them had a supply of wire, and a hammer and nails for occasions when there were no suitable railings for their work. They seemed to enjoy this occupation, and when Billy was hammering nails into some one's garden gate he would chant in time with his banging: "One, two, three, four, five, six! And one for 'is nob! One-and-six! Another three pints of the best! Where next, Captain?"

We seldom failed to make a sale, and few householders required much persuasion.

For what we were selling was a little enamel sign, only a few inches square, on which was printed in bold type:

NO HAWKERS, CIRCULARS, CANVASSERS.

Three-Fingered Billy 'who became a sort of personal guide to our tour.'

CHAPTER 17

I think of changing my vocation. I meet an unestimable person and am introduced to his unhappy partner. I decide to become a "pitcher."

SHORTLY AFTER THIS I became a pitcher and a waver-worker.

Ever since I had addressed the prayer-meeting at Ashton-under-Lyne the idea of pitching, of talking to the crowd, had appealed to me. Several grafters had told me that I would make a good crocus, and one or two of them had wanted me to row in with them on the markets. (A "crocus" is a quack doctor.)

But I had realized that it would take me some time before I should be an accomplished worker at anything, for my fortune-telling was by way of being a natural gift.

In the summer months I was making money with the tick-off, but the winter was no time to try out a new venture, and I had always put it off, although I felt sure that at some time sooner or later I should try my hand, or rather my voice, at some pitching lark.

I liked the idea of working hard for a few hours, and then being able to forget about graft for a while. Even when the weather was bad, a pitcher often got a day's work, I noticed, for he only required a couple of good pitches to make his visit to a market worth while. It might even be raining heavily for most of the day, but if it cleared for the final hour a pitcher could always get to work at a moment's notice and make a full day's money.

It was different with the tick-off. At the best this was a slow business. I found I was always at it. If I left my tent for a few moments I might lose a good client, and again I might have to wait for hours for the right person to come along.

Moreover, a successful fortune-teller should always be thinking about business. Some of my most profitable days had been on occasions when I never opened the tent. These were times when people approached me in hotels where I stayed, or sent their servants with a request that I should visit their houses.

Gypsies even make a shopping excursion a business trip. They seldom pay for their purchases, but tell the tale for them across the shop counter.

The tick-off is a fiddling game, and for steady money it wants a lot of beating, I think. But the time had come when I wanted to make more than a living. I wanted to make a lot of money and I wanted to become a pitcher.

After the last day on the knocker at Manchester we all parted company. Three-fingered Billy returned to Newcastle-on-Tyne because he said he could buy the best beer in the country there. He was holding enough money to buy about two hundred pints, and he was a happy man when he left us.

Joe went back to London and the others left for various parts of the country.

I spent several weeks working the tick-off as I made

my way down south, and it was a few days after my arrival in London that I knocked into Flash Jackson.

It was he who first started me on the waver.

I was crossing the road from Wyndham's Theatre to the post-office opposite when some one knocked into me. As I turned I recognized Flash.

I had first met him some years before when I had been promoting an Ideal Homes Exhibition at Southampton. This was during a time when I had been in my own business shortly after failing to get into Oxford and just before I became a cub reporter on the Cambridge *Daily News*.

Flash Jackson had worked the waver at this exhibition and he probably made more money out of the show than I did.

"Well, well," he said, shaking me warmly by the hand, "if it isn't Archie! Lord! I thought you'd faded away long ago."

It was a long time since I had been called by this nickname, but it took me only a few minutes to explain roughly what had happened to me since I had last seen him. My news appeared to delight him.

"That's splendid, my boy! So now you're one of us," he said patronizingly. "Lord! you were a prize mug in those days."

I began to remember Flash. He had been one of my stall-holders who had left hurriedly without paying his rent. However, I realized it was useless to remind him of this now.

"Well, you know, I packed the game in shortly after I finished with your show," he said. "I'm grafting the partner business now, but it isn't what it was. Believe me, a dishonest man can hardly get a living these days. Every Tom, Dick and Harry is on the make, my boy. Every one is getting wise. The West End is full of little upstarts who don't know the first thing about the business. They're showing up the game and cutting it to hell. Here, come and have a drink."

We were standing on the pavement near the Hippodrome and, talking as we walked, we made our way to the Queen's.

"Sorry, sir, I can't serve you," said the girl behind the bar when Flash ordered drinks.

He did not seem in the least taken aback, but turned to me casually.

"I had forgotten, my dear boy. Let's go to my club. The beer here isn't worth drinking, anyway."

I followed him outside, and, since it seemed impolite to do so, I made no more reference to the incident. Flash appeared to have completely forgotten it.

He took me to the Forty-Seven Club, which was in Gerrard Street and only a few doors away from Mrs. Meyrick's Forty-Three.

The club consisted of a large room on the first floor. Half a dozen tables lined the walls, and there was a piano in one corner. In the center was a small dancing space, and a bar occupied the other side of the room.

While I sat at one of the tables I discovered quite a lot about the partner business from Flash.

Of course you would not have found him under this name in the Buff Book, where he was described as a theatrical agent, but among his friends he was considered to be one of the slickest partner workers in London.

Flash was a crook, and there were two distinct sides to his business.

One was to find a partner with money, and the other was to lose the partner without losing the money. In spite of his grumbling he seemed to be doing very well indeed.

"I manage to find on an average half a dozen partners a year, my boy," he said, pulling at a cigar that smelt about as fishy as his business. "But some of them are more trouble than they're worth. People don't realize the amount of *work* attached to this game."

After a few beers he handed me a newspaper.

"That's my ad," he said, pointing to an announcement in the personal column. "What d'you think of it?"

I read:

Working Partner wanted. One prepared to learn Theatrical Agent's business. £300 needed to extend activities of going concern. Only live men need apply. Full particulars. . . .

"It looks all right," I said dubiously. "Is it a going concern?"

"Going concern? I should say it is!" He roared with laughter as he repeated my question. "It's the partner that makes it such an active business. You must come up to my office and see the fun."

I wondered why Flash confided so freely in me, but all grafters are like that.

I went up to see him two or three days later. He had a tiny office just off Leicester Square. It was a very small room, and the walls were decorated with photographs of famous actors. On his books were the names of some of the leading artists in the profession, and letters from less famous members of theaterland cluttered his desk.

A small advertisement inserted in a theatrical paper brought, he told me, enough correspondence and photographs to supply bait for at least half a dozen prospective partners.

I was in his office when one of these arrived by appointment. He was a stocky little man, and he looked as if he had spent a lot of his time abroad. He was deeply tanned, and his clothes fitted him awkwardly.

Flash appeared to be dictating a letter to "Dear George" . . . a five-hundred-pound-a-week contract . . . when the stranger came in.

"Ah, sit down, Mr. Peters. You'll find the cigars just on your left," he said. "I know you'll excuse me for a moment. I'm up to my eyes in work this afternoon. It's hard work for one man, you know.

"See that posted to Mr. George Robey right away," he added, turning to his secretary. "And get on to Moss Empires some time today and arrange for me to see that new German act."

I wondered what would have happened if the typist had posted the letter to "Dear George." Probably Flash Jackson's business would have changed from a going to a gone concern in a very short space of time.

But his typist was an expert in everything connected with Flash's business except typing, and anyway she had gone through this performance so often that she was not likely to make a mistake.

It was all new to me, though, and I thought it about time I made my departure.

"I say, Mr. Jackson, I know you're busy," I said. "I'll drop in tomorrow."

There was obviously not room for us all in the tiny office, and I hoped Flash wanted to be alone with his punter.

"There's no need to run away, Mr. Carstairs," protested Flash Jackson. My new name took me aback for a moment. He glanced from me to Mr. Peters and probably decided the occasion called for a private interview.

"As a matter of fact," he continued at last, "I have, as it happens, some business with Mr. Peters here which may take a little time. Perhaps it would be as well if I posted the contract on to you. You'll have nice time to read it over and perhaps you'll bring it with you tomorrow and you can sign it here."

This was all very disconcerting, and I was glad to get outside.

What exactly happened after I left I do not know, of course, but Flash gave me a pretty detailed account of the interview afterwards.

It appeared that the 'phone bell rang just after I left, and, after apologizing, Flash answered it. He spoke very clearly, he told me, so that the punter heard every word.

"Hullo. Glasgow call? Yes. What's that? Who? Oh, is that you, Fairfax? They want you to sign on for another three months? No, no, not a penny less than fifty a week, my boy! Make it clear to 'em. I'll write to 'em tonight. Yes, yes, leave that to me. Good-by, Charlie old boy. Not a penny less than fifty, remember. Yes, that's right. Stick to that, whatever you do. So long."

Replacing the telephone receiver, he said airily to the punter:

"There's no money *on* the stage these days, Mr. Peters, but there's a lot of money to be made *out* of the theater. Oh, a lot of money!"

This, he told me, he usually proved directly his new partner's money was safely in the bank.

He got the money, more often than not, because, although his method of impressing his punter was rather obvious once suspicion was aroused, he had a very convincing manner, and his rather disgusting schemes usually met with success.

For one thing the punter could not hear the voice that had spoken on the other end of the line, and this, of course, belonged to the secretary, using a call-box not more than three hundred yards away.

Flash told me all this very proudly some days later as we stood at the bar in the basement of R. E. Jones's, at the corner of Leicester Square.

"But how the devil are you going to get rid of him now that you've got his money?" I said.

Flash laughed and took a long drink.

"Leave that to me, my boy," he said. "I've never been known to fail. First of all I'll make him in love with the business. Hullo, Bertie," he exclaimed suddenly as a man squeezed past us to get near to the bar. "What are you having? Meet Algie, a friend of mine."

I wished Flash would leave my name alone. I began

to feel rather uncomfortable while I was with him.

Meanwhile he was welcoming the stranger like a brother.

"I've always said so, Bertie. You're the best comic in the business today," he said. "I'm going to do something for you some time."

For the next ten minutes Bertie, who, I discovered, last appeared in panto in nineteen-ten, seconded the first part of Jackson's statement.

"That's the sort of chap I'll introduce Peters to," said Flash when we were on our own again. "The town's full of 'em. Stand 'em a drink and they'll talk shop till closing time. When I've got Peters just where I want him I'll take him backstage somewhere. There are a few music halls in the suburbs where I'm known pretty well. He's never been backstage, and the first time it always gives 'em a bit of a kick. I'll talk to one of the boys about getting him a West End shop when he's worked out his contract. They'll stand for it. At the end of the evening Mr. Peters will think my work is dead easy."

This seemed simple if not salutory, but even now I could not see how Flash got rid of his partner.

"What happens next?" I asked innocently.

"What next?" said Flash. "Oh, well, he finds out that it isn't so darned simple as he thought. I'll send him along to see some big shot at a West End Theater. After he's been kicked out he'll return to the office wondering what he's done wrong and I shall do my best to cheer him up. I shall explain that in an agent's business a lot depends on personality, and I shall say that I know one can put a man on outside work too quickly. I shall point out that by mucking up some interview he might easily lose the firm some hundreds of pounds. So after this he'll have a basin full of looking after the office while I see to the outside. Before I've finished I'll have him addressing envelopes."

I was gradually beginning to understand the partner business. I saw that once the unfortunate Mr. Peters was convinced that he was quite unsuited to being a theatrical agent Jackson's job was not difficult.

"You see," said Flash, "the finish is usually like this. I say, 'Look here, Peters, you know the business is going to blazes. It was not a few pounds that I needed. I wanted a man to help me. And as it is—well, old boy, I can't say you're much of a help.' It always works," he said. "They're just straining at the leash to escape from their own failures."

"Yes, well, you're a blighter, Flash," I said. "Apart from the twist, I wouldn't have the heart."

He regarded me sadly.

"Archie, you're still a mug, my boy," he said good-naturedly. "I'm afraid you'll never make a wide man. In this world you're either a punter or a grafter, and if you're a grafter you've got to make the other man pay all the time."

This reminded me that it was his turn to buy the drinks and I said so.

"But of course," he said, and ordered another round. "No one can say that Flash Jackson is slow at ordering drinks. That's part of the game. But tell me, if a woman were to leave her handbag behind in your tent, what would you do with it?"

"Return it, of course," I said. "I'm a grafter, not a sneak-thief."

He stared at me. "Do you mean that?"

"Well, of course," I said.

He sighed, and a melancholy expression spread over his long face.

"You may be a better man than I am, Archie," he said. "But you're a lousy grafter."

However, this was not quite true. Flash Jackson is not a typical grafter. The West End has demoralized him.

As I parted from him I felt it was getting me down too. It stifled me somehow, and I wanted to get on the road again.

I had only been cultivating Flash because I wanted to find out about the hair waver, and he certainly told me all I wanted to know. He told me where I could buy the things. He also showed me how to work them and gave me as much information about the game as he could.

I appreciated this, because he certainly went out of his way to help me become a pitcher.

The hair wavers cost eight shillings a gross, and I sold these in a packet at three for a shilling.

Or rather, at first I tried to sell them.

CHAPTER 18

I start as a pitcher at Slough and visit Newbury, where misfortune overtakes me and a young woman with bobbed hair. I meet Alfie Holmsworth and am introduced to his Academy. The disastrous history of Gloria Eve, alias Miss Smith.

STAGGERING ALONG WITH a life-sized dummy head, a wig and a Primus stove, to say nothing of a gross or so of hair wavers, I visited the open air market at Slough the following Saturday.

I was fairly adept at working the things after a week's intensive tuition from the obliging if not altogether attractive Flash Jackson, but I had not then got my patter right, by any means, and I was nervous about "coming to the bat"; that is to say, I did not like asking for money for the waver. This, of course, was fatal, and I made but fourteen shillings the whole day.

Perhaps I ought to describe the waver. It is a tin cylinder, flattened slightly and sealed at one end, and to this a two-legged wire clip is attached. The hair is wound round the cylinder and fixed tight with the clip. Then a very hot iron pin with a wooden handle is thrust into the cylinder and after a minute or two the hair is really very nicely curled.

I do not know why I decided to work this particular line. Even Flash pointed out that I looked a bit tough for this type of work. I was never a delicate plant, and my life on the fair-ground had hardened me up considerably, so of course I did not look much like the conventional notion of a hairdresser.

Moreover, I am naturally an unhandy soul, so perhaps I might have chosen something more suitable.

However, the waver was reputed to be a great pitch getter, and the idea of addressing my punters by the score instead of individually attracted me.

At Slough I was very timid and preoccupied with the mechanical part of my demonstration, but when I had finished my first performance I had about twenty people watching me.

"Now," I said rather quickly, for I did not know how long the waves would stay in, "those of you who require the waver tonight can obtain them from me at our special advertising price of one shilling for the usual half-crown set."

I turned away for what was, I suppose, approximately five seconds while I picked up a packet of wavers from my suitcase, but when I returned to my crowd it had vanished and the space before my pitch was the one clear spot in the market.

This kept on happening, and at last I began to expect it, which was disastrous. The secret of coming to the bat, or price, I discovered, is confidence, but it took me a long time to get it.

I spent a whole month at the markets round London learning to pitch, and incidentally the secrets of the waver. It was very like my first attempts on the tick-off, and I had some lamentable failures.

Flash had told me to offer to wave any onlooker's hair free of charge, and one day, at Newbury, feeling particularly pleased with myself, I did this.

The idea behind this somewhat risky proceeding was that the offer would dispel any notion the audience might have that the wig on my dummy had been specially prepared in some way.

Unfortunately, at my first offer a girl with very short bobbed hair accepted my invitation and came out of the crowd.

I tried to put her off, but she was determined, and at last I set about it. It was the first real head on which I had ever experimented, and I suspected that the waver would not be so good on short hair.

My crowd grew rapidly, and it dawned upon me even in that moment of stress that a living model was the real crowd-getter.

When at last I put in the pin I had the largest crowd round me I had ever drawn, and as I looked at the girl sitting there smiling smugly with the waver stuck unsteadily on the top of her head I wondered what I should do if I burnt the whole curl off, as I had frequently done on my wig.

I looked at the crowd. It was still growing, and there was no chance of it wandering away before I took out the waver. I almost wished it would.

At last I took out the pin. My hand was trembling and I burnt myself. The wretched girl still looked happily self-conscious.

Unfastening the clip, I slipped the hair from the waver. To my joy it seemed to be a perfect curl.

Unfortunately, however, as soon as I released the end of it it sprang back and sat on the top of the sleekly brushed head like a corkscrew. It looked funny even to me, and I was hardly in the mood for humor at that moment.

There was a howl of joy from the crowd. The laughter, gusty at first, swelled into a roar which seemed to fill the whole market place.

The girl grew red first, then angry; finally she wept.

"It's all right," I protested. "I haven't combed it into the wave yet."

But the combing turned it into a sort of fuzzy pom-pom which still stood upright. It looked fantastic and awfully funny.

The girl peered at herself in her vanity mirror. Then she jammed her hat on her head and fled.

I did not make a single sale.

However, I went on pitching and cleared my expenses at Newbury, and for some weeks I continued to visit the southern markets.

During that period I saw more of Flash, and in a burst of friendliness he confided to me another side of his activities.

In conjunction with an old friend of his called Alfie Holmsworth he was engaged in the stage-training lark. Flash warned me that Alfie was a "low fellow" before he introduced him, which I thought was rather amusing.

Alfie certainly was a "low fellow." I had seen him

before at Wigan Fair when he had been running a kie show.

"Kie" is the name given to any sort of wild-man show. Alfie had been even wilder than his performers at Wigan, because his niggers would give extra performances in the town during their off hours, and this naturally spoilt a lot of the novelty of his show. People who had seen them dancing in the street for pennies often recognized them when they paid six-pence to see them as the Man Eaters in Alfie's show.

He fancied himself as a showman, though, and, like most people in the business, believed in giving as good a performance outside his booth as he did inside.

The niggers, dressed in loin-clothes and straw skirts, danced on the platform in front of the show, hitting tom-toms and making wild catcalls. One of them pretended to gnaw a huge mutton bone, and human skulls were arranged about the platform to heighten the illusion.

The main attraction inside the booth was the Dance of Death. Alfie used to break bottles in front of the audience and throw the pieces into a box, which was about six feet square and only a few inches deep. This was already filled with broken glass, and the niggers used to dance in it barefoot. Before the show the dancers used to rub their feet with resin and toughen them in a solution of alum and water.

Also, Alfie used to sprinkle the freshly broken glass round the edges of the box, and the stuff on which the niggers actually danced had had the sharp edges filed down and rounded off.

All the same, they gave quite an impressive performance. They were supposed to be hardly human, and to speak no language save an unearthly gibberish, in which they sang at the top of their voices.

I was in the booth one night when one of them trod heavily on a jagged piece of glass by mistake. This incident enlivened the show tremendously. Dancing about on one foot, with the other clasped in his hand, he let out a terrifying scream. His eyes bulged, and for a moment I thought he was going to spring at Alfie and the show was going to become really wild, after all.

It was evident that he was trying to speak, and the crowd leant forward.

"Hell!" he bellowed suddenly. "Damn you, Mr. Holmsworth! Ah've cut mahself!"

That ended the performance, and I did not see Alfie again in Wigan.

However, when Flash introduced him to me in London he looked more prosperous than usual. He was even fatter than before, was carrying gloves and a stick, and was smoking an enormous cigar with the band on. He seemed to be overjoyed to see me and explained his business.

Having adopted the incongruous title of "Professor," he appeared to be making a lot of money. When I asked him what he was professing he said he was professing to teach people how to become famous on the stage. His slogan, he said, was "Every one can act," and his principal line of sales talk, "You've got it in you and I'm going to bring it out."

"It," I discovered, referred to money.

We parted from Flash and he took me along to his

"Academy," a basement in the vicinity of Lisle Street. It was a bright but dirty room which had previously been used as a night club, and Alfie, the opportunist, had taken it over at a bargain price when the establishment had been raided by the police.

As we entered we were met by a plain, plump woman in the forties who was dressed in a travesty of the ingénue's costume in a musical comedy.

Alfie did not seem too pleased to see her, but as we walked on I heard him say pleasantly: "Very nearly, Miss Smith. But I don't want yer to spoil it. You're not quite ready yet. Just a few more weeks, and remember, me girl, watch them two top notes. When I do let yer go I want yer to go down with a bang."

Poor woman, she did.

I had the misfortune to be present when she made her first public appearance.

Alfie had a standing advertisement in the personal columns of a respectable but careless newspaper. As far as I remember it read something like this:

WANTED FOR FUTURE PRODUCTION: A few vacancies occur in a well-known stage-training Academy for young people of both sexes. Only those showing promise will be accepted. Stage engagement GUARANTEED when proficient. Apply for free audition to . . .

The only show of promise Alfie required, he told me, was the showing of his pupils' money and their promise to pay his fee.

The guarantee of work did not appear to worry him. The man who could handle a bunch of niggers, he said, could handle practically anything.

Most of his pupils lost heart and their money long before he was forced to find them engagements, but occasionally he was faced with a stubborn and defiant punter who demanded the opportunity he offered.

Miss Smith was one of these, and I was unlucky enough to be with him when she completed her training.

"I expected this to happen with this dame all along," he said casually after she had gone. "I'll fix her up, all right. Hand me the 'phone, will yer?"

He took the instrument and there followed a short conversation with the manager of a certain little music hall somewhere across the river, with the result that Miss Smith was booked for a week.

In all innocence I was present on her first night. It had never been known, I discovered afterward, for one of Alfie's pupils to have a second night.

The manager of the theater had a special board which he displayed outside the house after one of his conversations with Alfie. The legend on the board stated simply: TONIGHT: ALFIE HOLMSWORTH'S EXTRA.

Whenever this board appeared, it seemed, the management could rely on a full house, and Alfie's turn was looked forward to with excitement in the whole neighborhood.

As we approached the theater I saw a single vegetable stall outside the gallery entrance which seemed to be doing a roaring trade.

Alfie looked at it thoughtfully.

"I ought to have a tie-up with that fellow," he said cryptically.

But even then I was not prepared for what followed. I left Alfie and Miss Smith at the stage door and arrived in the theater in the middle of the first turn. The house, I noticed, was decidedly unsettled.

Two step dancers of the very old school were doing their best to entertain the audience with some very competent tap dancing. Dressed in seedy evening clothes, they impersonated a couple of drunks and capered about in perfect unison while the orchestra played soft music.

At its best it would have been a monotonous act, but the performers were dispirited and every minute the gallery became more and more rowdy.

The next two or three turns received the bird, although they were quite good of their type, and it dawned upon me that the pit and gallery were working themselves up for something.

When at last Alfie's Extra was announced there was a peculiar and dreadful silence for a few seconds.

This was followed by a great rustling of paper; then the smell of vegetables—tomatoes, and the odd, offensive reek of cabbage—permeated the theater.

What followed was a ghastly experience. I felt genuinely sorry for the unpleasant Miss Smith. Even if she had been good she would not have had a chance.

However, if an extra at this music hall ever managed to complete his turn, or even to face the audience after the first few minutes, then he did indeed show promise of becoming famous in theaterland, or, indeed, anywhere.

As the curtain rose, so did the house. It sounded as

though the gallery was going to descend in a body, and the stalls hastily took cover.

The orchestra stuck to their instruments, but it was impossible to hear them.

Miss Smith, who had adopted the name "Gloria Eve" for this occasion, stood defiantly in the center of the stage. Fortunately she had plenty of confidence. The curious thing was that nearly all Alfie's pupils had confidence. I am afraid he told them they were good and they believed it.

Whatever I think about Alfie, I give him credit for what happened next. He appeared from the wings in a mackintosh and, after several minutes during which all sorts of missiles hit the back curtain, he managed to get some sort of order.

"Now, look 'ere, boys," he said, beaming at the gallery, "I know you're all out for a bit of fun. We're 'ere tonight to entertain you, and it's a bit of fun we want you to 'ave. But I want you to give this little lady a chance. She may not be the type of artist you admire, but she's an artist nevertheless. Oh, yes."

The gallery began to get noisy again, and something red and soft just missed Alfie's left ear. It made a nasty mess where it hit the back cloth. But he stuck his ground and insisted on finishing what he had to say.

"Now, some of you 'ave brought a few bokays in with you," he said, "and you don't want to waste 'em. Well, that's okay with me. I'm not askin' you to. But I want you to be patient for a few minutes, boys. Just a few minutes. This little lady was goin' to give you a song . . . that's 'ow she opens 'er act."

He paused for a moment and glanced at Miss Smith.

"Well, boys," he said, "you may not feel like a song tonight. We'll assume that part of the act is over and I'll ask Miss Eve 'ere to give us 'er dance. It's a bit o' classical dancing, ladies and gentlemen, and it's very unusual. I'll first give you some idea of what it's like."

Alfie was a very fat man and he was bald. He probably weighed about seventeen stone, although he was very little over five feet high. Yet the house was comparatively quiet as he demonstrated to them. Alfie had a way with him.

Circling round the stage a few times, waving his arms and looking like nothing on earth, he finally stopped with his back to the audience and tried to touch his toes.

"Now when that happens," said he, straightening himself up, "we'll say the truce is over, but till then be patient, boys."

Gloria Eve was convinced that she was a dancer. Holding a dummy head of John the Baptist on a sort of plate, she glided up and down the stage in a most extraordinary fashion. As a burlesque it would not have been at all bad, but it was not a burlesque and somehow this all-important fact was obvious to every one.

To my surprise and relief the gallery threw nothing at first. There was a lot of laughter and a few cat-calls, but the dancer continued with an earnestness that was rather terrifying and which made me feel slightly sick.

At last the moment came when she bent to place the charger at the feet of some imaginary person facing the audience. She remained bending for some seconds, since it was the safest thing to do in the circumstances.

The moment she turned her back there was a terrific disturbance in the gallery and the stage was bombarded with every sort of missile.

Those still left in the stalls tried to reach an exit, but I fell to my knees between the two rows of seats and covered myself as best I could.

I never saw what happened to Miss Smith.

Although the gallery probably enjoyed themselves, it was a most unpleasant experience for every one else in the theater. I found I did not want to talk about it much afterwards. There was something demoniacal and brutish about that crowd in the gallery.

Flash Jackson and Alfie Holmsworth, of course, were not the only men in the stage-training lark, but the majority of crooks who conducted this business were by no means grafters. In fact, I believe it is conducted today by an unscrupulous but businesslike person who finds the glamour which surrounds the stage and screen an excellent decoy with which to attract unfortunate aspirants, and who conducts his business on very big lines.

Next time I saw Alfie in his office I asked him if he was thinking of starting a second-hand clothes shop.

"You mean all that junk over there?" he said, indicating a collection of hats, umbrellas and odd bits of wearing apparel that filled all one corner of the room. "Yes, that's all been left by pupils who ain't never took the trouble to come back and collect their belongings after their first performance. I've never 'eard of or saw 'em again. That's gratitude for you!"

I eventually lost touch with Alfie. He was always changing his business address, but as far as I know he may still be running the stage-training lark somewhere.

However, it must not be thought that all stage-training academies are conducted on these lines. Many of them are reputable institutions where much good work is done; but most businesses have their nefarious counterparts, and Alfie's concern was certainly one of the darkest of them all.

The 'tober' - Nottingham Goose Fair
National Fairground Archive

CHAPTER 19

I visit Newcastle Town Moor, where I become a mounted pitcher. I get into serious difficulties with a belligerent mob, from which I am rescued by my good friend Ezra Boss and his valiant tribesmen. I witness the stand of a Napoleon.

D<small>ECIDING THAT THE UN</small>-satisfactory influence London always has upon me, combined with my lack of skill at my new trade, was too much for me, I went north again, and here my luck gradually improved.

The general opinion of the grafters whom I met seemed to be that things were bad. But I was getting much more at home with my wavers and had worked up my spiel, or fanny, or tale, until it was practically nark proof; so that, as far as I was concerned, business was improving all the time.

A "nark," by the way, is the name for a heckler or rival grafter who tries to nark, or spoil, one's pitch.

At Flint market I suddenly got going and five-pound evenings became fairly usual after that. I found that my greatest difficulty was to get the right model. The waver was really astonishingly good on long hair, but on short hair it was hopeless; and the difference in the size of my crowd when I had a live model instead of the wig was extraordinary. So I had to find a woman with long hair to model for me before I could pitch.

When I stayed a week at a market or a fair I engaged a girl for thirty shillings or two pounds a week, but at single-day gaffs I had to rely on people from the crowd.

Sometimes there was a child with suitably long hair belonging to one of the other stalls or caravans whose mother would let me wave its hair if I paid it a shilling a time. I usually managed somehow.

I was getting quite good at this new sort of grafting when I worked at Newcastle-under-Lyne some few weeks after I left London.

When the market closed at nine o'clock I had taken just over a fiver. My throat was tired and I was hot and a little exhausted.

In a bar just off the market-place I met Tomlinson, and on his advice I took the bus to Crewe that night, and, catching the midnight train from there, arrived at Newcastle-on-Tyne at seven o'clock the following morning.

My luck was in when I met Tomlinson. Tired out by the irksome journey, but a little thrilled, as a grafter always is, to get into a fresh neighborhood where a fortune may possibly be awaiting him, Tomlinson and I looked out of the carriage window as the train passed through the dismal and poverty-stricken Tyneside district.

As we crossed one of the bridges which spanned the river we could see the quayside far below us. There were already signs of activity there, for it is on the quayside at Newcastle that grafters can work on a Sunday.

This was the biggest Sunday of the year, for it was the beginning of Newcastle's race week. The Northumberland Plate was to be run during the next few days, and the entire city was going to make holiday. The biggest fair in Great Britain was going to be held on the Town Moor, and grafters from every part of the British Isles invaded the town.

At the market in the Potteries on the previous day Tomlinson had been a herbalist, but he had traveled up with me to the Town Moor as a tipster. He was a thin, wiry man who wore glasses, a bowler hat and light gray spats. He had been on the road all his life, he said, and told me that he was apt to get weary at times.

Racing was his hobby. Whatever he took as a tipster he usually passed on to the bookmakers, and this, no doubt, was why he spent most of his time as a herbalist on the markets.

Leaving most of our belongings at the station, we carried the things we might need immediately to the quayside and set about claiming a position.

This was not as easy as it appeared to be at first sight. Although the quayside is supposed to be "free tober," it is in the hands of several "slags." The Newcastle "slag" is a distinct type, very different from the usual down-and-out who hangs about a market.

The Newcastle "slag" is the sort of man who makes up the personnel of the race gangs, and for a bit of silver he will pick a fight with any one. In fact, most of them looked to me as if they would pick a fight for the fun of the thing. They looked upon the quayside, which is in one of the toughest parts of the town, as their own property, and, sleeping out all night to claim pitches, they let them in the morning to the highest bidder.

While I was there, when they were not fighting among themselves they stood about in little groups, discussing whose stall should be thrown into the river next or how they were to get even with some unfortunate grafter who, they decided, was unsuitable to work upon the quay.

Directly we arrived a man with clothes too big for him and a face that needed a shave badly walked up to Tomlinson.

"Lend us a bob, Guv'nor," he said, and it was more of a demand than a request.

To my surprise, Tomlinson handed it to him without a word.

"Do you know him, Tommy?" I inquired.

"No, and I don't particularly want to," he replied candidly. "That's why I gave him the denar. I can use my fists if it comes to it, but one hasn't got an earthly with this mob. There are too many of 'em. It's best to hand over and say nothing. He'll remember it, though, and they're useful if there should be a bit of bother. They're a damned nuisance, I admit, but one has to put up with them."

Things got busy on the quay shortly after ten, and from then onward until two o'clock thousands of people arrived to listen to the grafters.

There were more men than women in the crowd, but the men seemed good spenders and bought my hair wavers and Tomlinson's tips without hesitation.

There was a holiday atmosphere about, and grafters had arrived from all parts.

Down at the far end, by the customs-house, there was a whole line of tipsters. Some were dressed as jockeys, although racing did not start until Tuesday. These insisted that they were going to ride, and no one seemed to think it at all odd that a thirteen-stone jockey should be dressed in full racing kit at midday on a Sunday.

Another tipster, who was called the Colonel, had a club foot and an enormous stomach. He had adopted the dress of a fashionable follower of the turf—several fashionable followers, by the look of him. His trousers would have looked better on a smaller man, and his threadbare swallow-tail coat might have passed unnoticed on a taller, slimmer person.

There were numbers of others. They all carried race glasses hung over their shoulders; or, rather, they carried the leather cases which had been designed to carry glasses.

Farther up, the Gray Brothers held a big crowd. There were three of them. Stripped to the waist, they did the usual strong man stuff, and sold a lotion which they swore would cure rheumatism.

The Delmo Brothers worked their second-sight act next door and sold tick-off charts at twopence a time.

I saw the Little Major, and with him was Napoleon Jackson, the colored man whom I had met at Mold. They greeted me enthusiastically, and the Little Major and I inspected the gaff together.

There were quite a dozen different colored grafters, selling lucky charms, "snake oil," and all sorts of medicines, and there were windbag workers from London and Scotland, while the R.O. boys from Liverpool were doing good business.

I think I saw all the people I had ever met on the fair-grounds, except Susannah and the Royal Gypsy.

The Little Major pointed out a strange-looking couple to me.

"Hullo! The Whizz Mob is here," he said. "I wonder what's brought them today. That's Little Peter, and the man with him is Black Diamond. They're two of the Birmingham Mob."

"Whizzboys," I knew, meant "pickpockets," and I wondered why men who wished to avoid attracting attention should dress so flashily. The Whizz Mob usually appeared on a race-course or gaff and then vanished as suddenly as they had come. Also, for obvious reasons, they did not as a rule advertise their arrival, so that their presence on the quayside caused some interest among the grafters.

At last I got down to work. However, I soon found that there was far too much noise and excitement for quiet demonstration that Sunday, and at last, in sheer desperation, I climbed on to the top of my stall.

This is known as "working mounted," and, demonstrating in this fashion with my feet in line with the people's heads, I found no difficulty in holding a crowd.

It was easy to get children with long hair out of my audience to model for me by offering them a shilling a demonstration.

My stall, which occupied a frontage of about twelve feet, I had hired from one of the "slags." It was ideal for this style of work, and I arranged to have it on the Town Moor during the week.

After I had had about half a dozen demonstrations in succession, Lionel, who was standing by my joint, shouted to me.

"You don't want to overdo it," he advised. "You've got all the week, you know. What about letting me have a gallop?"

Lionel was a tipster. I had never met him before, but he seemed a pleasant person, and I stood down while he had a pitch from my stall.

I took five pounds eighteen that Sunday, and I found I liked the waver. I could come to my bat roughly every ten minutes, and, although the work was intensive while it lasted, it was not the all-time job that the tick-off had been.

Tipsters and quack doctors, I noticed, often had to talk for an hour before they attempted to sell anything.

I found that working mounted took it out of me after the long train journey and the Saturday's work in the Potteries the previous day, but it gave me confidence.

This was the beginning of one of my most successful weeks on the road, and ever after this, whenever possible, I worked the waver mounted.

On the Town Moor I found that I was shouting for two hours on end with a crowd of between two and three hundred people watching me.

After the first day I arranged with a girl to become my model for the week. I paid her thirty shillings for this, and when she had to leave to wash out the waves and dry her hair for another session, I relied upon people from my audience. But, remembering the bobbed-haired girl of Newbury, I was careful to select only suitable people.

Wednesday was the most important day at the fair on the Town Moor, and I made just under eighteen pounds. On Friday I made eleven pounds fifteen shillings, and on Saturday fourteen pounds eleven shillings.

On the other days I averaged just over a fiver, so that, arriving at Newcastle with only a few pounds, I suddenly found myself with over sixty at the end of the week.

I had taken the money entirely in shillings.

I think the waver must have been new to Newcastle, or that my particular style suited the people, for it was not an exceptionally good week for the majority of the grafters.

Of course, I probably worked harder than any one on the fair. I realized that it would be a long time before I got another opportunity that promised so well, and as long as there were people about I went on working.

The one misfortune that every pitcher dreads happened to me on Thursday. I lost my voice. I was forced to rest when this happened, but on the Little Major's advice I drank a whole sixpenny bottle of olive oil every day after this for a long time.

All my old acquaintances seemed to have gathered on the Town Moor. Madame Sixpence was working hard and doing well, and there were nearly as many tick-off workers as there had been at Hull Fair, only of course they were more scattered.

The principal fortune-teller was Gypsy Lee. There were several Gypsy Lees on the Moor, but this woman, whose real name was Daisy Boswell, was queen of them all. She was an extraordinary-looking person, with very dark skin, astonishing eyes and a hooked nose. She was working from a saloon car quite near my pitch.

"Daisy's only just come out of stir," said Lionel. "I bet she got gelt out of the warders. What a woman! I wish I had her nerve. She'll be doing bird again before long, you see if she don't. She's what I call a wide chump. She can get more gelt in five minutes than any other tick-off will find on the tober in a week, but she don't know 'ow to spend 'er dough."

If she did not know how to spend it she certainly used to get rid of it. Whenever she walked into the nearest hostelry she insisted on standing everybody a drink, even if the place contained a hundred people; also she dressed extravagantly, but not fashionably.

On the Moor she appeared in a pair of tightly fitting boots, scarlet in color, laced to her knees, and although it was an ideal June day she carried a very expensive fur coat on her arm. She liked furs, she told me.

She liked diamonds, too. Her brown fingers were ablaze with them. She told me sadly that she had once had so many rings that she could not shut her hand, but that times were bad now.

She was ill then, and in fact she died about eighteen months after this meeting.

She was an extraordinary creature, and continued to tell fortunes until two or three days before she died.

When I saw her people stopped to stare at her as she walked along the street, and she liked them to do this. She was jealous of other fortune-tellers, and, although I had often talked with her before, she had always been a little on her guard when I had been working the tick-off myself. But as soon as I became a pitcher she was most friendly, and talked quite openly about her affairs.

I am afraid she was most unscrupulous in her business. She had been known to obtain several hundred pounds from one client alone, and of course this had got her into a great deal of trouble with the police.

Her last visit to prison had been in connection with a fur coat. She had been working at an exhibition, and one of her clients had come into the booth wearing a magnificent mink wrap. Daisy did not tell me the exact story, but I gathered that she told the woman that the coat contained an evil spell, and Daisy had offered to dismiss this if the woman left the coat in her charge. Unfortunately for Daisy, the client was a councilor's wife, and that gentleman was not at all superstitious.

Daisy Boswell did about three months in prison for this.

The fair people referred to three months' imprisonment as "a carpet"; a month's as "a wooden" or "a moon"; and twelve months as "a stretch."

I told her I thought she was silly. "Fancy hoping to get away with a thing like that," I said. "A person with your reputation can't just vanish into thin air with a fur coat worth a hundred or so and hope to get away with it."

She was seated in the back of her car, looking at me. Some of the fire had gone from her eyes since I had first met her, and she looked a little tired. But her personality was just as forceful as ever, and I have never met any one who had the same curious mesmeric attraction. I think she had some sort of hypnotic gift.

She nodded after I had spoken, but then her eyes blazed with that old enthusiasm that had impressed me so much before.

"You're right," she said. "But, young man, you ought to have seen that 'smother.' I did not think of anything else. Haven't you ever seen something that you wanted and as soon as you saw it nothing else mattered? I wanted the coat and I had to get it. That's all."

I left her sitting in the car looking rather sad. I am afraid she was thinking of her lost fur coat and wishing that one like it would come along.

That Thursday at Newcastle was a particularly tiring day. The Moor always got a bit rough towards the evening, and I should have packed up about nine o'clock, but I wanted to keep my average up and it was after ten when I finally decided to close down.

I was just about to come to my last bat when a drunken man lurched into my pitch and started to scatter the people about him.

This sort of thing often occurred, and in the ordinary way I should have tried to humor him. I used to work a joke into my patter, as a rule, and get the crowd laughing at the interrupter, but this evening I was unlucky. The man refused to be silenced.

The people in front of me were becoming very unsettled, and I realized that unless the man went away my pitch would be ruined. So I jumped down, and, catching him by the arm, tried to lead him off.

"Now, come along, old boy," I said firmly. "Get out of this."

But he was not to be dealt with as easily as that. He was an enormous person: a heavy north-country-man some four or five inches taller than I. He placed one of his hands on my chest and held me away from him at arm's length, and it suddenly occurred to me that we were going to have a fight.

Most grafters know exactly when and where to chin a man, but I have never accomplished this. I also have the misfortune to be rather a slow thinker.

"Look here," I said, but I got no further.

He caught my tie with his left hand and I noticed his right shoulder jerk backwards. Fortunately for me he was not quick, and I got as close to him as I could. His blow lost its force, and the moment he released his hold on my tie I hit out, rather wildly I am afraid, at his face.

I caught him on the jaw and he sat down. This was only because he was a heavy man, though; but for a moment I was quite exhilarated.

Only for a moment. The next thing I knew was that my ear was stinging as though it had been burnt. Some one from behind had let fly at me.

There was considerable force behind the punch, and, swinging round, I saw the man who had delivered it. He was a "slag" I had noticed on the Moor earlier in the week: a tall, bony individual with a drooping eye and enormous teeth set very far apart in his mouth.

This person evidently wanted a fight. I hit out at him and caught him on the cheekbone, but although I am not small and all my weight was behind the blow, I might as well have jammed my fist at a brick wall.

I ducked under his next blow and got one good punch in.

Then the crowd, which I had temporarily forgotten, surged in between us. This seemed to me to be an intervention of Providence, and I was a bit puzzled by it until I suddenly caught sight of Ezra Boss, my gypsy friend, amid the crush.

"Scarper and mind your smash, son," he whispered, and was gone.

As soon as he spoke I realized that the whole disturbance was probably a put-up job engineered so that some one could steal my money, and if this was the case I had certainly played right into their hands.

I glanced round me and realized that I was in the center of a crowd of at least a hundred people.

Before, I had been too excited to give much thought to anything except the man who had upset my pitch, but now I realized that by striking him I had set myself up as a fair opponent to any one who fancied a fight; and there were plenty of people looking for a scrap on Newcastle Town Moor.

The crowd was growing denser and more dangerous. The peaceable folk had fled, and those who remained seemed anxious to make the most of the row.

I made for my stall, but although it was only about six yards away it was some time before I could reach it. I had asked for trouble and I had got it.

A man I had never seen before seized me by the arm and swung me round to face him.

"What's the bloody idea?" he demanded, and crashed his fist into my face.

I went straight down. Staggering to my feet, I came up just in time to catch another blow to my chin which sent me down on the grass again. The world was completely black, and I remember that the grass felt comfortable.

I was just getting angry again when some one stumbled over me and a heavy boot was planted on my shoulder. I scrambled up. Blood was trickling down the side of my neck and my temple throbbed painfully. My eyes were full of blood, too, from a cut across my forehead.

I had just stood upright when I was nearly knocked over again by the falling body of the man who had hit me. Lurching against me, he sank to the ground and remained where he fell.

I stared at him and looked up to see Joe, one of the Bosses, was a few feet away, and in his hand he held a peculiar-looking weapon. Ezra had called his enormous family out to help me.

I discovered afterwards that his bludgeon was a heavy spanner wrapped in some felting and covered with an old sock.

A dozen or so gypsies had appeared, apparently from nowhere, and they seemed happy to have something to do. They shouted to each other in their strange language and hit out viciously on all sides.

One or two of them used their fists only, but the majority carried peculiar truncheons. These were made of rubber and bound tightly with thin cord. Although they were so flexible that they could be bent double, they were as heavy as lead.

The opposition was more organized than I had suspected. They were a very tough crowd, and one man bore down on Ezra, the neck of a broken bottle in his hand, the jagged glass gleaming wickedly.

Joe, however, dealt with him, and seemed to enjoy doing it.

Having been thoroughly knocked about, I suddenly felt angry, and I went for the next man who lunged at me. His blow glanced off my chin and I caught him in the wind with my left hand. As his chin jerked forward I hit him with my right. He went down beautifully, and I was almost sorry when he did not get up.

At last I reached my stall. The crowd was surging in front of it, but had not yet spread behind it. I was afraid when that happened the whole thing would go over.

I found my terrified assistant and told her to clear off to Madame Sixpence's wagon, where I could pick her up later.

She had collected my money for me and had it safely in her bag, and as the fight was still raging, she took it and slipped out of the back of the stall and fled.

I snatched up the best of my belongings and thrust them into my bag.

Out of the darkness I saw Ezra's brown face peering up at me.

"Make for our vardoes," he called. "Scarper! Quick!"

I ran with the rest of the gypsies, not knowing why or where we were going.

When we had covered some fifty yards Joe turned to me.

"One of our fingers took sights of the rozzers," he said.

By this he meant that some one had seen the police arriving, and I was surprised that we should be running away from them. I felt that if the police had arrived earlier it would have saved a lot of trouble. I did not feel in the least bit guilty.

But Joe knew more about these things than I did. The arrival of the police, I found, breaks up any sort of free fight, and when they come it is best for every man to get as far away from the scene of the trouble as possible.

The truncheons that the gypsies carried were illegal; but as a matter of fact when I talked to one of the policemen afterwards, he advised me to provide myself with one.

Our fight, I gathered, was a small affair. Although one man had to be taken to the hospital, no one was really seriously hurt, and the police did not make any charges.

"We know some of these men well," the inspector explained to me afterwards, "but we can't put our hands on 'em. Whatever you do to 'em, though, will be in self-defense; we know that. I should look out for yourself during the rest of the week."

I took his advice, and I also decided to take a few lessons in boxing.

"Fightin' never gets no one nowhere," Ezra said to

me seriously afterwards when we were talking by his wagon.

I agreed with him, but nevertheless I decided that there were occasions when it could not be avoided.

I also realized that if it had not been for the gypsies I might have had a pretty bad time of it, and I began to see their use in the tribe. Although they appeared to be always hanging about doing nothing, they proved to me that evening that they were ready for action whenever it should be necessary.

I was profoundly grateful that one of them should have been watching me at work, and I admired the expediency with which they all arrived on the scene as soon as the trouble started.

Fights were very common on the Town Moor.

The following day one of the Quayside Mob snatched Madame Enid's handbag, which contained all her takings.

Madame Enid had her tent pitched behind Napoleon's stall, and while he and her husband, Bert Armstrong, were working the muzzle, she was grafting the tick-off quietly from their pitch.

Business had slackened and they were going to pack up for an hour or so. The woman's bag was lying on the stall by her side and she was talking to the men as they shut up the joint.

She turned just in time to see one of the Mob snatch her bag and disappear. He had an accomplice, and although they separated, running in opposite directions, Napoleon saw the one who had the bag. He gave chase, and, as he was a good sprinter, soon overtook the runaway. The man dropped the bag and Napoleon picked it up.

When I heard the story I thought that was all there was to it, but the following day, just after ten o'clock, there was the devil of a row.

I had just come to my bat, and from where I worked, high up on the stall, I could see Madame Enid's tent. Something was obviously wrong.

Telling the girl to pack up, I hurried over, and pushing my way through a huge crowd I saw a most extraordinary sight.

Napoleon was standing alone in the middle of a large ring pitch. There was a clear space round him of about three feet each way, and the crowd was pressing round, snarling dangerously.

He was keeping it at bay with a hammer, round the head of which was tied a large white handkerchief. Over six feet high, he made a terrifying figure with his peculiarly shaped head and shining black skin.

I did not know what it was all about, but I guessed that the bag-snatcher had returned with a mob.

Unfortunately, it was impossible to tell who was an enemy and who a friend. I shouted to Napoleon, though, and forced my way through the crowd, and I saw several other grafters who, like me, were ready for action as soon as they realized against whom it was to be directed.

At the moment Napoleon stood alone. He was staring about him wildly, the whites of his eyes gleaming, holding back the swearing, muttering people with his hammer and saying nothing.

Suddenly he charged the crowd, which made way for him, and ran like a hare for the entrance.

A dozen or so tough-looking customers followed him, and it was easy then to recognize his opponents.

I and the other grafters charged after the Mob, but as Napoleon reached the tramlines the police got him and he was safe.

As soon as things had quietened down I called at the police station with Bert Armstrong and Mesdames Enid and Sixpence, and Napoleon was released.

The police had kept him there for his own protection, and it was not until I saw him that I realized in just what a predicament he had been. His enemies had been "mob handed," that is to say, working in a big group, and unfortunately, when he had hit out at one of the mob before I had arrived, the head of his hammer had flown off, leaving only the handkerchief tied to the harmless handle.

Luckily the mob had not realized this, and he had been standing there waiting for his chance to make a dash for it.

This sort of fight was often very dangerous, for when a mob gets to work there is no knowing what may happen.

I enjoyed the Town Moor, but I was not sorry when it was over. Although business was exceptionally good, it was hard work, and it was work under difficulties. But I had found how to pitch and had also discovered that there was quite a lot of money to be made at it.

My head healed rapidly, and I looked about for the next adventure.

CHAPTER 20

I make money, and go to South Shields, where I meet Sally. Sally adopts me.

Business had been so good at Newcastle that I decided to try my luck at some of the markets round about before I moved on. Every day I improved as a pitcher and my whole style of work gradually changed.

For quite a time I averaged over thirty pounds a week. I went out to make a lot of money, and, curiously, I usually got it.

Tomlinson decided to return to Crewe, where he lived, but I remained.

Gradually it dawned upon me that the secret of making money on the markets was to start early and work the entire time. This sounds very simple and obvious, but most of the market grafters had the firm conviction that it was no use pitching until the market was in full swing, and it took me some time to discover that they were wrong.

My model was my chief difficulty, and it was an ever-present problem. Sometimes I employed a girl by the week; sometimes I relied upon the children in the crowd.

Children, I discovered, made the best models.

They were much less self-conscious and were much more likely to sit still.

One day at South Shields, however, I was desperate. None of the employment agencies could help me and none of the other grafters had a daughter with suitable hair.

At last I gave up the search and decided to try one demonstration on the wig. It was the lunch hour and I felt that if I was going to keep up my average it was time I got busy.

As I lit my stove and prepared my joint a few barefoot children gathered round me to see what I was about. They were the usual rabble of ragged, inquisitive little creatures to which I had grown used in the north. Among them, however, I noticed a little girl who looked about ten years old, with long straw-colored hair bound in two plaits hanging to her waist.

She was an odd-looking child: her eyes set very wide apart, her nose short and broad, like the nose of a cat. She reminded me of a small white kitten, sleek rather than fluffy. She had the peculiar confidence of a kitten, too, and regarded me with stolid interest.

I offered her a shilling if she would let me wave her hair, and she accepted it readily.

Her hair waved beautifully, and my suckers were greatly impressed. She sat up on my stall, her dusty bare feet tucked under her chair and her hands folded in her lap.

I hardly noticed her at the time. I was very busy and she sat so still that she was as easy to work upon as any wig.

I did so well that pitch that I offered her an extra

two-and-sixpence if she would stay with me the entire afternoon.

"Ee," she said, "I'll 'ave to stay away from school."

It was the first time she had spoken, for our short conversation until then had been conducted, on her side at least, entirely in nods.

"Yes," I said dubiously. "I suppose that would be difficult?"

"Nay," she said. "I'll stay and have me hair waved."

I had a most successful day, and when it was time for her to go home it occurred to me that I might take her name and address in case I should return to the market.

She told me her name was Sally Fisher and that she lived in the slums. She went off very happily with her three-and-sixpence, holding the money very tightly in her small plump hand.

I forgot all about her. From South Shields I went to Stockton-on-Tees; but a week or so later, when I thought of going back to South Shields for the Saturday market, I turned up Sally's address and wrote to her parents, offering to pay her the same money as before if she cared to meet me at the market.

I did not expect her to turn up, for all my models were unreliable, but when I arrived about midday I saw her sitting on the pavement, patient and dusty and more like a white kitten than before. I discovered she had been waiting for me since nine o'clock.

She said very little, but climbed up on my joint as soon as I had put it up.

It occurred to me that it might be rather tedious for

her, listening to the same jokes every few minutes and remaining perfectly still for hours on end, but she seemed to enjoy it in a quiet, rather secretive fashion.

She had the gift of effacing herself completely. Although I was waving her hair I forgot all about her.

At that time I had taken up my abode at Stockton-on-Tees, where I had found some remarkably good lodgings, and at the end of the day I found myself wishing that I could be as sure of getting a good model in that district as I was in South Shields, and when I stopped for a rest I looked at Sally regretfully.

"I wish you could travel round with me," I said.

"Yes," said Sally. She made no other comment, and I started to pitch again. I had spoken casually, and thought no more of my involuntary remark.

During our next rest I asked her how old she was and she said "fourteen in a month."

I said I had thought she was younger than that, and she said she had seven brothers and sisters. Then conversation languished.

She was a silent person, but she was not shy or bored. It was simply that she naturally spoke very little.

At the end of the day she observed that she had a month's holiday in a fortnight's time. She also offered to play truant from school on Monday if I wished to work the market then.

This did not seem a bad idea. I had met the Little Major in the town and there were one or two other grafters staying with him.

So on Monday Sally and I went pitching again. She made herself extraordinarily useful. Without any instructions on my part she produced a clasp to fix the hair across her head whenever I had finished a demonstration, and when a punter gave me a note for a packet of wavers she had the change ready for me when I arrived back at the stall.

That night when I paid her and said good-by she did not go, but remained looking at me.

"What's up?" I inquired.

"If you'd like me to travel with you," she said, "will you call at the house and see my Dad? He and Mother think it's about time I got a job."

As I have said, she looked about ten, she was barefoot, ragged, and certainly did not appear old enough to do anything useful. The notion that in a month's time she might be expected to go into a tin works or some other inferno shocked me considerably, but I did not see what I could do about it. However, I did not want to hurt her feelings, and I told her to run along and that I would think about it.

I had done quite well. My takings on Saturday and Monday had amounted to over twelve pounds, and that evening I found the Little Major and Edwin, the Plant Food Wizard, at the Mariner's Arms.

Edwin was an extraordinary person. He sold some sort of artificial manure for aspidistras, and for years he had worked nothing but this particular line. It was white powder that he mixed himself, and he sold it in little packets at sixpence a packet.

He told me that the number of people all over the country who wanted to keep their aspidistras alive was amazing.

He traveled two fine specimens about with him, and

although I believe his plant food was quite good he was always potting new plants, since, as he said, they got knocked about a good deal on the road.

He was a pleasant, jovial soul, and he and the Little Major were among the best companions I ever met.

The Mariner's Arms is probably one of the finest hostelries in England. Most people know it better as Fred Wood's, after the proprietor, a retired champion cyclist.

The Little Major knew everybody there, and we made a party. Eventually I stayed the night and we sat up talking till the small hours.

In the morning I felt weary and disgruntled. I had had a sore head ever since my fight on the Moor, and the celebrations of the previous evening had not done much to soothe it.

On Tuesday morning I was full of new resolutions and I wanted to get down to work again and keep up my average.

Before leaving South Shields it suddenly occurred to me that my landlady at Stockton was one of the kindest and most sensible women in the world, and that she would probably look after Sally if the child's people were willing to let her come and model for me for a week or two.

It was rather a wild idea, I suppose, but I have never been blessed or cursed with much of that sort of imagination. I wanted to get on with my work and this seemed a way of doing it.

Finally I went to see the Fishers. I found the house at last.

It was in the most terrifying slum I had ever seen.

I thought I knew the East End of London pretty well, but nothing I had seen there even approached the street in which the Fishers lived.

There appeared to be no front door to the house, and, climbing up some steps at the back of the building, I came at last to the second floor.

There I was met by a pale, thin-faced woman with very black untidy hair, who stared at my feet all the time I was speaking to her. She had obviously heard all about me, though, and I was shown into a small kitchen-reception-living-and-(possibly) bedroom.

This chamber was quite clean, but there was hardly any furniture in it, and quite half a dozen small children played about on the floor.

Sally was among them, and she smiled at me, but did not speak.

I met Mr. Fisher. He was in his shirtsleeves and stockinged feet. Shoe leather was scarce in the Fisher family. None of the children, including a youth of about sixteen, wore shoes or stockings.

Mr. Fisher, a well-built, square-jawed man in the forties, sat on a stool by the fireplace and listened to what I had to say in utter silence. His head was closely cropped, I noticed, except for a little tuft of curls upon his forehead. The remainder of his poll might have been shaved.

He was obviously a very slow-thinking person, and he was slow in everything he did.

I liked him, and I was sorry he was out of work. When I offered him five shillings a week for Sally's wages he looked at me as though I were a millionaire. I am afraid the Fishers were very poor.

"When do you want her to start?" said Mrs. Fisher before her husband had spoken at all.

I explained that I wanted to start work at once, and that I would like to take Sally back to Stockton with me that night.

Mrs. Fisher hesitated, and I naturally thought that she might be alarmed, or at least dubious, about the propriety of the situation; so I suggested that I wire my landlady in Stockton.

But this, Mrs. Fisher seemed to think was an extravagance which bordered on lunacy. It was not the proprieties, but a nightgown that was worrying her, she explained, and it was the lack of this necessary garment that nearly prevented Sally from setting out in the world.

I realized that it would not be in order for me to offer to supply the deficiency, and Mrs. Fisher turned to her husband.

"D'you think I could borrow one of little Suzy's nightgowns from Lily?" she asked her husband.

That gentleman said that Lily had better lend it, and he spoke threateningly.

So it was finally arranged that Mr. Fisher should find out the next suitable train for Stockton and, calling for me at the tavern on the market-place, we should join the others at the station.

The whole of this rather extraordinary interview took about a quarter of an hour, and, leaving five shillings on the table as Sally's first week's salary, I climbed over a couple of infants who were playing wild animals on the floor and hurried outside.

Some few hours later, when Mr. Fisher, very ami-

CHEAPJACK

able after a couple of pints, and I, somewhat apprehensive of the responsibilities I had so light-heartedly undertaken, arrived at the station, the entire Fisher family had collected to see us off. It was the last train, and I was anxious not to miss it.

Sally seemed to be the least excited of any of us. Perhaps excited is hardly the term for my state of mind, but I was certainly bewildered by the Fishers. There were eight children in all, and Sally was the second eldest.

Mrs. Fisher was carrying one in her arms and her husband had told me that she was expecting another. Four children clung to my jacket and asked for pennies, and a very small boy held himself upright by clutching my trouser leg.

Sally and I obtained corner seats, and she sat opposite me facing the engine. Since it was the last train to Stockton it was a slow one, and for the first time I had a good look at my new assistant.

She was wearing shoes and stockings; her first, I suspected, for she seemed very conscious of them. They were not very fine shoes: brown rubber gym affairs, very new and yellow-looking.

Her threadbare coat was much too short, even for Sally, and over her straw-colored hair she wore a shapeless species of tam-o'shanter which was obviously not now the color it once had been.

Very wide-eyed and quiet, she sat stiffly in her corner, grasping a small papier-mâché portmanteau.

Now and again she opened this and peered inside, as though afraid that its contents might mysteriously have vanished. It contained, I saw, a parcel of sandwiches and a nightgown and nothing else whatever.

So Mrs. Fisher had been successful in her borrowing, and there was Sally, complete with food and respectability, the two things which were really essentials to the Fisher mind.

It occurred to me that I ought to talk to her. I did not know very much about children, and I tried to remember what would have interested me had I been her size.

"I'm afraid we've picked a slow train," I said at last, "but we shouldn't be very long now."

"I've never been in a train before," said Sally.

"Really?" I said, and there was a long silence. I couldn't think of anything else to say, and she sat quite still, staring in front of her, a completely inscrutable expression on her small kitten face. I gave it up. I had a great many plans to make, and I took out my notebook.

When I looked up again she was fast asleep.

Then and only then I realized that here was I, a feckless soul at the best of times, landed with the awful responsibility of a small child.

In the back of my mind I remembered that there were all sorts of regulations about feeding children. I knew they had to have a lot of milk, for one thing.

However, I relied on my landlady at Stockton to see to all that, although I knew that the responsibility was mine. I am afraid I looked at Sally as though she were some strange little animal of whom I had no very clear idea how to take care.

We did not arrive at Stockton until after half-past eleven at night, and I began to be a little anxious about my reception at my lodgings. My landlady was not expecting two of us.

However, I need not have worried. Mrs. Coleman, of Stockton-on-Tees, was a real motherly soul with a great experience of life thrown in. Her husband had been one of the biggest horse dealers in the north before the era of the motor-car. He had owned a circus and sold horses by the hundred during the war.

However, when I arrived with Sally I did not know the family as well as I did afterwards. I had only stayed with them a few days, and they were not used to me or I to them.

From that time on, however, their house became my home in the north. They were very like gypsies. They knew as much about grafters and the show people as any one in the world, and as time passed they gradually began to treat me as something between a favorite son and a star boarder, and I eventually found a kindliness in that household which I had never before known.

Mrs. Coleman rose to the occasion that night when Sally and I, weary and a little apprehensive, arrived upon her doorstep. Sally was taken off my hands, given a hot meal, a hot bath and a room to herself, all of which impressed her tremendously.

In the morning there was no time to be wasted and we settled down to work.

Stockton has one of the largest street markets in the north, and my toll was half-a-guinea, and for the hire of the stall from which I worked I paid three shillings.

From the beginning Sally was a startling success, and when I closed down just before five o'clock I had taken a little under ten pounds. This, for a week day, was extraordinarily good.

I gathered that the waver had not been seen in Stockton for some time, and Sally and I together were something completely new.

Working high above the people's heads, the whole street could hardly help seeing us, and we had such large crowds that the police were continually moving people on.

It dawned upon me that this market would provide me, and incidentally Sally, with a living for some weeks to come.

Of course I never made so much in a single day again in Stockton, but for weeks after this I made five pounds there every Wednesday.

After work on our first day at Stockton Sally and I went out on a shopping excursion. We got some shoes to replace the dreadful yellow gym sandals, and one of the other grafters, who was selling mackintoshes on the market, sold us a raincoat.

The hat was more difficult. Sally displayed a leaning towards feathers, but eventually we got something that was at once both striking and serviceable.

At Bishop Auckland market the following day we met the Wendon sisters, who sell cloth by the piece at their stall, and Jenny Wendon picked us out some very special dress material and promised to make it up for us.

So the following week, much to her delight, Sally had a Sunday frock.

CHAPTER 21

Sally and I go to Whitby, where the Little Major recounts to me his great plan to make our fortunes. The advent of the motor-car. The reappearance of Three-fingered Billy and the ancient secret of the "bugfat."

SALLY AND I CONCENtrated on markets near Stockton for the next six weeks. We returned to Mrs. Coleman's every night, and Sally grew sleeker and more like a little white cat than ever before.

There was one exception to this general rule, and that was when we went to Whitby one Sunday to work the regatta on the following day. It was my first visit to Whitby since I had gone there with the tick-off, and Sammy York and I had slept out all night in a shelter on the front.

Fortunately the weather was much better this year, and business was definitely good. The usual crowd was there, and soon after I arrived I knocked into the Little Major.

As usual, he was not quite sure what he was going to work, but was not lacking in ideas.

"Come and have a bevvy," he said as soon as he saw me. "I've got something I want to talk to you about."

Before I could do this I had to find lodgings and see that Sally was in safe hands. I explained this to him and we all set off together in search of a suitable lettary.

At last we found a place and I left Sally with the landlady, who promised to take her to the pictures. Then, having convinced myself that she was all right, I went off with the Major.

The responsibility of Sally's upbringing had sobered me down considerably, and I suppose I must have seemed a little paternal, if not the proverbial old hen, to the Little Major, for he looked at me in astonishment.

"It must be a terrible expense, a kid like that, and rather a nuisance as well," he suggested, and although I tried to explain how important a live model was to me he only seemed to think that I might have solved the difficulty more easily by getting married. The notion that any wife I chose might not like to have her hair waved continuously all day never seemed to occur to him.

However, when I considered the matter, this partial adoption of Sally did seem rather an elaborate way of going about the model question. But, curiously, in practise, it was a very good idea. With Sally I became one of the strongest grafters on the road, and I found that windbag workers and the R.O. boys no longer thought of pitching near me; in fact, other workers began to avoid my joint and I gradually grew to have no competition.

Naturally I selected a quiet position if possible, and of course there were times when I had my work cut out to hold my own, but I usually managed to do this, and the more often I was successful, the less competition I found in the future.

Of course, I am afraid I spoiled Sally at first. After a good day's work it seemed hardly prodigal to give her half-a-crown, but since she had never had any money at all of her own before, I suppose it was not very good for her.

Gradually she got used to it and would ask for it if I forgot to pay up. Whatever I gave her she spent at once, mostly on sweets and fruit.

At Stockton she went to the pictures every night, accompanied by one of Mrs. Coleman's elder daughters. I knew she was safe then and I could settle down to my own affairs. I am afraid I was not very good at bringing up children.

While the Major and I were having a drink at Whitby he produced his great idea.

"I've got a notion. It's a winner," he said seriously, "and I don't see why you shouldn't be in on it. You and I could wipe up a lot of gelt this summer if you felt like it."

I said I always felt like it, of course, but that as I was doing so well with the waver I was not really looking for a new line.

"Ah," he said, "but have you ever worked a cattle market?"

I said no, I had not; and he seemed pleased.

"That's fine," he said. "It's all new ground, then, and they're not bad in the winter either. We could have eighteen months' or more good work—a new market every day. That's the secret. To make money on the markets you must keep on the move the whole time. It's the fresh face that does it."

He paused and looked at me solemnly over his tankard.

"Ever tasted beer?" he said softly.

I stared at him. I seldom drank anything else.

He smiled. "Ah, yes, I know. But have you ever *tasted* it?" he continued. "We all drink it. It becomes a habit. But do we taste it? Some of the beer you get today, the sixpence-a-pint beer, isn't worth supping. There, son, that's my idea. You see, we haven't got much to beat."

His eyes were dancing with enthusiasm.

"Make your own beer. That's my idea. Think of the sensation we would cause on a market, with a big flash: 'DRINK MORE BEER.' And another: 'FREE BEER FOR ALL.'"

I grinned at him. The Little Major was always thinking out great schemes, but this one certainly sounded a good pitch-gatherer.

He was full of it, and continued with enthusiasm:

"Now, look here, son, we'd work a sort of crocus spiel, see? We'd tell 'em it's good for 'em. The poor blokes are so used to being told not to do this and not to do that that some one who told 'em to drink more beer for their health's sake would come as a real ray of light. See what I mean? Oh, it's a great idea! It's good because it's new, and it's new because you'll be selling something that every man wants."

He finished his drink, wiped his lips and leaned upon the bar.

"First we'd work out a spiel, something like these spread merchants use."

I nodded. "Spread," I knew, was the name given to a herbalist who sells a mixture of dried plants. He spreads these herbs out in front of him and lectures on the health-giving value of each.

The Little Major went on talking. I had never seen him so excited.

"Lord!" he said with fine enthusiasm, "if working chaps will spend a denar on lousy herbs that taste like filth and drink 'em just because they're supposed to do 'em good, surely they'll fall for the same sort of thing served up as beer? Look here," he went on, plucking me by the sleeve, "they can't buy beer in a pub today. It's all chemical. Chemical gargle, that's what it is. But what was the old-fashioned beer made of? The stuff that made Britain what it is today, or rather, what it was the other day? Why, malt and hops and yeast. What a spiel!" he said. "Malt, the body builder; hops, the appetizer; yeast, the laxative. I tell you, you can't beat it!"

The Little Major, whose head did not quite reach my shoulder and whose small hands fluttered nervously as he talked, reminded me of a very small bird flapping round a very large worm.

"You could put it over," he assured me, "and we'd cause a sensation wherever we went."

"But how do we come to our bat?" I said. It really did sound as though there was something in the scheme.

"Oh, it's simple," he explained. "First we work on the health business and then we glorify beer. We ask 'em if they've ever seen an anemic publican. We ask, where is there a finer bloke than a brewer's drayman. We give beer its due. First of all we praise all kinds of beer. Then we gradually shift it round to our special mixture.

"I tell you what," he added as a new thought occurred to him. "We might even give 'em a taster— just a little glass of some real strong stuff. Then we'd follow it up by coming to the bat with a rush. We'd give 'em a packet of stuff for a shilling that'd make a gallon of beer."

I began to laugh. The Little Major certainly had imagination, and I agreed with him that there was something about beer that had a wide appeal, and that most people would risk a shilling on the chance of getting good beer at three ha'pence a pint.

The Little Major was exalted by his own eloquence.

"This beer," he said, lifting up my tankard and looking at it with disgust, "this beer, why, there isn't a hiccup in a gallon of it. It's taxed to hell and that's what the working man has to pay for it. They've taken away his job. They've taken away his comforts. They've taken away his freedom. And now they want to take away his beer."

I smiled. I could see him arguing on the market that it was practically every man's duty to get drunk at least three times a week. I liked the Little Major. He got so interested in every new idea, and his fund of new ideas was inexhaustible.

I never went into his beer proposition seriously, though; nor did he. The next time I saw him he was just as excited about something else.

I had a very good day at Whitby regatta. I met many old friends, and among them Mad Jack, the gazer, whom I had not seen since Hull Fair.

He was in great form and had given up the Harold Lloyd novelty for a dreadful rubber hooter, which made a most appalling noise. With a card hung round his neck on which was painted "RASPBERRIES, ALL FRESH," he capered about the place as usual, followed by a crowd of little boys.

I found him rather disconcerting, for, whenever I came to my bat, it struck him as being humorous to demonstrate his own wares at the outskirts of my pitch.

Nevertheless, my day at Whitby was considerably more profitable than my experience with the tick-off in the same place, and on Tuesday Sally and I went back to Stockton.

We continued to work the markets round that city and I found that the responsibility of looking after Sally made me stick to my job and lead a sober, even respectable, life.

One day, at Darlington, I bought a car, and on the same day I again met Three-fingered Billy. It was odd that they should have arrived together, because through the one I spent most of my time that summer with the other.

The car, one of the old bullet-nosed Morrises, cost me fifteen pounds; or, rather, it cost me that sum to buy it in the first place, although it let me in for a good deal more during the two months I had it.

But a car of any kind is a great asset to the gaff hunter, and once I possessed one I wondered how I had managed before.

In this chariot I could travel my own board and trestle, and all sorts of paraphernalia necessary to my business, to say nothing of Sally and Three-fingered Billy, who became a sort of personal guide to our tour.

Among other things I bought an immense bookmaker's umbrella, which, in addition to being a very fine flash, made it possible for me to work when there was a slight drizzle.

Before I had this gigantic gamp it had been impossible for me to work in the slightest rain, for no hair, not even Sally's, would wave when it was damp.

Although it was not permitted on some markets, I always worked from the car where possible, and, although the old Morris was hardly an advertisement, a car of any description made a good impression on a market-place.

The effect was not so good, of course, when I had to get a number of "slags" to push us off before the engine would start, but as this only happened when business was finished it did not really matter much.

However, once the Morris started it usually went on, and it was a great boon to us.

At last I felt that the district round Stockton was becoming exhausted, and Three-fingered Billy suggested that we should journey on to Cumberland.

I was sorry to part with Sally, but she had a few weeks at school to make up, and at last I took her back to South Shields.

"I'll come back," I promised.

"Ee," said Sally. "All right. I'll be 'ere."

Three-fingered Billy and I continued the journey to Cumberland and spent a few weeks on the markets there. We centered at Workington and worked the markets round about.

Billy was glad to come with me.

"I don't seem to do nothing these days wot's any good," he said dismally. "I'm dead on the floor, and when you gets like that you don't seem to be able to get going again. I 'aven't 'ad a bit o' luck since I last saw yer on the knocker at Manchester."

Our tour was quite a success. Billy knew nothing about cars, which was a pity, since I knew nothing about them either, but he was useful in his own way.

Just outside Penrith I backed into a ditch and we spent nearly an hour trying to wedge the car up with logs, so that the back wheels could get a grip on something instead of spinning purposelessly in the wet mud.

When we were both exhausted and it looked as though we should have to walk to the nearest garage to get some one to tow us out, Billy had one of his few ideas.

He clambered into the ditch, set his back against a wheel, grasped the car somewhere and lifted it bodily on to firm ground.

"You can't beat the simple ways in the end," he said, as he clambered in beside me.

He still had his connoisseur's appreciation of beer, and this made progress a little slow at times, but we traveled about in the car until it died on us just outside Ripon one Thursday and I sold it to a scrap dealer for thirty shillings. It had been quite a good investment, though, and I was seldom without some sort of car after this.

Apart from making everything so much easier, it

enabled me to ignore distance, and when I was unable to get into one market I did not lose the day's work but motored on to the next.

Billy never liked cars. He was prejudiced, he said, and I sympathized with him. Cars and buses had ruined business at country markets. Billy looked back regretfully to the days when the whole population of a village used to turn out to see a fresh grafter, and when a fair visited a town practically the entire place had been saving up for it for months previously. The petrol engine had certainly changed all this. Villagers were now as sophisticated as townsfolk, and people like Billy were no longer a novelty.

"The game's not what it was," he said sadly one day when he had been enlarging upon this subject. "I can remember the time when beer was threepence a pint."

That summer, while he was with me, Three-fingered Billy was working the "bugfat." Although he had told me that he did this in the fine weather when I had first met him at Manchester, it was not until he joined me that I discovered exactly what this was.

On our first evening together I discovered that he carried in his bag a large newspaper parcel containing a huge mutton-bone and a decrepit-looking cod's head.

These struck me as being so extraordinary that I did not like to ask him about them, but when I saw him working on the following day I realized that these singular objects were nothing more nor less than his flash.

Billy at work was an extraordinary sight. He had used two empty orange-boxes as his stall, and on these he had affixed a pair of posters. One of these stated: "Where There's Dirt There's Danger." The other bore the simple command: "Kill That Fly."

Above the posters, and resting on the orange-box, were the mutton-bone and the cod's head.

Before Billy began to pitch he placed a little square of wax-like substance on top of each grisly relic. It was these squares he was trying to sell, I discovered, and he referred to them as "Scarperfly."

According to Billy, Scarperfly was a necessity in every home.

I had never seen him demonstrate before, and I watched his first pitch. It did not take long, but while he was working he put a lot of energy into his sales talk. His face was very red at all times, but while he was at work it looked as if it might explode. Thick veins stood out on his forehead, and his hands, which were never very steady, now shook as though with ague.

Most of his talk concerned dustbins. He enlarged on dustbins; he hung over them. I had never heard any one display such passionate interest in the things before.

Quite a number of people gathered to listen to him. I think, like myself, they were fascinated by the horrible display. There was something slightly sinister about the spectacle of the cod's head, with its open mouth and gaping eyes, and Three-fingered Billy in a bowler hat two sizes too small for him dancing about wildly behind.

Billy's spiel was threadbare; in fact, at places there were definite holes in it; but whenever he was at a loss for a word, or got tied up in one of his own arguments, he fell back on the touchstone statement: "Where there's dirt there's danger."

He repeated this story again and again, and the more often he said it the more its vital truth seemed to be obscured.

"I'll give anybody five pounds of my money," he concluded dramatically, pointing to the watery-eyed cod's head, "if you can ever find a fly settle where there's Scarperfly."

Oddly enough this announcement was impressive, for, although it was a hot summer day and the cod's head looked most inviting from a fly's point of view, not one, and there were enough in all conscience in the market, had settled upon this or upon the mutton-bone at any time during Billy's demonstration.

When he had delivered his guarantee he produced his stock and came to his bat. He charged threepence for two tablets and quite a number of people fell for it, although the "bugfat" was rather a slow money-taker, I decided.

At the end of the day Billy told me that he was satisfied if he took anything from a pound to thirty shillings at a market, as he avoided places where the tolls were high.

His gear cost him very little, he explained, and one evening after we had been traveling for some time together I discovered how very inexpensive it really was.

On that particular night, after a good day at Workington, he returned to our lodgings with several pounds of candles. Besides the mutton-bone and the cod's head he traveled a saucepan and some toffee trays, and these he arranged in a row on the kitchen table.

He explained that he was going to make up some more gear, and I offered to help him. There was very little for me to do, however, and in the end I settled down to watch.

Billy went about his work very methodically. Placing the candles in the saucepan, he melted them over the gas stove and then drained off the wicks, which he threw away.

This done, he stood looking at the melted tallow thoughtfully for some moments and then regarded me.

"I 'ad the bugfat blue the last time I grafted round 'ere," he said. "I think I'll make it red this year and call it 'Flyscarper.' Makes a bit of a change, don't it?"

There was really very little I could say, and I agreed with him.

From one of his many pockets he produced a small bottle of red ink, scattered a few drops into the saucepan and stirred the mixture. Having done this, he poured the colored wax into his toffee trays and when it had become firm he cut it into little pieces about an inch square.

"Well, that's that," he said with satisfaction. "What about a bevvy? They've got some wonderful stuff at a little place down the road."

I was mystified. "You've left something out," I said. "You've got to put something in it, haven't you? You've only got colored wax there. What keeps the flies away?"

Billy grinned and started to clean out the saucepan with a piece of newspaper.

"No, that's all, son," he said simply. "Yer now knows the ancient secret of the bugfat."

I had realized that Scarperfly would not prevent some of the diseases Billy had claimed it would, and that it was probably not the contribution to science that he had declared it. But it had never dawned upon me that it was quite the simple little fraud it was.

One thing still puzzled me, and at length I mentioned it, albeit somewhat diffidently.

"That cod's head and mutton-bone," I said. "I didn't see any flies on them during your demonstration."

"Oh, them," he said casually. "I readies them first. I soaks 'em in paraffin afore I starts. There ain't a ruddy fly livin' wot'll settle where there's paraffin."

He sighed and put away the saucepan.

"The good old bugfat!" he said, looking at the trays of pink perfidy. "It's all right in the summer. Nothin' to beat it. That is, when the summer is a summer. But last year it was cold enough for snow most days, and I 'ad rain for ten Saturdays runnin'. Why, I tell yer, son, I was 'ard put to it that time. The weather was so blinkin' umpty, d'you know what I 'ad to do?"

He looked at me and spoke with an earnestness that betokened truth.

"I 'ad to travel me own blinkin' flies about with me," he said.

CHAPTER 22

I am lost without a model. I acquire the Citroën and Sally returns. We observe Three-fingered Billy selling nerves of steel for a shilling. We meet Brother Adam; the service he did us. The Little Major and London Joe reappear and I hear a story, an explanation and a business proposition.

AFTER THREE OR FOUR weeks without Sally my model problem became acute again. I grew very weary of unreliable young women who got bored with the work and grumbled incessantly; while the inconvenience of finding casual workers on the market at the last moment was considerable.

At one fair in the north it looked as though my tober money would be completely wasted, and it would have been if another member of the Boss tribe—the Bosses seemed to be my guardian angels on the fairs—had not come to the rescue.

Gypsy Sarah lent me her small daughter Rachel for my demonstrations throughout the entire meeting. Rachel was fourteen, and her hair was that sort of black which seems to suck up the light. She also had the famous Boss beauty.

She sat for me in a crimson shawl and drew the crowds like the real showman's child she was.

When their caravan moved on, however, I was left as assistantless as before, and at last, in sheer desperation, I bought a Citroën of uncertain age but indubitable capacity and set off to South Shields to collect Sally.

She was waiting, as she had promised, and although my arrival was unheralded, the Fisher family greeted me with enthusiasm, and Sally, her Sunday frock sadly the worse for wear, clambered into the back of the car and off we went.

I still had Three-fingered Billy with me, and we three adventurers once again sped off to make our fortunes.

But the weather was not so good that month, and times were hard all over the country. On all sides we met with sad stories from hard-pressed grafters who found the game but a shadowy ghost of what it once had been.

No one, not even the quack doctors, found money easy to make.

One Saturday we met Ted Riderout and he was very disgruntled. Riderout was one of the most famous crocuses on the market, and he always traveled with animals. He was very fond of them and seemed to know a great deal about them. They made a wonderful flash for him, and, standing on the top of his stall, he would lecture first on their complaints and then gradually work his story round until he was talking about human maladies.

He sold some sort of skin salve for which he claimed the most remarkable properties, and he was the first crocus I ever saw who traveled a grizzly bear about with him.

When these two arrived on the tober together few other grafters stood much chance against them.

The last time I had seen Riderout he had parted with his bear and had come down via a small seal to a monkey. But when Sally and Billy and I met him near Newcastle all he had left were two guinea-pigs.

"Yes," he said despondently, "I've come down to this."

He was standing by his stall looking at the fat little animals in disgust.

"If ever I get on my feet again I'm going to buy a bear and stick to it," he said. "'Struth I am. To think I'd have to spiel for the best part of an hour about a poor little guinea-pig! It hurts me pride. I'm lost without me animals, I am. If something don't happen pretty soon," he added, replacing the guinea-pig in its box, "you'll see me pitching with a couple of blinking white mice."

We all sympathized with Riderout. Once a grafter has had a good flash he is inclined to rely upon it.

However, although business was not good, we ourselves did not do so very badly. Sally was magnificent. She had retained her quiet, almost secretive demeanor, and although the discomfort in which we worked was sometimes acute she never complained.

Since the weather was so bad, Billy gave up the bug-fat and worked the spread, and when he began to pitch after we had parted from Riderout, Sally and I watched him to give him a gee—that is, to pretend to buy from him, in order to encourage the punters.

He was worth watching.

Oddly enough, he was often quite successful with the spread, but when he got a good hand-out he always looked rather surprised. I think he had got so used to coming to his bat without breaking—that is to say, having a whole demonstration without finding a single punter—that when he did find a good market the excitement was too much for him.

All the time he traveled with me I never knew him to have a steady hand, but when he got excited, as he did on this particular occasion, this failing was accentuated and his hands flapped about all over the place like the wings of an imprisoned bird fluttering against a pane.

It made his work very difficult, Sally pointed out, and I agreed. However, he was always energetic once he got going, and before he had begun to work he had partaken of several pints of his favorite beverage.

"I can put more steam into it when I'm a bit lit," he said as we were helping him put up his joint.

But before he had finished his demonstration it was clear to both Sally and me that whatever he lacked as a crocus it was not steam.

From the very beginning he looked like one of Alfie Holmsworth's niggers dancing the can-can. His bowler hat was well on the back of his head, and his face was a horrific crimson. He spread the herbs out on a tray in front of him. I looked at these dubiously, remembering the ancient secret of the bugfat.

They looked to me like a handful of hay just before it has been turned for the first time.

Billy shouted to attract attention, and as soon as he

had one or two people watching him he produced a jug of hot water from beneath his stall and began to lecture on the properties of the disconsolate little bundle in front of him.

There was myrrh, he said, which was good for something or other; and sorrel, which gave people strength; and juniper-berries, a sovereign remedy for the most appalling complaints; and vervaine; and last of all rhubarb-root, which no doubt counteracted the ill-effects of all the others.

"Now," said Billy, his hand shaking so violently that he scattered most of his magical remedy over his stall instead of dropping it into his jug, "I'll make a man a man and I'll make a woman a woman. I'll make you eat well, sleep well, drink well."

His voice rose, and Sally and I thought he was going to burst.

"I'll make you spring out of bed in the morning like a two-year-old!" he roared at the astonished group in front of him. "And I'll make you sleep at night like an innocent little child."

On the last words, to my delight, he dropped his voice, and his eyes, watery at the best of times, filled with real tears. The curious thing was that Billy was genuinely attached to children. I remember traveling with him by bus from Sandbach to Crewe one day, and he was in great form, having taken two pounds at the market.

There were about a dozen children in the bus, and he gave them a penny each; or at least he gave eleven of them a penny each. At this point he discovered that neither he nor I had enough coppers to go round.

In despair he gave the last child a shilling, and then, realizing that the arrangement was not quite fair, he collected all the pennies back and gave the youngsters a shilling apiece.

The following day, when the pubs were open, he borrowed a bob off me.

However, at the moment "Professor Three-finger" was well away with his lecture.

"I'll give you nerves of steel!" he said, quivering all over like a badly set jelly. "Nerves of steel and stomachs of iron!"

He picked up his jug, scattering its contents wildly as soon as he touched it, and poured the remainder over a wineglass borrowed from the Spotted Dog.

"Ladies and gentlemen," he said, breathing like a steam-engine, " 'ere's 'ealth to you all!"

He threw the contents of the glass in his own face and gasped.

"Now," he said, "all this 'ealth for a bob a time. What about it?"

Sally and I stepped forward and gave him a gee, and quite a number of punters followed our example.

When it was over and Billy was refreshing himself in an attempt to get ready for his next spasm, I said, rather brutally: "You don't look the part, Billy."

He was not offended: I knew him very well. And of course I was right. It seemed to me that it was impossible to pretend that he did not look a wreck; in fact, at times it seemed wonderful that he could walk at all.

"If I were you," I said, "I should explain that I'd had a shock or something. Then you could say that it's thanks to your herbs that you're as fit as you are."

He shook his head mournfully.

"It'd only draw attention to it," he said seriously. "You don't want to mention things like that on the market. It makes people notice 'em at once."

While we were having this heart-to-heart talk Sally was minding my pitch, and at this point another grafter joined Billy and me.

I had heard a great deal about Brother Adam, and as soon as I saw him I recognized him from his many descriptions. He bore down upon us with hands outstretched and Billy greeted him with real affection.

Brother Adam must have been nearing seventy. He was a tall, heavily built old man who wore an enormous wide-brimmed hat, and looked more like the conventional quack doctor than any I had ever seen.

I saw him working afterwards; in fact, Billy and I stood to watch him. He had a paternal way of talking to his audience and periodically he referred to himself as "Honest Bro' Adam, a name that's cherished by both rich and poor."

He talked a great deal about religion and quoted the Bible freely, but he did not confine himself to this subject. He spoke a great deal about most things. His spiel lasted nearly an hour, and he discussed football, racing, the price of sugar and the appalling fall in the birthrate. He went into the terrible consequences of drink, vice and the dole, and referred to the Almighty as if he had actually seen Him that morning.

He seldom spoke about the herbs he was selling.

He came to his bat as a sort of afterthought, which I think it probably was.

He had been an officer in the Salvation Army, so Billy told me, and no doubt this accounted for his familiar footing with the Deity.

"God bless you. God bless every one of you," he said as he came to the end of his peroration. "May the light of God shine upon you tonight. Go home, you men, to your wives tonight to sleep the sleep of the healthy. Don't spend your time—valuable time, my friends: precious hours of freedom for which you have worked—don't spend these joyous hours in public houses, soddening your brains, sapping your energy and wasting your money. I ask you nothing. I give. I give you advice; advice worth more than all the riches in Christendom. I give you the secret of happiness, the secret of health and of right living."

When Billy and I met him afterwards in the Miner's Arms he drained his tankard and accepted another.

"This is the last round, boys," he said some time later as he ordered our drinks. "I've got to get on, and I don't hold with getting skint."

He believed in borrowing from himself, he told me.

"I've been on the road a few years, my boy," he explained, "and I've learned one thing. Never get right on the floor. You can't afford to do it at my age, and the game's a lot harder now than ever it was. I always believe in keeping some little reserve tucked away somewhere. Sometimes it's only half a bar and it's seldom over a phunt, but I never let bevvy break into it. If the game's bad I can always borrow a bob from myself."

Bro' Adam had very sensible ideas, but he very seldom lived up to them, I found. Whenever I met him after this he would greet me like a lost son, and I liked him very well. But he spent most of his time in public houses when he was not actually working, although the only effect alcohol seemed to have upon him was that he became more pompous and spoke more slowly.

Of course, he was hardly a religious man, but I think he often forgot that he was selling herbs and imagined that he was with the Salvation Army again.

As it happened, on this particular evening this peculiarity of his came in very useful.

Sally and I got down to work and we had just had two or three good pitches when the local branch of the Salvation Army itself arrived. Not unnaturally, this society was unpopular with the majority of the grafters. At all the good Saturday markets where every minute was valuable the Army had a habit of holding a band meeting, and although we mounted pitchers prided ourselves on holding our own with most people, a Salvation Army band takes a deal of shouting down.

On this particular evening they came in force, and we discovered that they intended to play for two hours. It was the best two hours of the day, and it was quite impossible for any of us to make ourselves heard once the hymns started.

There was not too much room, at the best of times, and this evening the place was overcrowded. Everybody was very disgruntled, and Brother Adam suffered with the rest of us.

Suddenly he left his joint and went over to them. We gathered round, for we guessed that he was a little tight and were afraid that there was going to be some sort of shindy.

However, nothing was further from Brother Adam's mind. The Salvation Army was composed of his long-lost brothers. He repented. He was converted. He addressed the meeting. He spoke as one inspired. Finally, he got every one so worked up that he marched off the market-place towards another part of the town and the entire meeting followed him, the band playing as they went.

We saw no more of Brother Adam that evening, but we all got an undisturbed night's work.

When Sally and Billy and I arrived back at the lodgings we found the Little Major had dropped in with London Joe. Sally was handed over to the landlady and put to bed in the same room as the other children, and we four sat round the kitchen fire talking.

London Joe was full of the bad times, but he was not very pessimistic. Times had been lousy before, he said, and proceeded to illustrate the fact.

"We were stranded in Ireland once," he said. "There was me, and Alfie Holmsworth, and one or two others, and things *were* bad."

He looked at me gravely.

"You may not know it," he said, "but Ireland has always been a happy hunting-ground for showmen, and when you find yourself right on the floor there it means something."

The Little Major nodded his agreement, and Joe went on.

"We'd had a cut at everything, but our luck was right out. We couldn't seem to do nothing right. Then, just as we was giving up all hope, one of our boys happened to see some grave-diggers at work in a churchyard. This gave Alfie an idea, and within the next few days we was able to pay up and get out of the town.

"We got hold of a rat—the place was runnin' with them—and after a bit of bother we managed to tie a lot of rabbit fur and stick bits of feathers all over it. Gawd! it did look a sight!

"We put this in the empty grave, and, leaving one of the boys to see that no one pinched it, we went off to start the glad news."

He looked at me with mild wide-open eyes.

"The tale went round like wildfire, and, just as luck would have it, the fellow whose grave it was to be had been a bit of a lad in his time and there was no two opinions as to what his soul was like.

"'There's a horrible little creature been found in Tim Murphy's grave,' every one was saying, and we said it too.

"We went along with a crowd from the pub, and there it was, all right, sniffing about at the bottom of the grave looking horrible enough for anybody's soul.

"Of course they're a superstitious lot, the Irish," Joe continued, and again the Little Major agreed.

"They were scared out of their wits, and Alfie was the one to offer to catch it. Then we *were* on clover! Once he had it, with proof as to where it had been found, we built up a tent and charged sixpence a time for people to see it."

He sighed.

"They make a rare do of burials over in Ireland," he said. "We had a real burster on the day of the funeral."

Hardly knowing what comment to make on this extraordinary reminiscence, I turned to the Little Major and asked him about his beer racket. He shook his head.

"It didn't come to anything," he said. "I've got a new idea that I'm going to work as soon as I've fixed up a spider woman show for Ernie Berners and his wife."

I had never been sure what a spider woman was, and I inquired about it.

"Oh, it's an old trick," he said. "One of the oldest illusions on the road. It's quite simple. You get a big frame and fix it up in front of a curtain. On a little ledge behind the frame you have a sort of rockery: a lot of plants and bits of grass and stuff. Then your girl—Mrs. Berners, this will be—puts on a sort of necklace of giant spider's legs. I make 'em very realistic. She stands behind the curtain and only her head appears in the frame. Then you fix up some slanting mirrors underneath and if you work it carefully it looks as though her head and neck end off where the spider part begins. It's very effective from the front. Punters have seen it hundreds of times, and their grandfathers before them, yet they still pay their sprasers. But that's not what I'm thinking about. I'm really going to make me fortune this time."

Billy and Joe exchanged a smile. The Little Major

was always going to make his fortune, and always had some new method by which to do it.

"I've met a man with a little bit of gelt," he said seriously, "and I think we're on to a very good thing. It's a bit late in the season, I know, but no matter. I've been thinking the stunt out for some time now, and this chap from the Smoke says he knows the right spot. It's somewhere on the main road between London and Southend—you know, one of those new arterial drags—and all we want is a little hut. The tober'll cost us practically nothing and we'll have it all on our tod."

"What is it? A tea-house?" I inquired. Somewhere between Southend and London did not sound a very lively pitch to me.

"No. Much better than that," said the Major cheerfully. "We're calling it THE LAST CHANCE. Thousands of cars and charabancs will pass us in the season, and every one will be a likely punter. Our gear will cost us next to nothing. For a few pounds we can buy up enough old swag to take a few hundred."

I think he saw that we were all a little unimpressed, for he went on hurriedly:

"What happens when you go to the seaside for the day?" he demanded suddenly. "Don't tell me; I'll tell you. You have a look at the sea: that's the first thing. Then after you've done that you have a basinful of fish and chips and perhaps a look round the amusement joints. Then you have a few bevvies and you probably buy a few souvenirs to take back to those at home. That's right, isn't it?"

London Joe and Billy agreed that he had described it to a T.

"Ah," said the Little Major, working up to his subject, "now about those souvenirs. You leave that till the last minute. And rightly so. You don't want to carry 'em about all day, and you don't want to spend all your gelt at once. You wonder if it'll last you out. Suddenly you find it's time to be getting back to the charabanc. There's a blinking rush—probably you've mislaid one of the kids—and either you or the old woman has stopped to have one last bevvy.

"Now, this is my idea. Whatever you've bought you must have forgotten somebody. You've probably got a butter dish with 'A Present from Southend' on it for your mother-in-law, and a bit of rock for little Alfie who couldn't be took because of 'is cold. But Gawd! You've forgotten all about sister Alice! Lumme, you must get 'er something."

The Little Major paused for effect, and also, no doubt, to get his breath. He glanced round at our admiring faces.

"That's where I come in," he said simply. "All the chara drivers'll know about my little hut. They'll get a commission. And at my little hut the people can buy just that sort of junk that they like to take home with 'em. Everything will have 'A Present from Southend' painted on it. Have you got me?

"People are not like us," he continued. "They never like to leave themselves skint when they're away from home. They're sure to have a bob or two on 'em. But once they're in the chara they feel kind of safe and they wish they'd spent that extra bob."

He leaned forward.

"You see," he said earnestly, "this joint of mine has got to be about four miles outside of Southend. For the first two miles they're still thinkin' of the joys of the seaside. But after they've thought about everything what's happened during the day they naturally start thinkin' about 'ome again. And it's then that they remember some one what's been forgotten.

"Then, just when they're thinking 'What the 'ell am I to do?' the chara stops at my joint and they read my flash: THE LAST CHANCE. And out I come to set their minds at rest."

He smiled at us.

"Think of the sudden relief," he said. "Why, at that moment they'd pay over the odds for a souvenir and there'd be no blinking arguing, either."

When we went up to bed he was still talking about it and had thought of marrying and settling down on the proceeds.

The next itme I saw him, though, he was half a mind to start a new religion, and earnestly tried to persuade me to foist myself upon the public as an unfrocked priest.

CHAPTER 23

Sally and I go south. The weather improves. I buy a new car and become "Professor X, the Mystery Man from the East." The winter again. I am tempted by security and fall.

THE DEPRESSION SADdened me, and I think Sally also, though as usual she made no comment nor indeed said anything at all.

She was an odd little person. I never succeeded in discovering what she was thinking about at any given time.

When we parted from London Joe and the Little Major I was still far from being broke. I still had the largest wad of notes I had ever possessed, but the season was getting late and in a month it would be Hull Fair again.

I felt that the northern district had been overworked, and, parting from Three-fingered Billy, who was due for one of his occasional trips home, Sally and I and the old Citroën, whose age was no reflection upon her powers, dashed to Crewe and from Crewe to Carnarvon.

Here was a setback. It was Saturday, the best day in the week, and the market was so full that I could not get in.

However, we met Napoleon Jackson, who advised me to try Blynafestiogg.

When Sally and I arrived I thought Napoleon had been unnecessarily facetious. There was only one other stall on the market, and there was hardly a soul about. This was in the afternoon, and it was obviously useless to start to think about work until the evening.

But at six o'clock I put up my bookmaker's umbrella and got ready.

To my astonishment, people appeared from nowhere, and before long I was grafting to a crowd of over a hundred. It was tremendous. People hurried out of their houses, and by seven o'clock the news had spread throughout the village.

A grafter, it seemed, was still something of a novelty in this little mining community.

When I packed up at nine o'clock and prepared for our drive back to Crewe, Sally sat in the car and counted my takings and we discovered that we had made over ten pounds.

The following day we dashed from Crewe to the south, the old Citroën blowing fire and steam like a war-horse, and Sally clinging to the side as she sat perched up in the back among a pile of gear. She was wide-eyed, and for the first time openly excited at the thought of her first glimpse of the Smoke.

Poor Sally! London disappointed her sadly. She said it was a solemn place, and not so happy as the great cities of the north.

I planted Sally on my slightly astonished sister

Marge, working quietly at her books in the country, and in that household she was a great success.

The weather improved, and we worked round Bury St. Edmunds, and afterwards I centered in Norwich for a week.

The sudden change in the temperature was extraordinary. The weather was perfect; if anything, a little too hot; but all things considered, conditions were as good as any grafter could desire.

I was no longer a novice on the road, and even when I arrived on a market which I had never visited before I was certain to meet some one I knew.

Towards the end of September I invested in a new car. The new models had appeared in the showrooms in Great Portland Street and I had a little money.

So when I drove into Hull for the fair a few weeks later I was driving a brand-new Morris saloon, and I felt as proud as if it had been a Rolls. My flash was complete. A new car, a live model and a lot of decent clothes.

But apart from these I possessed very little; in fact, I had about three pounds in the world, and as I drove up Walton Street the weather, which had been so good in the south, played me false again and a fine steady rain was falling.

It was Sunday when Sally and I made our triumphant entrance, and the gaff opened the following day. Most of the stalls were partly erected, and many people were about.

Borrowing a piece of chalk from one of the grafters, I claimed my old position opposite the barracks. Everywhere I went I met people I knew. The whole gezumphing world seemed to have gathered together: every one but Susannah.

There was something about the gaff ground which attracted the show people even when there was no business to be done. They stood about in little groups, heedless of the rain, and talked about their past successes and their future plans.

Every one seemed a little nervous about the approaching winter, but they felt that there was a week's work in front of them and anything might happen between then and the end of the fair.

I did not worry much. I felt I must average at least fifty shillings a day.

But the steady rain did not help matters, and those who had not grown accustomed to the life must have found the scene depressing. A fair in the course of erection, with steady rain falling, is one of the most dismal sights on earth.

Our worst fears were fulfilled. The rain continued. Business was terrible. Sally and I had pitch after pitch, often failing to sell a single packet of wavers, and there seemed to be no explanation of this, just as there had been no explanation for our good days.

Of course, it has always seemed surprising to me that we all managed to get a living year after year with the same lines. I got desperate at Hull. Something had to be done, and like most grafters, when in trouble I turned to the Little Major for assistance.

Although I had seldom seen him at work upon anything during the whole time I had known him, I knew that there was not a line with which he was not familiar.

We had knocked into him soon after our arrival, and I had little difficulty in finding him.

He listened to my story and shook his head.

"Well," he said, "what do you fancy? What about the stinker?"

I said I was on for anything, and he became enthusiastic at once.

"It's a fine idea," he said. "I wouldn't be at all surprised if the old stinker didn't win a race here. Flash—that's what the people want. Worked mounted from your joint it might just catch on."

As usual, the Little Major was much more interested in my affair than his own, and it was he who made all the arrangements and made it possible for me to open on the following day.

The stinker can be worked in a number of ways, and to those who know the fairs but not the grafters' slang it is probably better known as "The Mystic Writer" or "The Gypsy Queen."

The men who actually run this line often call themselves "spirit workers," although every other grafter in the vicinity sticks to the more descriptive term.

Specially prepared paper can be bought from practically any swag shop for this demonstration. This appears to be perfectly plain, but when placed in a dish which has been sprinkled with a few drops of chemical, a message suddenly appears upon it.

These charts are sold at a few shillings a gross, and on each, written in invisible ink, is a different character reading or fortune.

It is the chemical, which smells exactly like a stink bomb, that has earned the Mystic Writer its name.

Sally, the Little Major and I visited Woolworth's, where we bought a saucepan lid, a goldfish bowl, a tea strainer and some fringe intended for lampshades. We then returned to the gaff to prepare for my début as "Professor X. The Mystery Man from the East."

The goldfish bowl was to be my magic crystal. In this we put the top of the tea strainer, under which we had packed some cotton wool saturated in the evil-smelling developer.

The saucepan lid was a practical if unbeautiful necessity, inasmuch as it prevented the fumes from escaping from the bowl.

The lampshade fringe was used, the Major said, to give a mystic atmosphere to the whole business.

The magic crystal we placed on a small card-table on the top of my stall, and Sally sat behind it. Disguised in an old dressing-gown of mine, which made her look smaller than ever, she had some Woolworth pearls tied round her head and a mask partly covering her face. According to the Major, she represented Queen Zodiac, the Guardian of the Crystal.

It made quite a good show by the time we had finished, and, although it hardly won a race, it certainly enabled me to get out of Hull Fair with considerable profit.

Of course it had its disadvantages. Standing on the top of my stall, I shouted to the passers-by.

"Ladies and Gentlemen," I bellowed, "I have second sight! Most of you who walk up Walton Street before me are in the wrong job. Why? Is it that you do not possess the brains or abilities of your competitors? No! It is because you have not recognized some opportunity in the past. In every life there are times when luck is in. If we are prepared for these periods we must gain success.

"But there are times also when luck is against us, and it is then that we should avoid all forms of speculation and change."

It was fairly easy to attract a crowd at Hull Fair, and there was no difficulty in getting people to watch a free show.

As soon as I had a crowd I picked out some one and asked him to give me the date of his birth. After writing this on one of the prepared sheets of paper, which my audience saw was perfectly plain, I handed it to Sally and she placed it in the bowl. Then the writing would mysteriously appear in front of the eyes of my audience.

"There are no two readings alike," I explained truthfully. "Some of you may associate this with a machine you have seen at the seaside. You place a penny in the slot and in return you receive what is purported to be your character reading. You have all done this at some time or another, no doubt, and you have said to yourself: 'It is good fun.' And as fun it is undoubtedly good.

"But if I happened to push you aside as you were about to put your penny in the slot and I placed my coin in first, I would receive the reading which you ought to have had.

"How different is it," said I mendaciously, "with this, my magic crystal"—and I waved my hand towards my goldfish bowl. "First of all you must tell me the date of your birth, and then, by the aid of my magic globe of the zodiac, you will receive a specially written advice reading containing information about yourself which will amaze and perhaps terrify you.

"For this, ladies and gentlemen, I ask today the absurd fee of threepence. Threepence for a lasting record of your destiny!"

Unfortunately, poor Sally had not been rehearsed very well in her new rôle as the Mystic Queen, and she was sometimes rather slow in putting the papers into the globe. It was obviously most important that the saucepan lid should not be kept too long off the top of the goldfish bowl, for when this occurred the fumes rose and the smell was practically unbearable.

Whenever this happened I tried to ignore it and to continue hurriedly with my tale, but on one occasion it was quite impossible to pretend that there was not something wrong. The smell was horrific, and the crowd edged farther and farther away from me.

"I'm afraid boys have been playing with stink bombs round here," I remarked feebly at last. "But still, boys will be boys, I suppose."

But it was no good. I had to close down until the fumes had shifted.

Other stall-holders near me found work difficult when this happened, and Sally and I were not very popular for half an hour or so.

I never worked the stinker again after Hull, although it was very useful during that week.

On Saturday I was surprised to find how quickly money could be taken in thrummers (threepence).

After Hull we went to Carlisle to work the Cumberland round. I met the Little Major again there, and with him was a very bad-tempered Jewish fellow, whose name was Izzy Cohen. He told me his business, and the Little Major, who did not altogether approve of him, murmured to me that he was one of the cleverest lolly workers in the country.

"Lolly," I discovered, was the slang for shop.

Izzy Cohen opened shops in various parts of the country and sold them as quickly as possible, making his profit out of the goodwill.

When I met him he was furious with himself. He had opened a little sweetstuff shop in one of the little side streets, he told me, and had paid fifteen shillings a week rent. In accordance with his custom he had advertised for a buyer of the business, and after interviewing some fifty applicants the right woman had turned up.

It was just the place, she thought, for her little son Edward: such nice clean fittings, and in such an exclusive locality.

Izzy Cohen had obtained a deposit of three pounds in cash right away, and he had arranged to call that evening at the good woman's house, where her husband was to give him a check for fifty-two pounds.

He had called. He had got his check.

To me and the Little Major he described, with tears in his eyes, how he had slept that night and dreamed about an army of little Edwards all serving pennyworths of sweets to nice clean little children and wrapping the sweets in checks for fifty-two pounds, which were kept stuck on a nail among the beautiful clean fixtures and the nice clean boxes of chocolates.

But unfortunately for Izzy, he dreamed far too

long. He told us how he had looked at his watch and found it was nine o'clock. He turned over. Just five more minutes . . .

"I asked for it, my boy, I asked for it," he moaned, his little black eyes wet with real emotion. "I should have been there on the doorstep when the bank opened. I missed it by an hour. I strolled in at eleven o'clock and found the man had had a look at my lolly on the way to business and had decided that it was not a bit like the joint his wife had described to him. So he 'phoned the bank and stopped the check."

He was shaken with grief when he told us this story. I almost saw his point of view.

"When a Yiddisher gets caught napping like that, my boy," he said, "it's time he got spliced. I'm sick with myself, I dislike my own company."

As the weeks passed I was not too pleased with myself, either. The winter was rapidly approaching, and I had little saved for the cold months ahead.

I thought the first thing to be done was to take Sally home, but this was not as easy as it had first appeared. She had become part of my gear and showed no inclination to return to the slums of South Shields. She had been with me nearly six months, and had grown to look upon our business as something in which she had a share. She never argued; she hardly ever spoke. If I admonished her for visiting too many cinemas she ignored me.

I still had a vision of the dreadful tin works, too. I don't know why my mind harped on tin works. Perhaps because they were the only factories of which I had seen the inside.

"I'll take you back tomorrow," I said over and over again, but she said nothing and sat in the back of the car and looked at me with her old inscrutable expression, just like a small white cat.

I intended to take her back after the Carlisle run, but there were markets to visit and money to be made and she remained with me.

She was still the perfect model. Neither the rain, the cold, nor any of the hardships we had to put up with on the road upset her. She was always very quiet, very self-contained, and really hardly there at all.

We carried on for a while, and I took her home to my sister's for Christmas.

And then, just when I was looking forward to the bleak months of January and February, I received the offer of a really good job in London. It seemed madness to refuse it.

The time had come at last to settle down. I felt I had conquered the problem of making my living. I knew now that this bugbear, which had haunted my early life and threatened to give me a serious inferiority complex, was dismissed forever and that, come what might, I should never be afraid again of being a complete and utter failure.

But I had been thinking of becoming a more normal member of society for some time, and now this offer decided the issue. A comfortable, suitable job was open to me. I felt it was full of possibilities and that I should easily be able to keep it.

The last few weeks of the past year had been full of anxieties, doubts and uncertainties, but now a few words from a friend of my father had removed them all. I felt suddenly very much relieved.

Although the life of a grafter has its adventure, it was a tiring existence, leading nowhere and having no end, so I accepted my new job with a deep sigh of relief and the conviction that it was a godsend.

Punters at Hull Fair, 1935
National Fairground Archive.

CHAPTER 24

I take Sally home. I pause to say good-by and meet two very old friends. I hear of new fields to conquer. I am tempted. Sally knows best.

E̲verything was settled at the end of January. I did not require much time before I could take up my new activities. I had very few arrangements to make. Sally was my only responsibility, and I decided to return her to her family without any delay. There was no point in putting it off, I told myself, and when I mentioned it to her she took it in a manner that rather surprised me. She said nothing at all.

I thought possibly the idea of returning home with new clothes and a number of presents would appeal to her. Certainly she did not protest, but she asked no questions about my plans. Her own future she did not mention either.

We set off from London at dawn, and I worked at Banbury on my way up. I don't know why I did this, but I think I hoped to make my expenses. I was certainly not disappointed. Business was amazingly good, and I wished I had arranged for a week's run before finally settling down.

Sally was exceptionally quiet, even for her, and it was after nine o'clock when we arrived at Newcastle.

I had been traveling well, and I decided that not only Sally and I, but the car, which was very hot, needed a rest before we made the final jump of a few miles to South Shields.

After leaving Sally I intended to go on to Stockton to say good-by to Mrs. Coleman and her family before returning to London alone.

We pulled up at the Turk's Head, near the Bigg Market. I left Sally in the car and went in, hoping to find some of the grafters, since this was one of their great meeting-places. I felt I would have liked to say a good-by to a few of my companions of the road.

The bar was crowded, and, talking together in a corner, I saw the Little Major and Three-fingered Billy.

"God bless my soul!" cried the Major. "Look who's blown in! Where the devil have you sprung from?"

Three-fingered Billy looked pleased to see me, and he ordered me a drink.

"The game must be good, Billy," I said. "What are you grafting now?"

"The usual, son, the usual," he replied cheerfully. "I'm working the spread, but it's not much good round here. What are you doing, anyway? You ought to be at Leicester. We've just heard the market's workable and that would be worth something to you with your lark."

The Little Major took out a glass of lemonade to Sally while I talked with Three-fingered Billy. It appeared that there was now room at Leicester

Market, which was held on every day of the week, the big days being Wednesday and Saturday.

It had always been impossible to get a position here before, and the news was certainly important.

"You'd simply coin money there," Billy assured me. "Why, it'd last you right through the winter. I wish I could get down there, I'm telling you! Have you got the car outside?" he added wistfully.

Naturally I was interested, although the news was of no value to me.

When the Little Major returned I told them of my future plans.

"Well, I wish I could get a regular job," said Billy thoughtfully, adding after a pause, "in a way. But I can't imagine you settling down—'struth I can't. Why, the worst month's over, and we'll 'ave Easter 'ere before we know what's 'appening. 'Once a grafter, always a grafter,' you know. We'll see you on the road next summer."

Billy was wrong this time, I knew, but I liked to hear him make the prophecy. He went on to gossip.

I heard that Clarry had married Polly, and under the name of the Royal Rumanian Gypsy she was grafting in north Wales. He had knocked into them a few weeks before. They had asked about me, he said.

"All the boys are heading for Leicester. You'd have the time of your life there," he continued. "Tomlinson got a lift down there this morning with some blanket workers. I 'eard Madame Suzie was knocking it off there too, and Ezra Boss's wagon has been seen on the road."

It was closing time before we left, and Billy was

still trying to get me to change my mind and go to Leicester when we strolled out to the car.

The Little Major agreed with Billy.

"These chances only come once in a while," he assured me, "and when they do come you can't afford to miss 'em. There's room for us all in your jam, and if you don't stand me a drink this time next week—any drink I like to ask for—well, you're not the man I thought you were."

We stood talking by the car. Sally listened, but took no part.

"Why not give it a try?" said Billy, as if it was the simplest thing in the world to alter my plans.

As a matter of fact, when I came to consider it, it did not seem an impossible thing to do. I had changed my mind often enough before. But neither the Little Major nor Billy realized the full effect which an alteration in this scheme would have upon my life. It was probably only Sally who had any idea of the importance of the step they were urging me to take, and she continued to be silent.

I have since wondered if she was praying.

"I can fix you both up at my digs for the night," said the Little Major, "and we can make an early start in the morning. If we're going we don't want to leave it too late. Every one's heading for Leicester."

"As a matter of fact," said Billy, "I made sure you were there. Leicester's the talk of the gaffs. It's virgin ground all round there. It'll put you right in the market and the beer ain't 'alf bad there neither."

I liked Three-fingered Billy. He had always brought me good luck. But I knew that if I turned my back on my steady job now I was turning my back on the whole world of normal life, to which I might never have another opportunity to return. I might never even want to return. It seemed absurd to rush off in search of a few weeks' good work and so give up a whole lifetime of ordinary respectable occupation.

As I stood by the car I imagined all the old crowd collecting at Leicester, grafters whom I had not seen for years and others whom I had but recently left. Susannah perhaps, even.

Moreover, it would be pleasant to graft to people who had never seen a waver before, and it would be grand to be in with the others on a good thing.

But there was so much to prevent me from doing this.

"I'd love to set off right away with both of you," I assured them. "We could drive through the night. But—"

"But what?" insisted Billy. "You'll never give up the game for good. You'll be kicking yourself in a month or two for missing the chance of a lifetime."

"I've half a mind to go with you," I said, "but it can't be done."

Suddenly Sally spoke quietly and startled me, for I had forgotten her. There was an assumed casualness in her voice.

"There's enough gear in the back here to take nearly thirty pounds," she said. "It won't be much good to you if you don't sell it somewhere."

"I can take it back to the swag shop. What's the difference?" I said.

"The difference between thirty shillings and thirty pounds," she retorted.

I stared at her. She spoke with the quiet indifference of one who knows what she is talking about. I am afraid Sally had made a very careful study of my temperament.

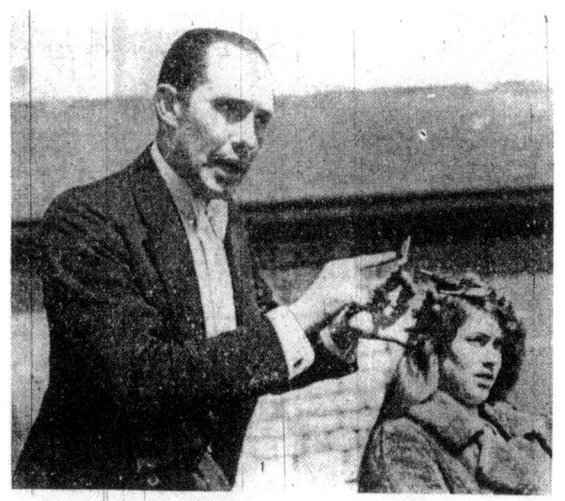

Philip Allingham selling lightning hair-curlers.

Tired Of Office Life: Now Makes £60 A Week Selling Hair Wavers

Headline in the *Sunday Express,* May 20th 1934.

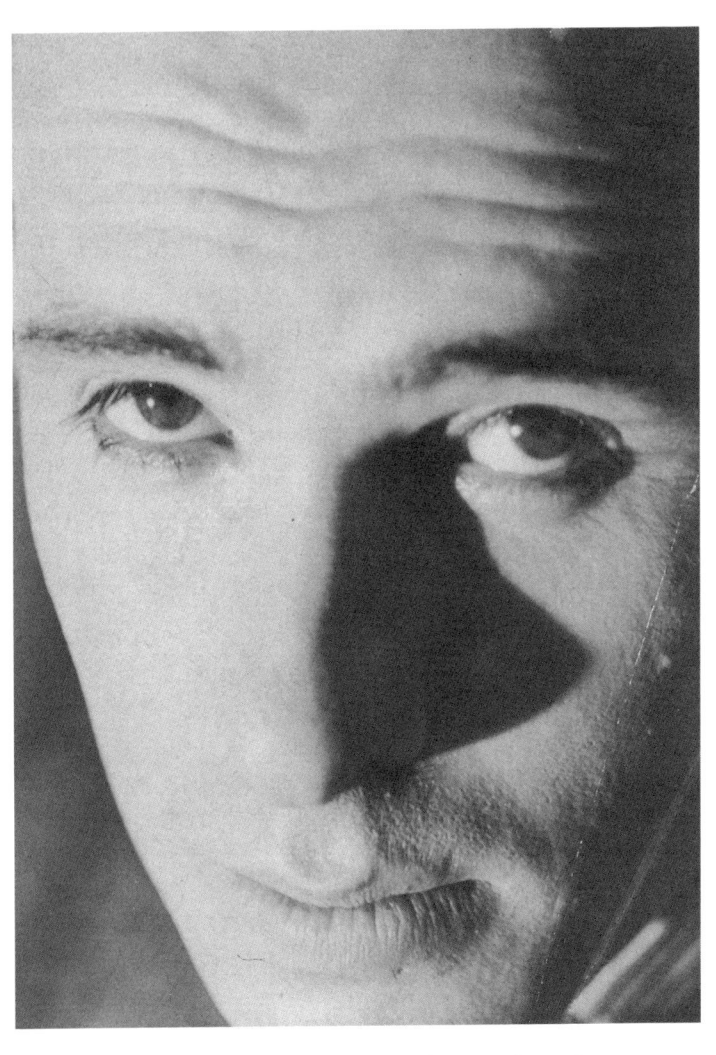

'Once a grafter, always a grafter, you know.'

GLOSSARY OF GRAFTERS' SLANG

Many of these words may be familiar to a number of people, but I have included all those that I had not heard before I joined the fair people and the market folk.

Some are rhyming slang, some Yiddish and some Romany, but together they make up the principal vocabulary of most grafters.

Abbreviations: RS: Rhyming Slang. Y: Yiddish, or words originated by Jews. ROM: Romany, or words originated by gypsies.

Apples (*Apples and pears*), RS: Stairs.
Bar: One pound sterling.
Half-bar: Ten shillings.
Barney: A quarrel; a fight.
Barker: One who stands outside a show at a fair-ground to address the crowd and persuade the people to enter.
Bat: Price. "To come to the bat": to mention the price.
Bevvy: To drink. A drink.
Bevvy'omey: A drunkard.
Bird: Jail.
Bogey: One who spoils one's game or interferes with one's pitch.
Bottle: "Not much bottle": not much good.
Brass (*Brassnail*), RS: Prostitute.
Bunce: Profit.
Burster: A very successful day or season.
Busk: To perform in the street.
Carpet: Three months' imprisonment.
Caser: Five shillings.
Charver, ROM: To despoil. To interfere and spoil one's business.

Chavvy, ROM: Child.
Clod: A penny.
Clobber: Clothes.
Coal: A penny.
Cobbler: A ball.
Cockernen, RS: Ten pounds sterling. A pen.
Collar-and-cuff, RS: An effeminate.
Crackers: Mad.
Crocus: A doctor. A quack doctor. A herbalist. A miracle worker.
Daisy (*Daisy roots*), RS: Boot. Shoe.
Denar: A shilling.
Dook, ROM: A hand. "Dook-reading": palmistry.
Dookering, ROM: To go around from door to door telling fortunes.
Donah: A woman.
Dropsy: Bribery.
Fanny: A grafter's sales story.
Feather (*Feather and flip*), RS: Bed.
Finger: A man.
Flash: A grafter's display. Anything to attract the crowd.
Flim: Five pounds sterling.
Flip, RS: A racing tip.
Fly pitch: A place in the street, market or fair-ground taken for a few minutes by a wandering pedler from which to make his sales.
Fly pitcher: One who makes a practice of selling his wares from fly pitches.
Funkum: Perfume.
Gaff: A fair or market.
Gaffer: A market master or fair-ground superintendent.
Gazer: A pedler who walks about a fair or market selling as he goes.
Gear: A grafter's stock or possessions.
Gee, Y: A grafter's accomplice or assistant who mingles with the crowd. "To give a grafter a gee": to buy something from him to encourage the crowd.
Gelt, Y: Money.
Gezumph, Y: To swindle.
Gezumpher, Y: A swindler.
Goy, Y: One who is not a Jew.

GLOSSARY

Groiny: A ring, a diamond or other precious stone when in a ring.
Grafter: One who works a line in a fair or market, as a fortune-teller, quack doctor, mock auctioneer, etc.
Homey ('Omey): A man.
Hole: A shilling.
Jam (Jam jar), RS: A motor-car.
Kettle: A watch.
Kie show: Wild-man or wild-beast show.
Kip: A bed.
Lakes (Lakes of Killarney; Stone lakes), RS: A lunatic.
Lark: A line (of business).
Letty (Lettary): Lodgings.
Lolly: A shop.
Lolly worker: A swindler who starts a shop and immediately sells the alleged good-will.
Lurk: An occasional customer.
Moll: A woman.
Mounted pitcher: A grafter who talks and demonstrates from the top of his stall high above the crowd.
Monkery: A district.
Moody: Gentle persuasion, blarney, flattery.
Moon: A month's imprisonment.
Mug-faker: A camera.
Munjary: Food.
Muzzel, Y: Luck, a charm. "To work the muzzel": to sell charms.
Nanty!: Cave! (Beware!)
Nark: (see *Bogey*).
Nicker: One pound sterling.
Palone: A girl.
Parney, ROM: Rain, water.
Peter: Suitcase, grip.
Phunt: One pound sterling.
Pitch: The actual space in the fair or market rented by the grafter or fair worker.
Pitcher: A grafter who addresses the crowd. One who shouts from his pitch.
Pucker, ROM: To talk.
Punter: A grafter's customer, client or victim; a "sucker."
Rattler: A train.

Rick: (see *Gee*).
R.O. (*The run-out*): A fake auction.
Rosy (*Rosy Lee*), RS: Tea.
Rozzer: A policeman.
Scarper: To go away. To run. To get out quickly.
Screw: To look at.
Shice, Y: An unprofitable undertaking. A wash-out. "To catch a shice": to have an unremunerative deal.
Slum (*Cough*): Cough lozenges.
Smash, RS: Loose money. Change.
Smoke, The: London.
Smother: A fur coat or overcoat.
Smudge: Photograph.
Snodder, Y: One who dislikes spending.
Spiel, Y: To talk. Or a tale, a set-piece. (See *Fanny*.) To gamble.
Spieler: A barker. A gambler.
Splits: The police.
Spraser (*Sprasy*): Sixpence.
Spread: "To work the spread": to graft as a herbalist with the herbs spread out in front of one and to lecture upon their properties.
Stretch: A year's imprisonment.
Stinker, The: "The Mystic Writer"; a fortune-telling device.
Suzie: Sixpence.
Tab: Cigarette.
Titfer (*Tit-for-tat*), RS: Hat.
Thrummer: Threepence.
Tick-off: Fortune-teller. This word includes any sort of seer or any method of fortune-telling, and dates from the time when grafters working this line sold cards on which were printed various conflicting statements, thus: "You are not married yet, but will soon be wedded"; "You will never marry"; "You will be poor"; "You will be rich," etc. The grafter looked at the hand of his client or into his crystal or ink, and put a tick by—or "ticked off"—the statements which applied. The client then bought the card. This was done to evade the law, inasmuch as the client was supposed to receive something for his money.
Tober: The fair-ground or market.

GLOSSARY

Tober 'omey: The toll-collector.
Tosheroon: Half-a-crown.
Tod: Own. "To be on one's tod": to be alone, or unmarried.
Two-ender: A florin.
Vardo, ROM: A wagon. A caravan.
Yock, Y: A fool, a chump.
Wide: Intelligent, informed, sophisticated.
Whizz mob: A gang of pickpockets.
Windbag: A mystery packet.
Wooden: One month's imprisonment.

Showpeople at Hull Fair
National Fairground Archive

Joyce and Philip Allingham, circa 1917.

Herbert and Emily Allingham by a 'vardo'.

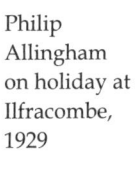

Philip Allingham on holiday at Ilfracombe, 1929

Philip, Joyce and Margery Allingham on Mersea Island, *circa* 1920.

Three Fingered Billy, Francesca Esposito and Philip Allingham, mid 1930s.

A souvenir photograph from Herbert Allingham's travels with his son, summer 1934 or 1935.

Pip Youngman Carter (at the back) and Philip Allingham at a party, early 1930s.

Margery Allingham behind the scenes at Robert Bros circus, early 1950s.

Margery and Philip Allingham in the garden at D'Arcy House, early 1960s

AFTERWORD
JULIA JONES

S_{ALLY} (not her real name) was more or less right about Philip Allingham. Or Allingham was right about himself. By the time he came to write *Cheapjack*, he knew that he wasn't going to stick forever in a London-based office job – because he already hadn't. Although the autobiographical action appears to be continuous, *Cheapjack* actually covers a four and a half year period. It was August 1928 when Allingham took his silk hat in hand and set out for Leeds and the Hunslet Feast: March 1933 when he handed the first draft of the book to his sister Margery at Viaduct Farm, Chappel.

Allingham had not been on the road full-time during that period: neither had he been 'a more normal member of society' without intermissions. He had spent weeks and sometimes months in fairgrounds and market places but he had also been employed as a manager in Madame Clara Novello Davies's voice training academy in rooms above the Aldwych Theatre. He had stayed there for the best part of a year, after which he had done occasional jobs with his advertising agency uncles, had developed an undefined business friendship with an entrepreneur called Hausemann and had hurried to the rescue in several family crises. These included his mother's breakdown in 1932 and several incidents caused by the drinking habits of his aunt Maud Hughes (of *Picture Show* magazine) and her husband Teddy Wood, a sporting journalist. When either relation (usually Wood) was made violent by whisky, Allingham would dash round in the motorcar of the moment, remove one or other to a place of safety and write whatever weekly copy was most urgently due.

Allinghams often wrote for one another: brothers and nephews produced copy for the advertising agency; nieces, sisters and brothers-in-law supplied articles and stories to Maud Hughes's cinema fanzines. Philip Allingham's father, Herbert, 'corrected' his wife, Emily's, serials and composed large sections of them. He did the same for his younger brother Claude on occasion and early in 1928 he corrected the 'blood' that Philip had written for the Dundee firm of D. C. Thomson. Herbert had been his daughter Margery's first editor though after her marriage, in 1927, she usually turned to her husband, Pip Youngman Carter, for criticism and advice.

By April 1933, when *Cheapjack* was handed to her, Margery Allingham was well on her way to becoming the most distinguished writer in the family. *Look to the Lady* (which she had dedicated to Philip under his Gypsy name 'Orlando') had been the US Book-of-the-Month Club choice for March and she was aiming even higher, in literary terms, with her current Campion novel, *Death of a Ghost*. However, Margery's bread-and-butter income still came from the anonymous silent film write-ups which she supplied weekly to Aunt Maud as well as melodramatic serials written pseudonymously for the mass-market magazine *Answers*.

There was no reason for Philip Allingham to feel inhibited about dropping his autobiography at his big sister's for an editorial wash-and-brush-up in rather the same way that he dropped his young assistants on her when it was more convenient for him to travel unencumbered. Both Sally (real name Jenny) and her younger sister, Susie, were accommodated by Margery in Essex when Philip was working elsewhere. She worried about their potential to annoy Pip and became positively obsessed by the challenge of de-lousing their long hair, a troubling necessity when one remembers that their job was to act as models for Philip's hair-wavers. When he was not near Margery, Philip would leave Jenny (or Susie or Nancy or Addie) in the care of a succession of landladies, with sufficient spare change for them to spend their evenings at the cinema while he went to the local pub or pursued other, more complicated, relationships.

Margery allowed her brother to take her for granted. They had grown up as close friends, playing and writing together, teasing governesses, learning party tricks and sometimes sitting up all night to talk. There had been a time, in her late teens, when she wished that Philip and she and a couple of others could all go on the road for a summer and perform some of the plays she had written. She loaned him money when she had it and worried when he stayed out too late. Occasionally her comments are somewhat patronising: 'Had a long talk with Phil on the West End and its evils. He seems very sensible.' (diary 21.6.1923, when Margery was just 19 and Philip 16½). Sometimes they quarrelled: she describes him when at school as 'a very unbearable young puppy' (diary 12.4.1921) and in a later moment of family crisis in 1937 as 'an antagonistic dynamo' who reduced her to tears before he'd been in the house ten minutes.

In the years after *Cheapjack* Philip grew more overtly bohemian and Margery more apparently county. Their essential sibling closeness survived. Although Philip had opposed Margery and Pip's decision to move to the grander location of Tolleshunt D'Arcy House, when he left his London home to join the Royal Army Service Corps in 1940 he despatched all his belongings for his sister to store without even notifying her.

Late in their lives Margery's secretary Gloria noticed how easily both Margery and her younger sister, Joyce, could relax with Philip. The brothers-in-law, Philip and Pip, incompatible in so many ways, always remained on good terms. Gloria remembers Philip Allingham as an unusually friendly and approachable person who made no distinction between staff and guests on his occasional visits to D'Arcy House. From her perspective as a young secretary this marked him out from many of Margery and Pip's other visitors in the 1950s and 60s. She describes him as 'unfettered'. Christina Carter, Margery's housekeeper, remembered his quick movements and rapid speech: the dramatic forcefulness of Francesca, his Italian wife.

The experiences described in *Cheapjack* were pivotal for Philip. He was twenty-two when, in his father's words, he 'took his destiny in his own hands and went on the road.' Before that he had suffered a succession of failures. He had been so unhappy at his prep school that he had persuaded his parents to take him away: he had failed the entrance exam for Tonbridge public school and been judged too 'backward' even to sit the Haileybury papers. Mild success at Forest School, Snaresbrook (the lower school prize, supporting roles in Shakespeare productions and a series of second places in running events) had not been sufficient to persuade him to stay there more than two years before transferring to a crammer in London.

His final academic disappointment was the Oxford Entrance Exam: the London crammer had 'guaranteed' success and Philip's unequivocal rejection appears to have come as a complete shock. His father, Herbert, immediately decided that he should go 'into business' but his mother, encouraged by her idol, the rumbustiously conventional Dr J. H. Salter, urged him to continue trying for Oxford. The University College authorities were adamant and Philip had to suffer the additional humiliation of having to write a letter to Dr Salter explaining that his examination failure was so complete that there was no possible appeal.

A string of jobs followed: all entered into with enthusiasm and energy, few lasting for more than a matter of months. The elegant explanation in *Cheapjack* that he 'tried my hand at everything it was considered dignified for a son of my family to do' glosses the truth that these were low-paid, junior positions, often undertaken for people who were themselves financially precarious. Philip's uncles, 'big Phil' and 'Tod' (Ernest) Allingham, who had learned the advertising agent's trade from their father, were fond of their nephew and eager to help. But the family agency no longer existed, the family newspaper had folded and, despite all their experience and their contacts, the uncles were finding it hard to survive in these depression years. They staged special marketing events – such as exhibitions of hairdressing products – but these were demanding to organise, tiring to run and yielded disappointing returns. Philip's subsequent exploits as a 'mounted pitcher', selling his packs of wavers directly into the crowd, can be seen as a more appropriate business model in hard economic times.

Discovering his own form of success as a grafter helped Philip emerge from the shadow of his older sister. Although Margery had made little impact on the academic world (even failing her LRAM) she had made her mark within the family from an early age. Her relationship with their father, Herbert, was particularly close and, although Philip managed to get along better with their mother, he seems also to have needed his father's approval. When the family was in London he frequently joined Herbert and Margery on the long walks they loved to take through the city at night. They would talk about the film, play or revue they had most recently seen (several in every week) or they would allow themselves to soak up the atmosphere of their surroundings, imagining what dramas might be being enacted behind the shuttered city windows.

Philip had also participated, with Herbert and George Hearn, in the series of séances on Mersea Island in 1921 when Margery seemed to function as a medium, developing the plot of her first novel, *Blackerchief Dick*, from the testimony of spirit characters. Philip was then 14 and had entered the experiments 'inclined to scoff'. He was swiftly converted and became an eager researcher into the historical truths that might lie behind Margery's ghosts.

When he returned to Forest School the following term, he joined the school debating society to oppose the motion 'That, in the opinion of this house, there is nothing credible in spiritualism.' He won. And he won again in the Easter term seconding opposition to a similar motion 'That, in the opinion of this house, belief in spiritualism indicates intellectual weakness.' The following year he was successful once more when he opposed the motion 'That, in the opinion of this house, self-interest not principle is the motive force that underpins society.'

School debating societies are conventionally thought as training grounds for future politicians – the president of the Forest School debating society at that time was sixth former George Dangerfield, who would later write an influential account of *The Strange Death of Liberal England* – but fairgrounds too require oratorical skills. Philip Allingham's young cousin, Michael, remembers watching him pitch at the Festival of Britain in 1951 and also in Shepherd's Bush market. He was amazed at the speed with which a crowd would start to gather as soon as Philip began to speak.

The early reviewers of *Cheapjack* routinely remark on the surprising fact of this ex-public schoolboy making a successful living as a grafter but, when Philip Allingham's background is looked at more carefully, he was not completely unsuited to the traveller's life. The money that had paid those school fees had already been earned from the pennies of working people. From 1909 his father, Herbert, had been writing fiction for flimsy comic-and-story papers that would have been read by many of the 'punters' who turned out into the market places to be entertained at Wakes weeks and on bank holidays.

As editor of the *London Journal* from 1889 – 1909 Herbert Allingham had told character from readers' handwriting or from the photographs that they sent in. He was used to boosting his correspondents' self-confidence and offering them advice on emotional dilemmas – skills his son later identified as his own basis for professional fortune-telling. 'I discovered that I could talk to strangers about themselves to their enjoyment,' he wrote in *There's Something In It!* a slim introduction to fortune-telling, published in 1936. Margery noticed this skill in her brother when she herself was telling fortunes at a garden fete in 1923.

Philip Allingham's immediate family members were bound to their desks by editorial deadlines but his aunt Grace had travelled the country in her youth, earning her living as an artiste in musical comedies. So, less successfully, had his uncle Claude – who, later in life, seems to have been direct-selling writing pads. The family veneer of middle class respectability was thin in places and several members nourished an unsubstantiated belief in a Gypsy ancestor (cf Margery's 1943 novel *Dance of the Years*). Herbert Allingham tended to romanticise the vagrant life, in print at least. 'There is no one under thirty so dead but his heart will stir a little at the sight of a Gypsies' camp,' he wrote in the year his son was born. 'We are not cotton-spinners all, or at least not all through. There is some life in humanity yet and youth will now and then find a brave word to say in dispraise of riches and throw up a situation to go strolling with a knapsack.' (*London Journal*, 1906)

Philip rarely stayed in any one place for long once his formal education was over. The first purchase he made in 1924 with the money he earned from the advertising uncles was a motor-cycle. Early in 1925 this was upgraded to a GN cycle car into which he crammed as many friends and relations as could be persuaded and set off on jaunts around the country. A new volatility came into the sedentary writing households of both Philip's parents and his sister. Herbert and Margery's diary entries were suddenly recording midnight arrivals and departures, breakdowns, smash-ups and unexpected visitors. Shortage of money eventually forced him to sell the GN, and his smart motor-coat, to Margery and his first months 'on the road' were spent travelling by train.

Once he became a pitcher (in 1931) and travelled with a regular assistant, as well as increasing quantities of stock, he was able to buy a proper 'jam' – first a Morris, then a Citroen. In the summer of 1934, when *Cheapjack* had become a best-seller, Herbert Allingham, aged 67, joined Philip and a motley assortment of fellow passengers in the latest vehicle, and set off to watch his son perform in market-places and fairgrounds from Cardiff to Blackpool – via Tonypandy, Newport, Neath, Carmarthen, Ellesmere, Manchester, Oldham, Huddersfield, Leeds, South Shields, Stockton-on-Tees – a roll call of the industrial heartlands where so many of his own readers lived and which he'd never previously encountered.

Cheapjack, however, had earned its success in the seven and sixpenny hardback market, not the penny papers, and for this Margery's covert intervention was probably crucial. The adventurousness, the observant humour, the naïve, experiencing mind were Philip's; the final stylistic polish was his sister's. She cut and shaped the manuscript, added its picaresque chapter headings, re-wrote the opening pages and at one stage (in chapter 18) took the story right away from the fairgrounds to include the painfully comic account of Alfie Holmsworth's stage training school. She kept an eye on the proprieties and added rhythm to some of the sentences.

As editor Margery showed a rare degree of empathy with the text but she was not its ghostwriter: authorship remains with Philip. His writing style is less reflective, less literary, than his sister's but his are the qualities of energy and directness that keep the reader swinging along through the story. They had written together as children and teenagers and he had worked professionally, if briefly, as a copywriter for Selfridges and a junior reporter on the *Cambridge Daily News*. His *Cheapjack* adventure had begun soon after his account of a brief amusing incident, 'My Hat', had been published in the weekly magazine *London Calling*.

This appears to have given Herbert Allingham the idea that if Philip were to collect material on his travels occasional, saleable, articles might emerge. Although Philip felt he had to slip away to evade his family, there seems to have been remarkably little opposition to his new career. His parents had probably been as worried about his future as he was. A few weeks before Philip had left London, Herbert noted that his son was 'a difficult chap to help'. That, however, was the only negative comment recorded in the course of what must have been a frustrating adolescence from a parent's point of view. Of course we cannot know what was actually said. Philip normally discussed all his latest projects at length with his father: it may be significant that, when he was setting off to Hunslet Feast in August 1928, he told his mother first.

Ever since Philip had bought his first motor bike Herbert and Emily Allingham had got used to not knowing exactly where he was. Herbert had always believed – rather against the evidence – that his son had 'grit' and, by the Christmas holiday of 1933, it was obvious that Philip had not only stuck out the hard times in his new profession but had brought home the currency that all Allinghams understood – words. Brother and sister had met frequently during 1933 and Margery had the final typescript of *Cheapjack* ready when Philip arrived on Christmas Eve, having driven through the night from Glasgow. Herbert read it a few days later. 'Phil's book surprisingly good and unlike anything else. May easily make a hit. Pip is taking it up to Evans tomorrow. My prayers go with it.'

Pip Youngman Carter, Margery's husband, was a commercial artist who would soon provide his brother-in-law's book with a charming cover. Evans was Dwye Evans, Margery's publisher at Heinemann. This company could hardly be bettered as first choice for *Cheapjack* since they had also published J.B. Priestley's *Good Companions* which had continued to be a bestseller ever since its surprise success in 1929. As the reviewer in *Everyman* commented later (8.6.1934) 'Anyone who has enjoyed the *Good Companions* will find here the raw material of that masterly effort.' Margery's agent helped organise publication in America, her friend Joe Gregory drew end-papers and she and Pip marshalled their marketing talents to ensure the book was widely noticed. There can be few other autobiographies that have been reviewed in both the *Tatler* and *The World's Fair*.

Margery felt deeply involved with *Cheapjack* but knew that

she must distance herself from the work if its essential truthfulness were not to be queried. 'Emphasised importance of saying stuff had not been tampered with by me,' she noted in her diary. And in the same entry 'Wrote Phil's article on Gypsies. Hope it will do.' When her father, presumably aware of the extent that Philip had suffered in the past from being overshadowed by Margery, took her aside and reminded her 'to let Phil have some of the credit for his book' she was hurt and angry. 'I seem to have got nothing but kicks out of the story and a great deal of hard work.'

She remained quietly proud of the book and, in 1951, tried to persuade Penguin to re-publish *Cheapjack* at the same time as they re-published ten of her Campion novels to make the Allingham Million. Nothing came of this and there were no more collaborations. In 1936 Philip published *There's Something In It!* a guide to fortune telling which also which entitled its purchasers to 'an Advice Reading and personal interview with the Author – London's leading Psychological Palmist' but otherwise he showed no further interest in writing. It was the experience set down in *Cheapjack* that had mattered to him, not the fact of having produced a book. 'I felt I had conquered this problem of making my living. I knew now that this bugbear, which had haunted my early life and threatened to give me a serious inferiority complex was dismissed for ever and come what may I should never be afraid again of being a complete and utter failure.'

Philip continued to travel and to graft in between spells of office-based fortune-telling. He impressed both Margery and Herbert by his increasingly professional wireless broadcasts, often written late at night after a day's work in a market. In 1935 he 'teamed up' with Francesca Esposito, a dark-haired Italian who told fortunes as 'Madame Francesca' and they later married. Philip took odd jobs in the North of England and reported on them for the BBC; he produced occasional articles for the *Evening News* and the *Daily Mail*. During the Second World War he served in the R.A.S.C. like his brother-in law Pip. He too emerged eager to settle to some serious peace-time career but, while Pip helped found *Soldier* magazine and then worked for the *Tatler*, Philip and Francesca built up their joint livelihoods as fortune-tellers. Michael Allingham remembers seeing Francesca gleeful over an £18 pile of half crowns earned from a session's fortune-telling and, when Joyce Allingham left the WRNS after 11 years service, she joined them to work temporarily on their stand at the Festival of Britain.

Together Philip and Francesca owned and managed a business called the Zodiac Circle. 'We're turning out a hell of a lot of stuff,' he wrote to Margery in 1953. 'Must be nearly 200,000 readings a year if I include the gear we supply to grafters. The other line – the Ancient and Modern Nature Preparations – is also holding its own and looks as if it will eventually grow into something solid.' The couple had no children but were generous to nephews and nieces. Philip was Michael Allingham's favourite cousin. He offered immediate support after Michael's father, 'Tod', died and regularly took Michael and his mother out to sumptuous West End shows and dinners. At one period he used to arrive driving a Rolls Royce. Those half crowns must have continued heaping up.

After Margery died in 1966, Joyce Allingham was overwhelmed with the responsibility of running Margery and Pip's business affairs and appealed to Philip for help keeping their brother-in-law constructively occupied. 'You will say "Well, what can I do to help?" The answer is "Nothing at the moment but put up with Pip – but not at any price. For God's sake tell him the stuff is not good enough. He can do it ... I can only deal with Pip if he pulls his weight where his work is concerned.'

All three of the Allingham children believed strongly, if idiosyncratically, in the power of work. Philip supported Pip by employing him. Bizarrely, the sophisticated Colonel Youngman Carter, ex-editor of the *Tatler*, member of the Garrick Club, the Lords' Taverners and the Amicable Society of Old Blues, wine-writer and debutant crime novelist, found himself commissioned to produce astrological copy for the *Woman's Weekly* diaries of 1968 and 1970. 'What's wanted is One hundred words (100) only about Capricorn and Aquarius subjects, and one hundred and twenty about each of the other ten zodiacal subjects. 1,400 words in all. I can type this from your writing … if you can let me have the copy,' Philip wrote.

Pip and Philip had had such fun dashing around London together at the time of *Cheapjack's* first publication. 'Suppose they're only young once,' Margery had written rather grumpily in her diary. Now Pip tried again to get *Cheapjack* republished as a paperback but his agent, Graham Watson, met with no success. The book was not sufficiently edgy to attract the 1960s publisher: the brothers-in-law could not recapture their naïve energy and youthfulness. Philip was living separately from Francesca, alone, but with a new girlfriend. In 1969 he underwent a painful operation for stomach cancer and knew he would never recover. He made his Will, took careful precautions to ensure that his body would not be discovered unexpectedly, shut himself in his flat and committed suicide.

In her letter to Philip, pleading for help with Pip after Margery's death, Joyce tried to explain what impelled her to persevere with their brother-in-law. 'When Marge died a passage from one of her unpublished works came into my mind. "The most important legacies in the long run usually turn out to be unfinished business and nothing material at all ... one can inherit what appears to be pure trouble until one discovers the life in it."' Pip Youngman Carter also died in 1969, Francesca Allingham in 1980 and Joyce in 2001. Joyce left her own material and immaterial legacies both to me and to the Margery Allingham Society. This paperback re-publication of *Cheapjack* has not been pure trouble: I hope the editorial apparatus we have added to this edition manages to enhance, not obscure, 'the life in it'.

Francesca and Joyce Allingham with actress Enid Stamp Taylor. 'I discovered that certain people to be interviewed, actresses especially, told me much more about themselves if I told their fortunes instead asking direct questions.' (Philip Allingham *There's Something In It!* 1936)

ACKNOWLEDGEMENTS

Lesley Simpson and Barry Pike of the Margery Allingham Society supported this project straightaway. Lesley's technical skill with scanner and camera has been invaluable as has her constant availability and interest. Vanessa Toulmin has been generous with her knowledge and we are grateful to her colleague, Ian Trowell, at the National Fairground Archive for the time he spent selecting photographs from their collection. Susannah Coates at Forest School searched diligently through old school records and Nigel Cochrane is always ready to assist in the Albert Sloman Library at Essex University where the Margery Allingham and Pip Youngman Carter Archive is now situated. Staff at the Newspaper Library, Colindale, gave practical assistance and Sean French provided an elusive article from the *New Yorker*. Ian Boyle (Simplon Ship Postcards) and Ken Crow (Southend Museums) found photographs at short notice. June Turner and colleagues at the Essex Book Festival were immediately ready to help promote the new edition. Without the experience and painstaking attention to detail of our neighbour, Roger Davies, the book would probably have remained in the realm of good intentions. We would also like to thank Geoff Fisher of Anthony Rowe for his advice and patience. The recollections of Gloria Greci and Michael Allingham confirmed our impression that Philip Allingham was a generous, unconventional and likeable person. He dedicated the first edition of *Cheapjack* to his clients. We hope that it will give particular pleasure to Michael Allingham and Fortuna Lepers.

PHILIP ALLINGHAM'S
PSYCHOLOGICAL READING OF YOU

**Face the Truth—
It's in your Face!**

The Caricaturist, like the Physiognomist, sees only the outstanding facial characteristics. And with a few strokes of the pencil he can capture a person's true character far more accurately than any photograph can do. Note the exaggerated chin (indicating an **argumentative** streak); the wing-like ears (restlessness and love of travel); high cheek bones (obstinacy); thick lips (love of pleasure); high forehead (comic vein), and the inquisitive nose (born to ferret out the truth).

Have a look at those around you through the eyes of a Physiognomist. With my help you can read them like a book.

An Impression of Allingham by that famous Artist, Hyne

Assisted by Madame Francesca, the world-famous Psychic Medium. Madame Francesca has assisted at seances in Paris, Naples and London. She has brought happiness, health and security to thousands. She is ready to solve your most personal problems. You may have heard Allingham on the wireless over a score of times. His articles on Psychology, Palmistry and Astrology appear daily in your newspapers and magazines. His gramophone records on Astrology completely sold out. In the Foreword to his latest book, "There's Something In It," that distinguished lady, Madame Clara Novello Davies, mother of Ivor Novello, writes: "I know Allingham possesses some strange psychic gift." He is not a Prophet, but an Adviser, experienced and full of sympathy and understanding. Leave your troubles behind you with him.

NOW ALLINGHAM IS HERE TO HELP YOU.
At-a-Glance Individual Reading.

This is only claimed to be a sample advice reading and a very concise record of your outstanding characteristics. Do not judge yourself by one characteristic alone, but by taking all the various tendencies marked on the chart below, you will be able to form a fairly accurate reflection of your *true* self. This chart is intended to assist you to develop your talents and to overcome and avoid your faults. For more detailed work (a personally cast Horoscope or Astrology Reading; a Phrenology Chart; Palmistry Consultation; a Graphology Record; or a Numerology Reading), see me privately (appointments can be arranged now), or write at any time to Philip Allingham, 34, Duke Street, St. James's, London, S.W.1. Needless to say I am your confidential adviser.

You are now about to read Madame Francesca's honest opinion of yourself. Possibly it may not be flattering, but for this very reason it is an opinion well worth having. Turn over, gentle reader, and discover the worst!!

Souvenir of "Adventures of A Cheapjack" Lecture.

At-a-Glance Character Reading

By

Madame FRANCESCA (Mrs. Philip Allingham)

YOU POSSESS .... PER CENT. PERSONALITY
YOU HAVE .... PER CENT. SEX APPEAL
YOU CAN MUSTER .... PER CENT. DRIVING FORCE..

READ ONLY WHERE MARKED

Your Lips denote:

Discontent.
Easy-going nature.
Love of pleasure.
Determination.
Ability to lead.
Recklessness.
Cautiousness.
Reliability.
Sensitiveness.
Love of authority.
Keen sense of humour.
Originality.

Your Nose denotes:

A keen business sense.

You're a man who knows what he wants— and gets it!

You may not say much—but you're thinking all the time.

Here's a nose which knows a thing or two!

You're good company providing you get your own way.

Here's a nose which isn't easily put out of joint—adaptable and a good mixer.

A nose with a keen appreciation for good wine, good food— and people who aren't too good!

You're easily led—if it's in a direction you want to take.

What a detective you'd make! Trust you to nose out the facts.

Quite the bar-maid's idol! A sight for a publican's sore eyes.

Your Eyes—

See all but disclose little.

Eyes that show sympathy and understanding.

Your eyes suggest you're a bit of a saint and a bit of a devil all rolled into one.

You're a trifle lacking in self-confidence.

You're rather nervy, erratic, difficult to handle.

The eyes of a serious, intellectual person.

The eyes of a flirt.

Eyes that were meant to smile—let them!

Mischievous eyes—if given a wink, you'll take an eye-full.

These eyes won't miss much—you see the world and enjoy life.

Suspicious eyes—you seldom see the best in people.

Eyes that show disillusionment—you've seen unhappiness.

Your Chin denotes:

The ability to lead.

An inventive streak.

Extraordinary determination.

Weak will-power.

A tendency to philander.

A chin that can take what's coming!

A jolly personality.

A chin that'll see many a close shave!

An argumentative nature.

Lack of patience—a hard task-master.

The strong square chin of the born leader.

The sharp, pointed chin of the intellectual.

GENERAL SUMMING UP—

The Proud Man—One who has accomplished much and knows it! She's a lucky woman who gets him—and he knows that too.

The Prompt Man—One who always says the right thing at the right moment. Women adore him!

The Careful Man—One who takes out two women at a time—you believe in safety in numbers.

The Reckless Man—One who always says what he thinks—even to a woman about her hat.

The Rare Man—One whose car doesn't (conveniently) break down while seeing HER home—who never says his wife doesn't understand him—who doesn't say it's her mental companionship he wants most of all.

The Stingy Man—One who arranges to meet his girl *inside* the dance hall.

The Optimistic Man—One who believes all women are bad till he finds them out.

The Honest Man—One who knows a lot about women—and still likes them.

The Shy Man—One who thinks of all the right things to say—just *after* he has said good-night.

The Amiable Man—One who listens patiently while SHE discusses the other men in her life.

The Foolish Man—One who never takes a chance.

The Envious Man—One who says he has no time for women.

The Popular Man—One who mixes his drinks and his women, but never loses his head—nor his heart.

The Clever Man—One who never takes a woman at her face value.

NOTES ON CONTRIBUTORS

PROFESSOR VANESSA TOULMIN is Research Director of the National Fairground Archive. She comes from a Lancashire showland family, and completed her PhD researching the social history of travelling showpeople. Her publications include *The Winter Gardens Blackpool: the Most Magnificent Palace of Amusement in the World*, *Electric Edwardians: the Story of the Mitchell and Kenyon Collection* and *Pleasurelands: All the Fun of the Fair*.

FRANCIS WHEEN is a journalist on *Private Eye* and a regular broadcaster on Radio 4's *News Quiz*. His books include biographies of Karl Marx and Tom Driberg, the best-selling *How Mumbo-Jumbo Conquered the World* and, most recently, *Strange Days Indeed*.

JULIA JONES is the author of *The Adventures of Margery Allingham*. Her PhD thesis *Family Fictions: the Working Life of Herbert Allingham* can be read on www.golden-duck.co.uk. *The Salt-Stained Book*, the first volume of an adventure trilogy for children, will be published in 2010.

THE MARGERY ALLINGHAM SOCIETY can be contacted on www.margeryallingham.org.uk or by post via The Secretary, 28, Parkfield Avenue, Amersham, Bucks HP6 6BE

The Author